SEMINARS
THE
EMOTIONAL
DYNAMIC

Advanced Presentation Skills
for Financial Professionals

3rd Edition

By Frank Maselli

Published by
The Frank Maselli Company, Inc.
www.frankmaselli.com

THE FRANK MASELLI COMPANY, INC
Advanced Training for Financial Professionals

Published by The Frank Maselli Company, Inc.
Franklin, Massachusetts

ISBN 978-0-578-00946-9

Additional copies my be obtained at
www.frankmaselli.com
or by calling 800-231-5272.

Ask us about volume discounts.

Dedicated with love to my wife Rebecca and my daughters Gerilyn and Rachel. You are the true "emotional dynamic" in my life.

Also dedicated to you...the thousands of financial and investment professionals out here who struggle every day to help clients realize their dreams. You are remarkable people and I'm proud to be part of this wonderful industry.

Table of Contents

Preface P1-2

1.   A New Approach. 1

2.   11 Great Reasons to Do Seminars. . . . 7

3.   Defining a Great Seminar. 19

4.   Seminar Basics 24

5.   The 9 Critical Emotions 29

6.   LIKE 34

7.   UNDERSTANDING 57

8.   RESPECT 84

9.   CONFIDENCE 101

10.   HAPPINESS. 118

11.   FEAR 140

12.   ACTION 149

13.   CHANGE 164

14.   ENTHUSIASM 172

15.   The ReCap. 185

16.   Mastering the Q&A Session 188

17.   The Emotional Close 206

18.   The Seminar Circuit 211

19.   Generating Attendance 218

20.   Stage Fright 234

21.   The Instinctive Speaker 239

22.   Courage & Conviction 245

Appendix A1-7

About the Author

PREFACE

What's New in the Third Edition?

Since the second edition of this book came out in 1996, it feels as if a lifetime of changes have taken place in the world and in the financial services industry specifically. The core philosophy of The Emotional Dynamic has remained the same – I doubt that will ever change, but some of the techniques required a little updating.

There's a new chapter on **The Basics of Seminars**. I added this just to be certain we were all moving forward from common ground.

You may also notice a new approach to understanding and using fear as an emotional motivator in a presentation. In 1996, it was necessary to scare the heck out of an audience just to wake them up from their euphoric slumber. Today, people are scared witless and need a whole new level of comfort and confidence.

There is a new chapter on **The Instinctive Speaker** which discusses the Kolbe test and how your natural action Modes can impact you as a speaker.

In the **ACTION** chapter I've included a whole new appointment-setting process that should really help you. It works very well in the light of more modern client fears and attitudes. And it sends the right message about you and the professional level of service you provide.

I've re-written nearly every aspect of this book, but my commitment to seminars has never been stronger than it is today. Not only will they help you grow your practice, but they will enable you to reach out and save a lot of people from financial ruin. Despite the tough times we face, seminars remain one of the most powerful tools you have in your professional arsenal.

Thank you!

There are so many people who make it possible for ideas to reach the paper, but let me highlight a few who have influenced my path.

Michael Conn was my first branch manager at Dean Witter in Baltimore who encouraged me to try public seminars about a million years ago. He saw something in me that I didn't even know was there. That may actually be the definition of a great manager. Thanks Mike!

The legendary Bob Donato taught me to respect and take great care of the financial advisors under my command. I've tried to live by those ideals. His lessons were far ahead of their time and his wisdom, warmth and humor are with me every day.

Let me add a special thanks to Jorge Villar and the great team at Response Mail Express in Tampa. They created Seminar Success University and asked me to be the "Dean." So now I get to put people on "double secret probation." I've never met a sharper group of marketing experts who are more committed to seminar excellence.

Most of all…I'd like to thank my wonderful wife Rebecca and my daughters Gerilyn and Rachel. Writing a book and being on the road takes a lot of time away from family, but they have stood behind me all the way. When I told my daughters I was writing a book, they were thrilled at first…until they realized it wasn't a new Magic Tree House or Berenstain Bears. Maybe someday.

Chapter 1

A New Approach

"Fortune favors the brave."

Virgil

There has never been a better time in history to reach out with seminars and really help people!

Hollywood could not have written a better script for someone aspiring to grow a business...and I'm assuming that's you or you wouldn't even be reading this. More people need guidance with their money than ever before, and you owe it to them and to yourself to get out there right now.

Seminars are not the only way to grow, and they certainly aren't the easiest or cheapest way...but they might be the most effective and enjoyable marketing and communication activity you have. And there's nothing wrong with having a ton of fun while you work.

This book is going to take you into a world very few people get to visit — a world of excellence, passion and ideas that could change your business and your life forever. You're going to learn skills and techniques that could revolutionize the way you think about yourself and your profession.

Where no one has gone before

Even though we are going to cover some of the basics of seminars, this book is intended to be the advanced class. The entire concept of the emotional dynamic is very different from anything you've seen on the subject of presentations or public speaking. In this book, we will examine seminars from the audience's perspective and explore what is going on in their heads while you're doing the presentation. What specific feelings are evoked when you say and do certain things in certain ways? How are they reacting to you and how can you encourage specific emotional responses that lead to better message reception and better business results?

This emotion-based analysis is critical to understanding why some people become clients and others do not — why some events produce tremendous business results and others are a waste of time and money — why a handful of professionals are building huge practices with seminars, symposiums. workshops and events while the vast majority will swear to you that seminars don't work.

We will look at all aspects of the seminar process, from the initial invitation to the follow-up, in the light of its effect on the audience. When you are done with this book, you will have learned strategies and techniques that very few people in this industry understand. By focusing on the emotional mind-states of the audience, I hope to change the way you think of seminars and human communication. This understanding will dramatically boost the success of your events and will give you a massive competitive advantage in today's crowded industry.

This is a big job, but when it's over, you may be surprised at how enjoyable seminars can be and how quickly you will be able to adapt these ideas to fit your own style.

What is a "seminar?"

Whenever you stand up and talk to a group of people…it's a seminar! This allows for a wide variance in the size of the group or the specific format of the talk. You may be the only speaker, you may be part of a group of presenters, or you may be hosting a guest such as a portfolio manager, wholesaler or research analyst. The audience may have come specifically to see you, or you may be a guest speaker at an organization such as the Rotary, Kiwanis or Lions Club.

It might be a ten-minute presentation to a pension committee or a 20-hour, multi-week adult education course at the local college. It might also be a tele-conference or a webinar conducted over the phone or the internet.

Whatever you call them is fine by me. I know many folks who eschew the word seminar and prefer *workshop, symposium, get-together*. Use whatever name fits your approach.

Audience size has little bearing on the fundamentals of great presentations. The skills you will learn in this book will be most helpful with groups ranging anywhere from five to five hundred people. They will also help you with one-on-one presentations, or a "micro-seminar." You may even find that they add new life to your phone calls as well. It's all one unified field out there — the principles of great communication are identical with only marginal variation for the venue.

Who should be reading this book?

I come from the investment world…so my primary target audience for this book is financial advisors, planners, wholesalers, accountants, insurance agents, portfolio managers, bankers, client managers and mortgage lenders. But the principles in here are universal rules of group communication and should help anyone who speaks to people in a persuasive capacity. You could be a CEO, a teacher, minister, pharmaceutical rep, or an attorney. Maybe you are a leader of a community organization and want to inspire your volunteers. Whatever the need, if you speak to people this book will help you!

Topic neutral

Some of you may be doing investment or financial planning seminars, some mortgage or long-term-care seminars. I've even worked with one guy who sells adjustable beds! It doesn't matter. The topic itself is immaterial. The skills in this book transcend topic. They will help you no matter what you're talking about. Of course, it's nice to have something interesting to say but my only rule for seminar topic selection is… **talk about whatever gets you really excited!**

It's that excitement and passion which will inspire your audience…that's what they will remember long after the facts and statistics are forgotten. It's that energy that will cause them to bond to you.

Roll your own

I'm not a huge fan of store-bought seminars with one caveat. As long as you can get excited about the material…it's OK. I find that when I create my own seminar it's easier to build that enthusiasm in from the ground up.

Some of you may have no choice…you can't build your own seminar. Maybe you're too busy, or compliance won't let you or you don't have the technical skills with PowerPoint and other graphics programs. There are many reasons that you may be doing an off-the-shelf package. There's nothing wrong with it…just make sure you learn the material cold and can deliver it with passion.

Creating a seminar may seem like a daunting task, but it's really a lot of fun. It's mainly a matter of observation and organization. Once you know the basic theme, you break it down into bite-sized chunks and begin collecting ideas from a diverse group of sources including wholesalers, product marketing materials, industry publications, news media, books, articles, other speakers, portfolio managers, analysts, economists, etc. This involves cutting out articles, scanning important magazines and wire stories for facts, quotes and statistics developing what I call a seminar "story book." The good news is that our industry fills your inbox with more information than you will ever need. You will never starve from lack of ideas or data in this business.

The act of creating your own seminar leads to another, equally critical benefit for you…you will become a much smarter, more capable professional than your colleagues or competition. This is because you not only have to know lots of stuff but you have to know it well enough to TEACH OTHERS! That carries a massive added responsibility that many people shun. Embracing this responsibility will set you above the crowd and dramatically improve the quantity, quality and enjoyment of your business.

"My market is saturated with seminars!"

Seminar overload may seem like a problem, but you *want* a busy seminar market. That means people are interested and it gives you a chance to stand out by comparison. In any field saturated by mediocrity, there is a burning desire for excellence and that will be you. No more boring sales pitches – you are going to deliver professional, dynamic, educational and motivational programs that truly help people reach their most important financial goals.

Think about the seminars that are occurring in your city or town right now. If you haven't been to one, I strongly urge you to get out and see what kind of weak, low energy, confusion is being perpetrated on the public. The majority of advisors doing these **"Sominex Seminars"** are working by the old rules. They have no clue what the audience is feeling from one minute to the next. Consequently, they're being shunned on follow-up calls and ultimately converting only 5%-10% of attendees into appointments. They're also having trouble filling the room.

By contrast, you will fill every seat and probably have to turn people away at the door. Your follow-up receptivity will be excellent and your client conversion rates will climb to as high as 80% or 90%! That is what an emotion-based approach can do for you.

Most seminars stink

I have been to thousands of seminars in my career and I would say that 75% of them were terrible! Like a tool mishandled by an unskilled artisan, these events wasted time, money and effort, and generated no positive results for either the presenter or the audience. Now you might think I'm a harsh critic but I'm not. In fact, I'm a great audience. I'm one of those people who really roots for the speaker to do a great job. I smile and laugh at all the right moments. I ask great leading questions. I'm the perfect shill and yet, I've been shocked by the low quality of these presentations.

It concerns me that major financial firms could allow their representatives to get up in front of a roomful of existing or potential clients and deliver such a weak message and poor image. Quality control in the public presentation environment is a life and death necessity and it's sorely lacking. Most firms focus their attention on the compliance aspects of seminar design. They strictly limit the creative process as a risk control measure, but they do nothing to assist in the delivery of the message leaving their reps to struggle with that most important element on their own.

I saw fundamental deficiencies like poor grammar, low energy, lack of preparation, unreadable visual aids, misprinted handouts and an uncomfortable physical environment. Most of these seminars were deathly boring or very overt sales events. Some were too thin in factual content, others too heavy. Many were confusing, badly organized and hard to follow.

"But my seminars are already great!"

Maybe you are already an excellent speaker…someone who really knows what to do in front of a room. If so, I salute you. You are probably giving top-quality, emotion-packed, value-added seminars and setting appointments with the majority of attendees. Keep it up. You're on your way to tremendous success if you're not there already.

The only suggestion I can make is: **don't get complacent.** I urge you to keep training and expanding your skills. Even the best public speakers have to freshen their material and sharpen their delivery periodically or they risk going stale. I've worked one-on-one with scores of top presenters and they are all amazed when we discover the bad habits they've developed over time. We all do it…even me.

> *A while back, I discovered a bad habit in my own presentations. It's a quality I call "strident delivery." I listened to myself on tape and was stunned by how intense and overpowering my tone of voice had become. It was making me sound angry and this was not my intention at all. A quick tape review caused me to make a simple but critical shift in my style.*

For the rest of you who are not yet great — you can be. All it takes is some knowledge, training and a bit of creative flair or personality. None of this is beyond you. Some people are going to be naturally better at it than others, at first, but everything in this book is learnable. No one is born a fantastic speaker. The vast majority of top presenters are self-made with little or no formal education. Now you've got an edge and a coach. So read on!

No theory...only real-world insights

The entire emotion-based approach may seem very new or advanced, but nothing you will read in here is theory. I've done all of it in a public seminar forum. There are no clever paper concepts. All of it has been proven in the field under a variety of stressful and difficult circumstances.

Initially, you may be quite uncomfortable with many of the things we're going to discuss. That's OK. Give yourself time. I'm asking you to think in a new way and that's not easy. Some of these techniques may seem strange or too difficult to try. That's OK too. Even if you pick up one thing, one idea or tool you can use, you will see positive results almost immediately. That feedback will compel you to speak more often and thus quicken your advance.

The ideas you will read here come from three primary sources:

- *35 years of public speaking experience and over 10,000 presentations.*

- *Decades of research into the field of interpersonal communications.*

- *Direct observation and study of thousands of public speakers and presentations.*

Over time, you will be able to modify and perfect these techniques to fit your specific needs and personality. The result will be much more powerful events, happier clients and a more successful business!

Chapter 2

11 GREAT REASONS TO DO SEMINARS

"It is not the strongest of the species which survives, nor the most intelligent…but the one most responsive to change."

Charles Darwin

Seminars are definitely not the easy road.

As much as I want to convince you to do them, I realize they are not for everyone. This book is not going to show you how *easy* seminars can be. It might make the process more of a challenge, but I will give you the tools to conquer that challenge. Ultimately, the decision to include seminars in your marketing and educational game plan should be based on your personality and business style. If you *are* going to do them, then do the best seminars you can. Be the absolute best in your market and reap the tremendous rewards that come with superior performance.

One of the things that make financial seminars so challenging is that they blend elements from several public speaking formats. Great presenters need the conviction and charm of a politician, the empathy and persuasion of a preacher, the energy of a motivator, the knowledge and technique of a teacher, the quick wit and courage of a stand-up comic and the powerful dramatic skill of an actor. Unlike each of these other presentation mediums, however, seminars carry the added burden of having specific, measurable goals.

The units of measurement may be dollars as in assets under management, fees or commissions. They may also be things like community awareness, referrals or good will. Whatever yardstick you prefer, there is one basic goal of any investment seminar:

Get the audience to believe in YOU!

Once an audience buys you, bonds to you and connects with you…everything else falls into place. I'm hoping you share this belief because there are still some folks out there who think we are in the product business and they insist on pitching stuff at seminars. That's a tremendous mistake. Any product you try to sell at a seminar gets in the way of the only "product" you ever need to "sell" to anyone…yourself!

Seminars certainly are wonderful educational events that offer people valuable financial advice and skills, but the real power of this medium from your perspective is that seminars place you, literally and figuratively, right at center stage. You are the focus of attention, admiration and awe. There is simply no other communication modality that carries as much potential for your success as the public seminar.

1 - Position yourself as D.S.B.

This stands for Different, Smarter, Better and it's the essence of marketing in any competitive service industry. In the world of financial services, there is massive commoditization of products and providers. The typical investor has no clue who you are and why you're different from any other advisor.

There are a few exceptions to this — companies that have carved out a specific niche in the public's mind. But most investors think of this business as one gigantic ocean of financial information. Whether you work at a large company or you are an independent practitioner, the need for you to differentiate yourself from the crowd has never been greater than it is today.

Seminars will help you stand out and help your prospects and clients answer two critical questions: *Why should I work with you?* and *What makes you special?* The ultimate answer to these questions is probably some combination of your personality and professional skill. As a medium of communication, seminars afford you the best opportunity to get that message across. Whether you use them as a full-time element of your marketing strategy or only as periodic special events, they can generate tremendous results.

A seminar allows you to showcase yourself in the most powerful light. They give you a chance to display several positive attributes in front of a room full of people. For example, you can be…

> *trustworthy, smart, witty, articulate, commanding, confident, funny, warm, entertaining, enlightening, inspiring, technically*

skilled, intelligent, worldly, charming, experienced, friendly, energetic, authoritative, powerful.

It's nearly impossible to highlight these characteristics over the telephone. You might hit a few in a face-to-face appointment, but that's more a time for listening than for talking. In reality no other form of communication lets you transmit as many powerful messages with more intensity than a seminar.

Client relationships change over time and the attributes that won you the client may not be the same as the ones needed to keep the client. At some point in the relationship, it becomes critical to move beyond D.S.B. and demonstrate that you truly care more about the client than any other financial professional they've met. But it takes time for people to recognize the depth of your concern. You have to start by getting the client on the books and D.S.B. is a good way to begin.

Being different and better or being *perceived* as such by your clients and prospects will be your initial ticket to success in a crowded world of financial advisors. Seminars give you the best opportunity to do this.

2 - Seminars help you grow your business

In nearly every service-based business, there are only two ways to grow….

- *Get new clients*

- *Do more business with existing clients*

Seminars help you do both! They are certainly not the best idea for every advisor, but if you like to speak in public, they may be the greatest business-building technique you could ever use.

I could make the case that the best way to get *new* clients is referrals. I love referrals and I've written a book called **"Referrals The Professional Way"** which introduces an exciting new philosophy and set of strategies for mastering this very misunderstood process. But when you think about referrals for a minute, you will see that even though they may be #1 for getting new clients they do very little to expand your relationship with *existing* clients. Because of that, they are not the overall winner for building a business.

Seminars help you deepen your existing client relationships over time. They help you cross-sell (or cross-*solve*) with a variety of services and solutions. They help you increase retention and improve client performance. The industry statistics vary depending on whom you ask, but the numbers I've seen that relate client retention to cross-selling are fascinating.

Studies indicate that the length of a client relationship depends on how many different types of business they've done with you. A client who owns one investment or financial program with you has a 35% probability of sticking for five years or more. A client who owns two things – 65%, and a client who owns three things will almost never leave you…a 90% probability of retaining for five or more years!

I'm not talking about Google, Microsoft and Intel. That's not three things. I'm talking about broader product or service categories. But the stats are remarkable and the best way to deepen the relationship is to expose the client over time to a wide variety of investment and financial programs that meet their needs and solve their problems. The seminar or "event" format may be the most effective and enjoyable way to do this.

3 - Make your people smarter

Seminars give you a chance to teach people important strategies that can help them make better decisions with their money. You can also help them ward off the scams and fads that do serious damage to their long-term success. You can reduce the emotional impact of the media and help them truly understand what they are doing.

If you are a reverse mortgage or long-term care expert, there may be a lot of educating that needs to take place before someone is ready to make a decision. Both of these topics are complex and there is a lot of confusion out there. You are dealing with deep emotional issues and people will often choose to do nothing rather than ask themselves the tough questions that they may need to face about their future.

The seminar forum gives you a chance to tell your story from start to finish. You can take people on a systematic journey that calms their fears and simplifies the process. You can give them a stronger decision-making framework and help them understand their choices. And you can do it in a group setting where people facing these decisions will feel less vulnerable.

Some advisors don't like the idea of educating clients. They tell me, *"If I make my people too smart then they won't need me!"* Folks…please don't worry about that. First, it's not going to happen. The vast majority of people with money today have figured out that they need professional advice. They are not coming to your seminar in hopes of stealing a few tricks and running off to do them on-line.

Second…even if it did happen and someone said, *"Thanks for your ideas. I'm going to do them all myself,"* You dodged a bullet! Someone like that is probably not going to be a good relationship anyway. A good rule is never work with people who think they're smarter than you are. That's a short road to hell. You will be fighting a daily battle for respect and appreciation and life is too short for that. I tell people like this, *"That's wonderful and I wish you the best of luck. The ideas are superb, but the precise execution and the monitoring is another story. You may find that more challenging. So when you get serious about your future…come back and see me. I will be here."*

4 - Systematize referrals

We all love referrals, and seminars will help you get more of them. For financial professionals, there is nothing better than getting regular, high-quality referrals from your top clients. But asking a high net-worth client for a referral is the toughest thing you will ever do and most of your referral training is dangerously wrong. The techniques you've been taught, such as *"I need your help to grow my business,"* or *"I get paid two ways…"* make people feel uncomfortable, call for very bad timing and send the wrong messages about you and the success of your business. I strongly recommend that you learn some new skills and you should read my referral book.

A strong seminar program is a cornerstone of the "Event Referral." This is a relaxed, non-threatening, educational venue that requires very little effort or risk on the part of your client. All they have to do is bring a guest. The client doesn't have to tell them what a great guy you are or how much money you made them. There is no sharing of personal information or any selling that might endanger the client's relationship with their friend. The friend gets to make a completely independent decision about you based on your success in the seminar.

If you do a great seminar, the client will naturally want to take credit for "discovering" you, which is wonderful. The referral had a chance to see you in top performance mode and is eager to start their own relationship. If you stink, the client has "plausible deniability" and can divorce themselves from the referral process with very little loss of prestige.

Also, referrals often tend to dry up in tough market environments. Not only might you have fewer happy clients, but you may be more reluctant to ask for referrals when your clients' portfolios are declining. Seminars, being an educational tool, are just as effective, even more so in tough times. This could keep the stream of new clients from evaporating. **The toughest times are actually when your seminars will produce the best referral results!**

5 - Reach across generations

Imagine that you are a twenty-five year old advisor trying to build relationships with fifty- and sixty-something high net-worth investors. You have tremendous natural barriers to effective rapport. These clients may see you as a child who can't possibly solve their problems effectively.

A seminar can quickly place you on a higher level and help you gain the credibility you need to reach out to these people. If you are able to do something powerful and intelligent in front of that audience, the entire age issue fades away and you can move forward based on your ability.

The flip side of the age issue is equally tricky. Maybe you are a sixty-something advisor trying to bond to the thirty-something children of your top clients. A seminar gives you a chance to prove you are fully versed on the latest ideas and services our industry offers....not a "geezer" who pushes the "old-school" techniques. You can also display an appreciation of *their* life goals, which might be quite different from those of their parents.

6 - Enhance or re-gain credibility with the public

To put this in delicate terms...the financial services industry has a pretty choppy image with the public. Depending on the state of the markets or the latest scandal on Wall Street, we may be held in moderately high esteem or rank somewhere below Taliban stone mongers.

A seminar gives you a chance to tell your story and build your own personal trust and credibility. You can use this either to separate yourself from Wall Street, if need be, or to stand out as one of the good guys in a marginal crowd.

People know they need professional financial advice but they are jaded and confused about whom to trust. The media pushes meaningless information and hypes short-term market activity that is very counterproductive to successful investing efforts. Only the wisdom that comes from experience, training and full immersion in the disciplined processes of planning and investing will help clients reach their goals. Guess what...YOU'RE the one with this wisdom!

7 - Educate your people

A major full-service investment firm surveyed their top clients recently and asked, among other things, *"What do you want most from your financial advisor?"* The number one answer expressed by over 83% of the respondents set everyone back in their chairs...EDUCATION!

Look I realize this is hard to believe. You have clients who completely trust you. If you *tried* to educate or explain stuff to these clients you're likely to hear, *"STOP! You don't have to explain every detail. That's what I hired you to do. If you think this is right for me...then do it!"*

Those are magic words because it means you've completely sold yourself to a client and your relationship is great. But ask yourself this, *"Have I built this level of trusting relationship with more than a handful of people and then with the heirs of my best clients?"*

You are infinitely more likely to build a solid relationship with the best investors through direct, face-to-face contact. A seminar allows you to provide the education they're demanding AND sell yourself at the same time. This transmission of wisdom helps keep the assets in place.

Seminars add the extra dimension to your business that will form a high-touch communications link between you and your people. A comprehensive seminar program can also be used in conjunction with a good newsletter to accomplish the ongoing education.

8 - Leverage your time

Time is your most precious commodity. You simply don't have enough to do all the things you need to do so finding ways to make it go farther can be a major boon to your business. Seminars allow you to maximize "brain-time." This is defined as those few seconds when a person is actually paying attention to you...brain fully engaged.

Just for fun, let's compare a seminar to cold-calling. How much brain-time do you get during the typical phone call? I've calculated roughly 15 seconds! That's it. The rest of the time they are thinking about their day, whatever stuff you interrupted or trying to get off the phone without getting body slammed into some product.

So multiply that out:

30 contacts a day	=	7.5 minutes
5 days per week	=	37.5 minutes
4 weeks per month	=	2.5 hours
12 months per year	=	30 hours

One entire year's worth of phone work equals 30 hours of people paying attention to you. It's depressing!

Do one seminar per year, put thirty people in a room for one hour and you have achieved the same amount of focus as an entire year on the phone. Imagine if you wanted to do one seminar per *month*...think about the impact that could have on your business?

You want further proof? Imagine yourself doing a seminar in front of a room full of 30 people. Now suddenly imagine the room is empty and you're doing the exact same seminar with each person in the audience...except now over the phone and one at a time.

Could you possibly have the same conversation with each individual? *"Hey Bob I want to talk to you about estate planning. Got an hour? Yeah, just sit there and listen to me for an hour and take some notes. OK...here we go..."*

I could also make a subjective case that calling to invite people to an educational meeting is much less threatening and stressful than trying to sell a stranger something over the phone. Thus you will enjoy it more and therefore be able to make more calls in the same amount of time. That's what I call psychological leverage.

Seminars will not only be more fun for you but the quality of your message can improve dramatically. The business leverage you achieve by putting a bunch of people in front of you at one time is enormous!

9 - Tap into the group dynamic

Whenever you put two or more people together in a room something happens. They stop being individuals and they become part of this vague social structure called a group. Their behavior changes in subtle and sometimes dramatic ways.

They often become more aware and attuned to the reactions of people around them. They begin to react to you based not only on their own impulses but on their perception of the other people's reactions. They will check themselves in the mirror of the crowd to judge the appropriateness of their reactions.

If others are laughing, they will laugh. If others are smiling and nodding, they will smile and nod. If others are feeling enthusiastic about you, they will feel the same way. It works like a charm and it cannot be duplicated in any venue other than with a roomful of people. By understanding and tapping into the emotional flow that's controlling this behavior, you can influence not only individuals, but the bulk of an audience all at once!

I'm simplifying this quite a bit for our discussion here. There are many aspects to a group dynamic that have been studied by experts for decades. You should also know that the group dynamic isn't cast in stone nor does it always work to your benefit. For example, if people see others looking bored and eager to leave, they will begin to feel bored as well. If someone feels confused, they will check to see if others look confused and if so, they will begin to feel more confused and annoyed at you for confusing them.

> I was a guest speaker at a company meeting once and a speaker prior to me opened his talk with a really sarcastic comment about the company. It was obviously a joke, and I thought it was funny but it bombed big time. The audience didn't laugh and you could tell the guy was in trouble.

> As the seminar went on, he started to relax and he actually was very good. His stories were great, his humor eased up a bit and was quite funny. But the audience never warmed up to him. Why? Because they were still punishing him for the opening joke! No one wanted to be the first to break the unspoken agreement to make him suffer...and so despite his very strong finish, the group dynamic worked against him. As individuals, they would have forgotten the comment and moved on very quickly. But as a group...they couldn't. Not without offending each other. It's scary how this stuff works sometimes.

10 - Create a social environment

People generally like to socialize with others. It's a natural human instinct and the seminar can be a great way to tap into the positive energy that is created in a friendly, social environment. Let's say you're doing some kind of dinner event at a nice restaurant. There's a nice setting, good food, relaxing conversation, meeting new people, sharing thoughts...it's all good stuff and it puts people in a great mood to hear your story.

I'm not saying that everyone likes social events. There are some prospects who would never attend a seminar. But it's a self-selecting mechanism. The people who don't want to come aren't coming! This is not a mandatory socialization like an annual company party. This is totally voluntary, so the people who come to the event are predisposed to have a good time and to be in a good mood. That is a huge advantage over other forms of prospecting. I don't know many folks who sit at home all day hoping for the phone to ring. *"Oh boy...I hope it's a cold call!"*

11 - Have lots of fun!

There is something magical about standing up in front of a roomful of people and leading them on a journey of discovery. Maybe it's an ancient human instinct we have for telling stories around the fire. I don't know what the source is but I do know that I love to talk to people and that passion has been with me as far back as I can remember. Certainly some part of that came from growing up in a big Italian family. At Sunday dinner, you had to speak up boldly or you didn't get fed. And I didn't miss too many meals.

If you feel that way too, you will have a lot of fun with seminars…and having fun is a great way to grow a business! In fact, having fun may be the *only* way to grow the kind of business that comes close to your potential. Fun and success are directly correlated. The more fun you have the more successful you will be at whatever you're doing.

That goes against most of the success lessons I learned early in my career. People told me that I had to beat my head against a wall to succeed. I had to suffer, to struggle, to fight. They said, *"You've got to get a lot of no's to get one yes!"* Then some manager told me, *"If you are willing to live for three years the way no one else is willing to live…then for the rest of your life you will live the way no one else CAN live."* I didn't even know what that meant, but it sounded profound. I bought it and I tried it without much success and even less enjoyment. Then with the help of a bold young manager named Michael Conn, I discovered seminars and the rest is history.

Chances are you enjoy speaking too and you are probably pretty good at it already. You have some natural talent, but now it's time to take that skill to a professional level. This is where we harness your innate ability and love of attention and turn it into something you can control for maximum results. Now you can reap the dual income you get from seminars: the growth of your business and the enormous psychic gratification from doing something you love and are good at!

You ask, *"Frank…can you really build a successful business by doing something you love to do?"* My simple question back is, **"Can you do it any other way?"**

I attended a program called Strategic Coach founded by the brilliant Dan Sullivan. If you've never heard of Dan…you need to. His program is not just for financial professionals, but for entrepreneurs of all types. It arms you with specific skills and ways of thinking about business and life that will alter both in very positive ways.

One of the most powerful concepts Dan's program discusses, is the that of "Unique Ability" or "UA" for short. I will simplify his definition of UA by describing it as something that falls within the center of three circles of skills and abilities.

Circle One: *Things I love to do*

Circle Two: *Things I'm really great at*

Circle Three: *Things that make me money*

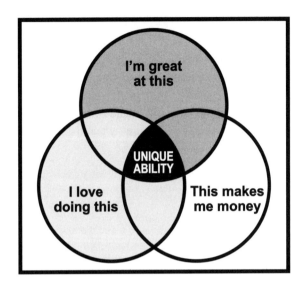

Somewhere, these three circles meet and overlap. In that zone of overlap lies your Unique Ability.

In Strategic Coach, we spend a lot of time thinking about our UA and then a lot more time on the second critical question — *Once you've found your Unique Ability, how can you build an organization around you that allows you to focus your time and energy on it?*

For many of you that UA is some variation on the concept of TALKING TO PEOPLE. If you spent more of your professional time focused on meeting with and talking to people, you would be immeasurably more successful.

Placing yourself in front of as many people as possible should become the central organizing theme of your entire career. You should build your world around this goal and direct energy toward building a team of people who do everything else — allowing you to focus on meeting with thousands of people each year.

I am living proof that this can work. After many years, I've been able to strip away nearly everything that is NOT my Unique Ability. This frees me up to be more focused and powerful and ultimately produces a great deal of enjoyment.

Do you have a choice?

It's tough to grow a practice today. Competition in our profession is ferocious and it's getting worse. The complexity of the investment world has grown exponentially and clients are bombarded by vast amounts of investment misinformation leading to confusion, uncertainty, bad decisions and horrendous performance.

Your seminars will be high quality, fun, inspiring and enlightening events with no sales pressure – exactly what people want. You are going to blow them away and the benefits to your business will amaze you. Sure, there are other ways to build, but when you look at all of the techniques and balance them out with your innate abilities and passions…you may find seminars are right at the top of the chart. So stop worrying if they are right for you and try them!

Chapter 3

DEFINING A GREAT SEMINAR

"It is a rough road that leads to the heights of greatness."

Lucius Annaeus Seneca

Wonderful things happen to you when you get great at something!

Being goal-oriented, most of us would say that the ultimate measure of a seminar is the amount of business done as a direct result of the event. But a seminar is not only a revenue-generating tool. It's a critical step in the continuous process of building trusting relationships with both prospects and clients. Sure, you might generate some business right away, but most people are not ready to make a commitment right there. That does not mean you've failed. Instead, you need to broaden the measure of a great seminar to include other things that lead to longer-term business success.

Success is more than a packed house

Defining a seminar solely by the number of attendees is a mistake. It's like measuring a football team's success by the total weight of their players. When I ask a rep, *"How was your seminar?"* I hear, *"It was awesome. We had a hundred people!"* That's nice, but what did you *do* with those hundred people?

I'm not saying that crowd size isn't important, but it's what you do in front of that crowd that matters. How you challenge, excite and inspire them will determine the ultimate success or failure of your entire seminar effort. I can't tell you how many times I've been in the audience of standing-room-only seminars filled with intelligent, motivated prospects only to see that tremendous potential wasted by an inept speaker.

So what makes a great seminar?

Right now, with no added training at all, you are probably capable of doing a pretty good seminar. But pretty good is not enough. This book is about becoming fantastic. So what does that look like? How do you measure the power and impact of a seminar. I use the following yardsticks:

▪ *Appointments*

The most immediate and useful measurement is the number of appointments set with members of the audience. Appointments are a direct payoff…instant gratification…the psychic *"ka-ching"* of our business.

You should use the seminar event to create interest in a concept and credibility in yourself. Then you follow-up with a personal appointment at which you may probe and profile more deeply or actually invest the assets for a qualified client or prospect. Once you get them to sit for appointment, your odds of doing business soar astronomically.

I will count the number of appointments set within four weeks of the event. This four-week time frame is not arbitrary. Experience has shown that beyond the four week mark the prospects have cooled off to the point where the memory of the seminar alone is usually not sufficient to bring them in for an appointment. You will need to re-light the fire in them.

Keep in mind that the cool-off time for an ordinary seminar tends to be much shorter than for one of your SUPER-seminars. An average seminar may see people cooling by the time they reach the parking lot. Four weeks assumes you're doing some very good work up there.

At some point you will get good enough and your seminars will become so powerful that people who attended seminars months or even years ago will convert to clients. Imagine someone calling you out of the blue, *"You may not remember me but I came to your seminar last year. My advisor just retired and I was wondering if you had some time to meet with me."*

It happens, believe it. It's a powerful feeling that will bring a tiny tear to your eye. People change, and so do their relationships with financial advisors. If you've placed yourself in their minds as a value-added professional who knows his stuff, when change does come, they will remember you.

My personal goal is to set appointments with a minimum of 50% of the room right there at the seminar! I'm going to show you how to go even higher than that, but let's start with a reasonable number.

▪ Referrals

Here's the scenario: one of your top clients attends your seminar. They have never given you any referrals in the past, but after the seminar, they tell you about a friend that might need your help. The client agrees to call the fiend and set up a meeting with the two of you. This is a major success!

Referrals are a very emotional and dangerous process for the client. By doing a great seminar and using the emotion-based techniques you are going to learn here, you will have paved the way for those referrals and the flow will come much easier.

Or how about this? One of the seminar attendees is so impressed by your presentation that he invites you to speak to his company's investment club or their pre-retiree group or his Elks Lodge. Here the referral is another seminar and another chance to reach new clients. The effect can begin to snowball.

During every seminar, you should mention that you are available for special speaking engagements or as an "emergency speaker" to fill in on short notice in case they have a cancellation. If anyone in the audience is a member of an organization, club, company, or any other group that might be interested in a similar presentation or a customized event, you would be happy to visit them. You might even want to include your "program menu" in the handout kit. This menu is a listing of topics on which you can speak. It doesn't need to be too elaborate, but it should contain some exciting and thought-provoking titles with a brief description of each seminar including the approximate time you need.

▪ Public & group awareness

Let's assume that you're prospecting in a small to medium-sized town or in a local retirement community. You're doing a seminar but you're also cold calling and mass mailing to get business. This is part of a strategy called "farming" an area where you use a multi-layered marketing strategy to penetrate a region.

The local newspaper or community newsletter carries a story about your seminar. (A story that you submitted as a press release.) This could be a very powerful aid to your "farming" effort. Not only will some people recognize your name from the article but you can include copies in any mails you may do and refer to the event and the article during any cold calls you make.

The key to remember is that public awareness doesn't just happen...you are in control and must *make* it happen. Your seminar is an important event but you've got to make it easy for the local media to help you by sending press releases, biographies, announcements, photos, etc. Naturally, this works better in smaller communities, but there's no reason you can't divide a major metropolitan area into smaller sub-sets for "farming" purposes.

Group awareness is also a major benefit of seminars. Let's say your target market is printers. You speak at the New Jersey Printers Association meeting and *The Printing News* carries a story about you in their next issue. This becomes a strong connection when you talk to other printers. If they missed the story you can send it to them.

It says you're an insider, you're one of them. Your receptivity within the group goes through the roof. You get invited to their national conference. You get on their advisory board. You write a special investing column for their monthly newsletter. It just goes deeper and deeper until everyone in that group knows who you are and what you do.

▪ *Stature in the community*

How would you like to be the advisor to whom everyone in your community with serious money turns to for help and advice? Seminars are the way. If this is your goal, you're probably going to need to do a regular, on-going series of events. One way is to teach an Adult Education class.

I know what you're thinking. *"Serious money doesn't go to adult ed classes!"* Wrong...Boy Wonder! Just you wait and see. I guarantee you that this is going to become one of the biggest industries of the next few decades. Business sage, Peter Drucker said recently, *"The continuing professional education of adults is the No. 1 gross industry in the next 30 years."* This is a wave you might want to catch.

I used to teach a seminar on investing at the local community college. Nothing special here...many advisors have done this. What I did, however, was slightly different with dramatically improved results. I looked through the college course catalog and saw that all the "basic" courses were taken by other instructors, so I changed tactics and titled my course **"Advanced Investment Techniques."**

I advertised it in the catalog by saying *"This is the course your advisor doesn't want you to attend!"* I effectively declared to the community that I was superior, I was the expert ABOVE the other instructors. I teach the *"graduate"* course. People with serious money come to my course. I'm different, smarter and better than all the other advisors.

I immediately leap-frogged all the other financial advisors in the adult-ed program. Did I frighten some people away? Sure, but I attracted a better group of prospects and captured people who had just completed a basic course with another advisor. One man had just been thrust into a new job as the manager of a $260 million pension for a local manufacturing firm. He needed help and had just take the "Fundamentals of Investing" course but needed more. Even though I didn't get the pension account, I did get several personal accounts of key people in the company based on my relationship with him.

Whenever I talked to anyone in the community during my other prospecting efforts, I mentioned that I taught the advanced course at the college. This carried added weight and led to significant business that would never have otherwise come my way.

▪ Elevated relationships

Let's say that you've done a little business with a particularly tough new client. Maybe she's done a couple of trades or has given you a little money to test you out. She's always seemed a little resistant to your ideas or your approach and reluctant to open up. Suddenly, after the seminar, she is more responsive to your probes about her financial needs and agrees to a one-on-one meeting.

I'd call that a huge victory! Here, the seminar has helped elevate the quality of the relationship and brought this client closer to you. It has helped you mine the gold in your own book!

Don't let others define your success

Some of you may have to deal with a branch manager or a supervisor of some sort. My best advice is don't let them judge your seminars solely by the assets, gross fees or commissions you generate. Seminars are a process. Be sure they understand that this is a long-term commitment on your part and that you expect them to be your partner in this effort.

This is especially true if you're just starting out. It may take three or four seminars before you bring in a single dollar of assets. Both you and your manager need to be prepared to stay the course. The results will all come if you stick to your game plan.

Chapter 4

SEMINAR BASICS

"Some people try to find things in this game that don't exist; but football is only two things – blocking and tackling."

Vince Lombardi

Let's do a very quick review of the basics to make sure we are on the same sheet of music.

I told you we are the advanced class, but I first want to share a few simple rules that will help you with your seminars. Don't violate these…they are proven, tested and will keep you out of trouble. Then we can build a more powerful methodology together.

Rule #1: Know your material cold

Not only will this help you appear like the expert you are…but during the seminar, you want to focus the vast majority of your attention on the audience…not on the presentation itself. If you are clicking the slideshow wondering what's coming up next or what you are going to say…you cannot devote the proper level of attention to the people.

The audience will guide you throughout the event. They will tell you when to speed up, slow down, re-cover a critical point, stop and hammer home an emotional message, use more or less humor…everything that's critical to the best seminars. The slides and the content…believe it or not, are secondary.

Focus on them! Be so totally confident in your material so that your passion overcomes your instinctive nervousness. To go in unprepared is asking for trouble…or diminished results at best.

Rule #2: Arrive 90 minutes early

Something is going to go wrong with your event and if you show up ten minutes before you're scheduled to speak…you're screwed! What could go wrong…you ask. It could be anything from the room setup to the noise level to the projector not working, the air-conditioner is busted, etc. The hundred variables that make up a great event could all decide to conspire against you at the same time and you would be powerless to correct them.

If you have a staff that handles details like this make sure that they arrive early. All of this is designed to take the pressure off you and allow the "delicate genius" (thank you George Costanza) to prepare mentally for the performance of a lifetime.

Rule #3: Make your guests feel welcomed

The whole Host / Guest relationship is a good metaphor for the seminar scenario. As the host, it's your job or your team's job to make people as happy and comfortable as possible. This means a warm greeting at the door, escorting them to their seat, handling special requests, making sure they can see the screen, etc. It also means touches like valet parking, clear signs to the room and other items we will cover in greater detail later.

For now, it helps to remember that these people have given you a precious gift by attending your seminar. They've invested their most valuable commodity – time. And you owe it to them to go the extra mile in charm and civility.

Rule #4: Keep it simple

One of the biggest problems I see with seminars today (and have for years) is overly complex content that leaves the audience scratching its collective head. I know we work in a complicated world and the technology of high finance is jammed with facts and statistics. But I'm telling you…people don't care. And worse, the more you try to baffle them with rocket science the less they will like you, understand you and want to work with you.

We are going to discuss this in great detail in the chapter on Understanding, but you must learn how to explain things in simple terms if you want people to grasp your message. That means using stories with simple morals, common analogies, easy-to-read graphs and charts, visual builds and several other techniques designed to make your talk accessible to civilians.

The purpose of the seminar is not to overwhelm them with details, it's to clear up the confusion and fear people have about the world of money. To guide them out of the storm you need to be as clear and visible as a laser beam.

Some advisors deliberately try to talk over the heads of the crowd in an effort to show how much they know. This is a mistake. Your audience is sitting there trying hard to understand what you're saying and how it relates to their world. Don't make them struggle to do that. You've probably heard the acronym WIIFM – What's In It For Me?

Let them know why you are discussing certain topics and how those topics and ideas will affect them personally. Make it meaningful to them. Connect the dots *for* them. The better you do this, the more deeply they will bond to you and the more likely you will be able to help them succeed.

Rule #5: Get the audience involved

I love audience participation. It gets the creative juices flowing. It really can help people understand complex concepts and it's a lot of fun. It can also be a catalyst for tremendous laughter if you do it well.

I like to engage the audience in targeted exercises in the form of games. One of my favorite is The Price Was Right. This is where we take a look back at a year, say 1978 and compare the prices then to the price today on several common items like cars, houses, milk, bread, postage stamps, etc. A simple game like this can really generate a lot of energy in the room. It drives home to critical points I want to make about inflation and everyone has a great laugh.

The two dangers of audience participation are doing it too early and too often. Early in the seminar I want to maintain tight control of the room. If you start to solicit input too soon you may get a lot more than you really want. Too often tells them that you really don't have much content and you're using these games and their feedback to drive the body of the talk. Ultimately, they came to hear you, the expert, not to hear themselves talk. A limited use is all the spice you need to perk up your event.

Rule #6: Don't sell products...sell yourself

Anytime you start pitching a specific product or an investment strategy at a seminar, you radically reduce the number and the quality of appointments you will set from the event. You are putting a product ahead of yourself, and you are the only sale that should be made at a seminar.

"But Frank...I don't do comprehensive financial planning. I have one product to sell and that's why I do seminars."

OK...the rules are slightly different for you. Maybe you do need to spend more time discussing the specifics of your product or service. But even if that's true, the chances are that you are not the only person from whom they can buy that product or service. You have competitors who might be cheaper or have something more appealing about *their* product. I'm telling you that you are still selling yourself at the seminar. So don't make the entire evening a product pitch. Use the same emotional dynamic to connect to that crowd and they will end up choosing your product *because of you!*

Rule #7: Follow-up immediately

People always ask me how long they should wait after the seminar to make their follow-up calls and set appointments...24 hours...48 hours? How about ZERO hours!

Follow-up starts immediately. It needs to be built right into the seminar and we will get deep into that subject later. If you wait 24 or 48 hours the people will have forgotten they even *came* to a seminar. People are busy today. They have a hard time remembering what they ate for breakfast. How will they recall the way they felt at your seminar two days ago? So strike while the iron is hottest and it will never be hotter than when they are right in front of you.

But you need to do this in a professional way. A heavy-handed approach would send the wrong message at the event. We are going to discuss a specific appointment setting process that you can use at the end of the seminar and it will help you tremendously. But remember the whole seminar and the entire emotional dynamic is designed to get you in front of people in a one-on-one session. The strength of the total seminar process is what will determine your success in the follow-up.

Rule #8: Have fun!

You've got to love this game or it will be over before it starts. Seminars are a blast and your enjoyment during the presentation will be contagious.

I probably am preaching to the choir here, so I won't overburden this point. But if you truly love speaking to groups...let that passion come through. Let the audience see that you are deeply excited by the topic and the act of speaking. You are most vibrant when you can help people learn stuff that can change their life. Let them know how much you appreciate their time…not by saying those words…but by the quality and intensity of your effort.

And if you're down, tired, sick, stressed or any of the other negative energy conditions that we are vulnerable to…you must learn to control it and master it before you go on. The old saying in theater is, *"The show must go on!"* That is true for seminars as well. It might be your worst day, but it has to be their best evening…so gut it up!

Those are the basics as I see them. Stick with these and you will be ready to go to the next level.

Chapter 5

THE 9 CRITICAL EMOTIONS

"Emotion is the chief source of all becoming conscious. There can be no transforming of darkness into light and of apathy into movement without emotion."

Carl Gustav Jung

The essence of a super-successful seminar is your ability to create, tap into and control a specific pattern of emotions in the minds of the audience.

It is these emotions that will move them to action, not logic, not statistics, not facts, not great investment ideas — although all of these are used in the process. If you hit all nine, the people in that audience will probably trip over themselves in a rush to work with you. If you only hit five or six you will still be effective but the level of success drops as you reach fewer of these emotional goals.

This ability to create emotion in an audience of virtual strangers and, simply by the power of your message, motivate them to take decisive action, may be the highest level of human communication. It's a set of skills that can be attained only through proper training and experience.

In the following chapters I will break the seminar process down into the emotional building blocks that underpin the entire communication process. Then we will go into greater depth with each emotional condition and how you get there. When we're done, we will have carefully reviewed every major aspect of the seminar process from the invitation to the follow-up. You will be ready to solo.

Most seminar training programs discuss the presentation process in chronological order: Opening – Body – Call to Action – Close. We're doing it this way instead because the emotions will give you the *reasons* for doing what you must do as a presenter. Actors call it the "motivation." If you understand the emotional goal, you will transcend the rote memorization of presentation mechanics. You will begin to react creatively and intuitively. THAT'S...when things will start to really happen for you. You will understand for example, how your opening and close are emotionally connected and how you use similar themes to effectively do both. You will see why using humor in the opening is not the same as during the Q&A. It's this critical "why" that makes all the difference between an average seminar and a fantastic one.

An emotional overview

Let's take a quick look at the nine critical emotions that comprise a great presentation. As you stand in front of the audience, these are the things you want people to feel.

Like

Most critically, you want the audience to like you as a person on an instinctive, "gut" level. People do business with people they like. That's an accepted axiom of our profession and it should be the primary overt and covert goal of your seminar. If you achieve none of the other emotional objectives, getting prospects to like you will still leave you with a chance to follow-up and get them in for an appointment. The good news is that most audiences are predisposed to like you. They want you to do well...so you're starting with a slight advantage.

Understanding

You want your audience to have a clear understanding of your message without distortion or confusion. There's nothing better than when someone comes up to you after the seminar and says how clear and understandable you made everything. You've gone a step toward de-mystifying the world of money and you must be really smart to do that (or so they'll think!)

Respect

As a financial professional, you want your audience to have respect for your skill and experience. They must believe that you are someone who knows the intricacies of the financial world and can solve their problems. As a speaker, you want them to perceive you as different and more dynamic than other presenters they've heard.

Confidence

You want them to feel confident in your abilities, knowledge and judgment and have a sense that you are an expert. You want them to trust that you have their best interests in mind. You also want them to have greater confidence in their own skills and decision-making ability. This self-confidence is a magnificent relationship builder.

Happiness

You want your audience to enjoy the seminar experience and to have a great time while they learn. Also, they should feel happy about themselves for having taken the time to come to your seminar. You want to create an air of excitement and fun throughout the event. You also want to use humor where appropriate to stimulate memory, relax the audience and build rapport. Humor isn't easy, but it's a critical concept that we'll discuss in detail.

Fear

Your goal in a seminar is not to scare people…it's to make their fears go away! Years ago, during the bull market of the 80's and 90's, I found it necessary, as a presenter, to use fear as the primary motivator if I wanted people to take action. But that has changed as investors have become more confused, markets have grown more complex and the economic and geo-political landscape has become less certain.

Today, the people who come to seminars are already scared. As a presenter, you no longer need to create fear…it already exists. Instead, focus on clarifying the fear and directing it toward a positive outcome. Speakers who do nothing but frighten an audience in order to sell a product have no place in our industry. Unfortunately, scare tactics still work, particularly with vulnerable groups like seniors, but they are wrong and should be eliminated.

Action

You must outline and gain agreement on specific action steps as a solution to their problem AND you must motivate them to actually do something! Getting someone to do something is a very emotional process. Inertia is a comfortable state that is hard to break out of. Make it as easy as you can for them by doing all the emotional "machete work."

The ultimate action step for most seminars, is to set an appointment and we will cover the appointment process in detail.

Change

People hate change. Many would rather stay in a bad relationship or with a weak financial plan than switch advisors or alter their portfolio. You want your audience to recognize the need for change in their present situation and to understand that change is a normal and healthy part of any financial strategy. If they already have advisors, you want them to believe that changing to you has a specific set of benefits.

Enthusiasm

You can actually add two more E-words if you like: Energy and Excitement. These three are very similar. You want your audience to feel them and to do so, you must transmit them yourself! These will not only enhance your message and the quality of the presentation but they will boost your credibility as an expert. People respond to passion. They can immediately tell the difference between a speaker who is just reciting words and going through the motions versus one who is totally in love with their topic. With these three emotions you can move mountains.

There's a simple acronym for this set of emotions that should help stimulate your memory.

LURCH FACE

Lurch was the stoic butler from the old television sitcom The Addams Family. He was played by the a talented, though under-appreciated actor named Ted Cassidy and he very rarely spoke. His one memorable line was *"You rang?"*

Actor Ted Cassidy as Lurch

Why do we need an acronym? Well it sort of worked out that way but acronyms in general are great memory joggers. It's hard to recall a list of nine items, but a simple word can bring them right back to you.

The sum of these nine emotional mind-states is the overarching super-emotion known as:

TRUST

This is the ultimate emotional goal of the seminar process…but trust is too big to understand. It's one of those multi-faceted emotions that involves liking, respect, confidence and all the others mentioned above. I highlight it because it's the one word clients most often use to describe their own emotional state. You need to be aware of it as the defining condition and objective in their minds. During the entire seminar process they will assay their feelings about you and come to an emotional decision *"I trust him"* or *"I don't trust him."* There is only one good outcome.

Now the question becomes, *"How do you create these states of mind in the audience?"* It's time to get into the nine emotional steps. Let's examine in detail, some of the specific emotion-evoking mechanisms that you can use in your next seminar.

Chapter 6

LIKE

"Getting people to like you is merely the other side of liking them."

Norman Vincent Peale

There's an old saying in Italy, *"It doesn't matter how many dragons you slay...what matters is did you go home with the princess?"*

You may not be the smartest or best financial advisor in town. You may not even have done a particularly good seminar. Let's even go so far as to say that you completely failed to achieve every other emotional condition in this book. But, for some strange reason, the audience walks out feeling as though they like you. You could still see very positive results from the event. You will still have a chance to connect on a deeper, more personal level. They will take your call and many will even agree to an appointment.

If they DON'T like you they will find some reason on a conscious or subconscious level not to do business with you. They won't say, *"I don't like you!"* but you might hear, *"I'm really happy with my advisor."* Or *"I'm just not ready to make a move now...I only wanted information."* But the truth will be that somewhere, deep inside, they decided you are not the one.

Getting the audience to like you is a process that flows through the entire seminar. It permeates every aspect of your presentation and involves the organization of the event, the nature of the content, the energy and enthusiasm you display, the general tone of your voice, the use of humor and a whole list of other variables. But it starts with…

An exciting topic

Do a seminar on a concept that gets people's attention and is on their minds. It shouldn't take more than a minute to come up with ten interesting and timely ideas that people would want to learn more about right now. Then you can narrow that list down to the ones that get you the most excited and that you're qualified to teach without a lot of extra research or effort.

Then, you have to come up with an interesting way to phrase your idea and build your title and supporting language. Beware of using excessive hyperbole or overly-dramatic wording to frighten or excite people. You undermine the audience's trust and your own credibility when you try to terrify or bedazzle them. You simply want to say things in a memorable way that gets the message across with some emotional impact.

I'm no advertising copywriter, but here are some examples of possible ways to say the same thing. These are only my suggestions, you may have many more ideas...so use them.

Typical: Saving For Retirement

Option 1: America's Retirement Crisis & Five Ways to Avoid It

Option 2: Retirement Peace of Mind How to Get it & Keep It

Option 3: Protecting Your Retirement in Turbulent Times

Option 4: Forty Years in Retirement...Are Your Ready?"

Typical: Stock Market Investing

Typical: Understanding Managed Money

Option 1: The 7 Secrets of Professional Investors

Option 2: Dow Jones 25,000: Is It Possible?

Option 3: Bull or Bear - What's Next for Stocks & Why?

Typical: The New Tax Law

Option 1: Taxes Hurt...You Can Stop the Pain

Option 2: 22 Ways to Save on Income Taxes...RIGHT NOW!

Option 3: How to Say 'No' to Uncle Sam & Survive

Typical: College Savings with 529 Plans

Option 1: Why Johnny Can't Go to College

Option 2: Win Your Kid a Full College Scholarship —
Five Strategies for the Athletically Challenged Child

Option 3: The Grandparents' Greatest Gift: Graduation!

These may not be the best ideas for headlines but the key is to catch their interest fairly quickly. I don't think you can expect people to wade through paragraphs of stuff to get excited about a seminar. Once you have picked an exciting topic for your seminar, the next step is to develop...

A great invitation

The seminar invitation is the critical first touch...your initial contact with the audience. It has the difficult task of cutting through the mental clutter everyone has these days. Your idea needs to grab them and compel them to respond. So devote yourself to crafting a great invitation...it makes a huge difference in your overall success.

By the way, I am assuming you are using some kind of written invitation. This is not the only way to get people to attend, but it is, by far, the most common and cost-effective. So if you are serious about seminars, you are probably going to need a really strong direct-mail invitation process.

Which mail format?

There are many types of mailer invitations you can use ranging from simple postcards to full-color packages. Each one has pros and cons, but the first decision you will probably make is whether to hire a company to do the mailing for you or do it yourself. That is usually a function of budget, time and expertise.

If you go to Google and type in "seminar mailers" you will get 82,000 responses and find hundreds of companies that do this kind of work. In our industry, there are roughly five serious players in this space. I've looked at them in detail and have built a great working relationship with the folks at Response Mail Express in Tampa...which should tell you something about my favorite marketing format, but we will get more into that later. For now, let me just talk about the invitation in general as a tool to start the liking process.

Whichever mail format you use...

Your invitation must have certain elements or characteristics. Failure to consider these detracts from your appeal and may cause someone to immediately dismiss you and File 13 your invitation.

▪ Easy to read

All critical information must be presented in clear, easy to understand format. Don't make people struggle to find things like date, time, location and RSVP instructions. These should be visible from arm's length.

I also like bullet points that tell me a little about what I'm going to learn at the event. I don't need War & Peace, just five to ten quick ideas that get my juices flowing and pique my curiosity.

▪ Visually engaging

Give them something interesting to look at. Make it clean, professional and fun. Use color, simple pictures and graphics that evoke a feeling of success and enjoyment...or that tell a story in some way. Remember, the invitation is "selling" people partly on the event and partly on you too. I have to be willing to read it before it can do that.

▪ Easy to reply to

Ideally, you should give people a toll-free number they can call that is manned 24/7. The easier you make it the more likely they will reply. If you are using a return mailer, it should be a pre-addressed, postage-paid, business reply piece so they don't need stamps.

You may also include a web reply site. This is quick and useful for most folks but there are many potential attendees who are not comfortable with computers, so don't make this your only option.

▪ Your picture

Why not...assuming you're not going to frighten anyone away, but please use a professional photographer. There is an art to the "headshot" that can't be captured by your 12-year old with a digital point-and-shoot. Not only will a pro photographer make you look good with lighting, depth-of-field, camera angle, backgrounds, and PhotoShop...they can capture that twinkle in the eye that says to your audience, "I have a secret!" If you are serious about your business, get this done right.

If you work with older audiences, (the WWIIs and the Ike Generations,) remember that these folks place a tremendous emphasis on traditional family values and on teamwork. Depending on what compliance will allow...I would include a picture of my actual family or, at least, my professional team on the invitation. This might also depend on the market you're in and the demographic you're trying to attract.

For example, I probably wouldn't use my family in Manhattan or Los Angeles, but I might in the South or Midwest.

▪ *Quotes from previous attendees*

This is huge! People love to read reviews. If you think of a seminar as being similar to a movie or a play you will understand what I'm about to suggest.

When you read a movie review in the newspaper and you see *"Two Thumbs Up!"* from Ebert & Roper or *"A Blockbuster Smash Hit!"* from the New York Times, what goes through your mind? Chances are you may be a little more excited about seeing that movie. It's a well known fact that people like to know they are making a decision that others have already made and enjoyed. It's human nature. So why not use this to your advantage.

On your invitation, include some quotes from happy past attendees like:

"The most fun I've had in years."

"This was a highly stimulating and enlightening evening."

"I've been to seven seminars this year and yours was better than all of them put together!"

"Totally enjoyable...and no sales hype!"

These are actual written comments I've received from my own public seminars over the years. I've included them in subsequent seminar invitations.

To get great quotes, all you have to do is ask for them in a creative and fun way. When you do a seminar, you should always hand out an evaluation form. There's a sample in the appendix. On the bottom of the form I leave several spaces for COMMENTS and I say the following to the audience:

> "Folks, please take a moment to fill out the evaluation form. Your input is very important to me and especially your comments on the bottom. I use your comments to make these seminars better each time...so any thoughts you have about tonight's seminar would be greatly appreciated."

> "BUT...if you don't want to take the time to write any comments, just turn over to the back. I've written several comments there, just check off the one you like!"

This always gets a laugh...especially when they read the comments I've written which are super-hyperbole quotes like:

> "Greatest seminar since Moses came down from the mountain!"

Invariably two things happen: They check off one of my "comedy seed quotes" which is nice. But even better…they read the comedy seed quotes, turn back over to the front page and write something that's even better. I received two great quotes from Merrill Lynch Financial Advisors:

> "Climb Mt. Everest and at the top you will find Frank Maselli teaching FAs how to grow their business!"

and my favorite…

> "Next to the birth of my children, this was the greatest event I ever attended!"

How great is that? You can bet your boots that I use this quote on nearly every seminar invitation. I have a file drawer filled with these now.

Don't miss this opportunity to power-ize your invitations. Subliminally, you're setting the tone for the event. People will begin to like you before they ever set foot into your seminar simply by virtue of seeing that others have liked you in the past. Getting endorsements and favorable comments about your seminar is easy and it pays big dividends.

If you question the validity of this idea, just take a look at the movie pages in your local paper. You will see many such "blockbuster" comments, but a closer examination will reveal a clever Hollywood trick. Many of these movies quote reviews from some obscure source like the Online Hollywood Reporter or The Cinema Sound Bite. Many studios will even pay a second-tier reviewer for commentary.

Now you can't get Roger Ebert to review your seminar, but any comments that might get someone to think. *"Hey this person seemed to have a great time…maybe I would too,"* is all you need to get the crowd started toward liking you.

Make people feel welcomed and comfortable

The liking process starts with the invitation but then it continues with several other elements that you might not normally consider. I call these "comfort items" and they are very important. Some may sound crazy to you, but ask yourself how you would feel if someone did these things for you? I think you'll see the benefits.

▪ *Valet parking*

Before the seminar even starts…what is one thing that each person in the audience will have to do? Park their car!

So here come Ma & Pa Kettle driving into the parking lot of the seminar facility. Sure enough, if you've picked a location like a hotel or a restaurant, the place is busy and there's no parking anywhere near the front door. Maybe it's hot outside or worse...it's freezing cold, raining or sleeting! They parked 200 yards away and can barely see the main entrance. They slip on the ice. They curse and swear. They're getting wet or starting to sweat. Slowly, mild negative emotions begin to build. Who needs that?

Why not reserve parking? Talk to the management of the facility. Very often, they will be glad to accommodate you. Cordon off a block of spaces as close as practical to the door and then add the magic touch — hire a parking attendant for the evening to direct your people to their reserved space.

"Good evening. Are you here for Mr. Tentpeg's investment seminar? Park right here!"

Wow! Can you imagine the image you've created in the mind of your guests? Your role model for this should be DisneyWorld. Disney knows that confusion is a negative emotion which impacts the quality of your visit. They take what could be the worst part of your visit — parking a million miles from the front door with a hundred thousand other cars — and they make it FUN!

Now you probably can't have a tram carry your people in from the Winnie The Pooh parking lot, but the emotional message of reserved parking is big and powerful. If you wish, you may even want to make a humorous quip about the parking at some point in your presentation. I might say something like...

"Did everyone find our special parking area OK?"

[everyone murmurs "Yes"]

"We were going to name our parking lot Goofy Green like they do at Disney World, but considering our topic tonight we thought instead we'd call it Bernanke Blue!"

If you're going to go through the trouble and expense of creating this image by reserving spaces and hiring a valet, you might as well shine a small spotlight on it.

▪ *Lots of directional signs*

If you're doing the seminar at a restaurant this usually isn't an issue. But let's say you decide to hold it at a hotel. Ma & Pa Kettle have made it into the lobby and now they're looking for your seminar. But there's no sign. Or if there is a sign, it's in six point type or on one of those absurd video monitors.

So they creep awkwardly up to the registration desk and try to get someone's attention so they can ask *"Where's the investment seminar?"* knowing all the time that they're going to be made to feel stupid and uncomfortable by some clerk who is obviously busy and annoyed. Again, negative feelings before the event begins – not good! Have big signs and lots of them. Twice as many as you think necessary. Signs everywhere with arrows. Signs in the parking lot and at all possible entrances to the facility. People don't always come in the front door.

A sign is much more than something that directs people to the room. It's a symbol of organization and professionalism. It's an emotional buoy that says *"Thanks for coming and we welcome you with open arms!"* which starts the event off with the proper message.

A strategically placed sign also is free advertising to non-attendees wandering around the hotel lobby. Many times, I've had walk-ins come to my seminar just from the sign they saw in the lobby. You never know who you will bump into in a hotel lobby. Quite often, you will find business travelers who have little to do but head up to their room and watch TV. If your topic is compelling and your sign says, "Open to the Public, Refreshments Served," you may snare a few big fish. I caught one recently who invited me to speak at his company!

Avoid the last minute, magic marker on the yellow pad type sign. And since you may not know which way to point the arrows until you get there, make ten signs each with right, left, and up arrows to cover the contingencies. Then laminate them for a professional touch. You're selling yourself with every detail here, so spare no effort.

By the way, be sure to collect all your signs before you leave. You don't want to annoy the facility staff by leaving a bunch of signs hanging around. Show everyone that you are a class act, including the facility management.

▪ Decorations

Think about it...you've never been to a special event of any kind that didn't have some type of decoration. As a bare minimum, you need a nice big banner with the name of your firm for a backdrop along with an American flag in a stand. The subliminal message is self-evident.

The facility should provide table-coverings and the flag. They will often have the white linen with the side drape for the tables. Be sure they drape only three sides of the table leaving open the area where your legs go. Next to Indian Ocean barnacles, few things in life are more persistent than lint on your clothes from an improperly draped table skirt.

It's OK to have some fun with decorations. Anything you can do within reason and budget to create the feeling in their minds that they are coming to a special, exciting and enjoyable event is great. I've used balloons, pennants, set-up displays, table tent cards, streamers, and enlarged photographs on the walls.

▪ *Lighting*

Lighting should be bright enough for people to see your visuals and take notes at the same time, but not so harsh as to cause glare. Test it out. Sit at a table and try to read the screen and write a note. If your audience cannot see both you AND their own notes, they will get annoyed.

Avoid rooms with *only* fluorescent lighting. These throw off a cold, hard color that makes you look pale. They also can interfere your wireless mouse. Often, a facility will supplement the ceiling fluorescents with incandescent ceiling lights, sconces, chandeliers or rim lighting. Get to the sight early and mix the lights so that you have a proper balance of visibility and drama.

Avoid dark rooms. If the room is too dark, they will either get a headache or fall asleep. Darkness saps energy. You're not likely to get much audience interaction in a dark room. It's hard for you to make eye-contact or read their faces. You might miss valuable audience cues this way.

Do not backlight yourself. Avoid standing in front of windows or reflective surfaces. I attended a presentation at a beautiful country club on a Saturday morning. The room had a great view of the golf course and the speaker thought it would provide a nice back drop to his presentation. Instead, we couldn't see him at all. The brightness of the view drowned him out and all we saw was a dark shadow where his face should have been. If you insist on a bright background, or have no choice, be sure to light yourself from the front with a hooded flood or a spot light.

Another bad lighting technique is often seen where a speaker stands behind a lectern with her face lit only by the note light on the stand. This is far from the ideal presentation format, yet it's extremely common in those massive slide show presentations we've all attended. If you find yourself in this situation, insist on a spotlight or overhead key light that will make you completely visible without interfering with your projection screen.

In an ideal world, you would create lighting that adds a sense of drama to the presentation. If you ever find yourself in a position to deliver a presentation from a stage or custom-lit facility, you can really have a ball. Lighting makes for an exciting show. The proper design and use of theatrical lighting can enhance every aspect of your presentation.

If you start doing really big seminars, (over 500 people) or doing televised presentations, it will be worthwhile to hire a lighting director to set the lights for the event. Big rooms tend to swallow light and video shoots require lights that are a different color temperature than stage lights. It's a whole science...believe me. But we'll leave this for the post-graduate class.

▪ *Music*

I always like to have music playing in my seminar room before I start my talk. It is a well-known fact that certain kinds of background music have a positive, subliminal effect on people. It can put them in a happy, responsive frame of mind. Retailers have found that music actually makes people buy more. Gambling casinos actually tune all their slot machines to the key of C because they've learned that this is the most relaxing sound.

You might use non-vocal selections from the classical or light jazz category. Depending on my audience, I will use some vintage Sinatra or big band swing which seems to promote a positive mood. During one stretch of seminars, I actually created a musical theme that I would play before and after the presentation. I took selections from Broadway shows and movies that all had money in the theme. This was a lot of fun and set a great tone. It showed effort on my part and drew several comments from the crowd. Hey, it was unique and they appreciated it.

Whatever music you select should be played at very low volume — enough to be heard but not too loud as to interfere with conversations. Naturally, you don't want any music playing during your talk, unless you're doing a multi-media presentation where music is integrated into the presentation itself.

If you *are* doing multi-media, please invest in some good speakers. You can buy a pair that connect directly to your laptop or your iPod. That works fine for small events and rooms. As you move into larger venues, you will need a more elaborate system.

Few things are worse than bad sound, so be sure your system is up to speed. Often, hotel sound systems are old and crackly, so it's wise to invest in your own amp and speakers. I would never trust my multi-media show to anyone else's sound system.

There are several great software programs that will allow you to mix music into your PowerPoint presentations. I use one called ***SonicFire Pro*** by Sonic Desktop Software. You can find them at www.smartsound.com. They offer an entire library of different types of royalty-free music and a "maestro" program that will let you compose a musical piece of any length and type to fit your needs. It's easy and fun to do! They also come out with new tracks all the time which you can download and use immediately.

Always have food

There is some concern in our industry today with the "free-lunch" seminars, particularly within the senior market. Regulators are scrutinizing these events fearing that unscrupulous practitioners are luring retirees to their demise by offering a hot meal. Bernie Madoff and his $50 billion Ponzi scheme they ignore, but they want to close down your buffet line. It's absurd, but absurdity is often the nature of regulations in a hyper-sensitive environment. So if you want to avoid the dinner or lunch seminar for a while…I could understand that decision. For the sake of this discussion, however, I will assume you are doing high-quality, informative seminars and not trying to manipulate or coerce people into bad investments. So let's talk about food purely from an event standpoint and leave the ethics to others.

Good food generates greater attendance

There is a huge body of evidence that says holding a meeting at a 4 or 5-star restaurant will draw a bigger crowd. You may not think you can afford the $75 - $100 per head of a Ruth's Chris or a Palm, but seminars are an investment in your business and should produce a multi-fold return. If you made $50,000 every time you spent $10,000…you would never question the value of that investment. It would be better to do fewer seminars at nicer locations that to blanket your market with invitations to Denny's.

Even if you're not planning to offer a full meal with the seminar, you should still serve food of some kind. It is essential to put people in the right mood. As a minimum, I would have some individually wrapped snacks, nuts, soft drinks, bottled water, juice and coffee. You will have to develop your own approach to this but I honestly believe that doing a seminar without something to eat is a huge mistake and sends the wrong message about you. I don't care if it's just cookies and Cool-Aid…I want something to nosh on or I'm not going to be a happy camper!

You can also use food to enhance your seminar message. I did seminars on global investing and a nice accompaniment to that topic was to have a multi-national blend of snacks. You can find these in the international aisle of any supermarket and they can be a lot of fun. Even better is to provide some popular American snacks and highlight that they are made by Unilever, or Nestle or some other foreign company.

Another (slightly different) way that food can enhance your message is at a wine tasting. The guest host for these events is usually a wine expert of some kind and they will often talk about the wines you've brought to sample. They will be able to discuss various blends of grapes used by the vintner to create certain flavors. This gives you a perfect segue into the world of investing. After all, we blend different investment styles to create the customized portfolio. Except that, unlike a wine, which is mass-produced, we create a unique "taste" specifically for each client's palette. It works!

Avoid crunchy or noisy foods like tacos or messy foods like chips and dip that interfere with the audience's attention or ability to take notes.

Certain types of food reveal something interesting about the host. I attended a program where the snack foods were all healthy, granola-type, yogurty things with fresh fruits and natural ingredients. There wasn't a Twinky within five miles! The lunch was a balanced and light fare of fresh fish, chicken, veggies and whole grain rice. All of this was intended to convey a message of health and good nutrition implying that successful, intelligent people who would attend such a training program would naturally want to eat this way. There would have definitely been something incongruous with their theme if they had served pizza, burgers and fries and had chips and candy for a snack. Of course, by the second day I found this great little Philly cheese steak place a few blocks away and was happy.

What about alcohol?

Obviously, if your company has a policy about alcohol at seminars…stick to their rules. But if there is no formal policy, I would suggest you avoid alcohol entirely. Not only do you have a liability risk, but you could run into audience control issues and it's just not worth the effort.

Obviously at a wine tasting, alcohol is a featured element of the evening. These can be tremendous fun…but you must be on guard and you might want to brief the wait staff to be alert to over-indulgence. The people you are inviting are not likely to abuse the situation, but you never know. So use your judgment and err on the side of caution.

Reducing costs

Serving any kind of food can get expensive, but the facility may be willing to work with you to control refreshment costs. If you plan a series of seminars, let them know you plan to be back every month – they may cut you a break on the grub.

Skimping on food is not a good option. I went to a breakfast seminar once where the host was so cheap that they served donuts CUT IN HALF! Imagine this...*half a donut!* That would not be the right message to send your prospective clients.

When should you serve the food?

You have a few choices here, each with certain advantages. The most common format I've seen is to do the presentation first and feed them afterwards. This lets you avoid the dilemma of talking while they are eating and while the wait staff is serving. It also means that people can't skip out on your presentation after the meal. But it has one major drawback...it tends to put people in a bad mood because they have to wait for the meal. Exactly at the most critical part of your talk, they are getting anxious and starting to look at their watches wondering, *"When is this guy going to finish so we can have dinner?"*

I prefer the hybrid format of feed—speak—feed—speak. It goes like this: I will have bread and other appetizer items pre-set so that they can start eating something as soon as they sit down. After everyone is seated, I am introduced to the room and I do a power opening for no more than ten or fifteen minutes. This is a "teaser" of the seminar that gets them excited and eager to listen to my talk. Then we eat dinner. During dinner, I may table-hop and talk to people just to get the mood of the room and warmly welcome folks individually. Then, after the main course is finished and cleared, I will step back up and conduct the main body of the seminar. When I'm done, we will have dessert and coffee.

The mood created by this hybrid approach is much more friendly and enjoyable. By letting them eat dinner before the body of the talk, I can ensure that they are in the best frame of mind to listen to my story. The teaser introduction prevents them from leaving after dinner and the overall pacing of the event is more natural and relaxed. This may also alleviate some of the regulatory issues since people are free to leave after the teaser and the meal if they wish. No one is bound to stay for the seminar just to eat.

You may want to try different structure to find the pattern that works best for you. If you decide to speak first before eating, just remember not to drag your talk out too long. Waiting too long for food has a way of really annoying people. Trust me...I know eating.

Aroma

There is evidence to support the claim that in addition to music and lighting as subliminal stimuli, aroma can play a big part in creating a frame of mind in your audience. Just as you might use an air freshener in your home, you could lace the air with pine, vanilla or citrus. A recent study from the University of Michigan reported that a large percentage of men respond to the aroma of cinnamon rolls in a very positive way.

The first time I experienced this was going from Los Angeles to New York on the now defunct MGM Airlines. This was the most opulent and comfortable travel experience you could imagine with only 35 seats on the entire plane! The highlight of the trip were the fresh baked chocolate chip cookies. When they brought these out you could see everyone come alive. You would think no one had ever seen a cookie before. There was something about the smell that put us all in a great mood.

So, being a student of human nature, I tried this at several seminars. Somewhere near the end of the Question & Answer session, before my conclusion, my assistant would bring in some fresh cookies. What a powerful impact! It also was a great way to say *"Thanks for coming,"* and seemed to spark very strong positive emotions in the crowd.

If this aroma thing is too much for you just be sure the room doesn't smell bad. Cigar Aficionado may just have held a Big Smoke in your room. It's a handicap you don't need.

Sight, smell, sound and taste all add to the feeling of well-being and warmth that you want to create in the seminar. None is so critical that you can't survive without it, but with a little effort, you can reap major subconscious rewards with an audience that really likes you.

The genial host

You also get people to like you by first liking them. Before the seminar even begins, people are milling around looking you over. They can probably guess that you're the speaker because you seem to know many people, you're shaking hands and you're the only one wearing a suit...subtle clues like that.

Let them see you with a smile. You are genuinely happy that they came. Frankly, for many of you it's a downright miracle, so let that joy show through. Appear friendly, warm, cordial within the context of professional decorum. Take care not to overdo this, however. If you appear too happy or too friendly you may come off as "slick" like a "friendly" used-car salesman. You're not here to be "one of the guys," but rather remain in control as the professional who is the center of attention.

Don't get bogged down with friends or existing clients. I've seen it happen a hundred times. Mildred Gotbucks walks in, whips out her latest account statement and monopolizes your time with the saga of her lost dividend. You are not there to handle specific client problems or be buttonholed into private conversations. With a gentle reminder, most people will realize this and gladly wait until the "post-seminar social," to handle specific questions. But if not, this is where a good assistant can really help.

Have the assistant by your side during this greeting period. If any problems arise, you can hand-off to her. Politicians, military leaders and CEOs never go unaccompanied into a "greeting zone." Someone is always attached to them whispering names and deflecting potentially embarrassing situations. Besides, it looks impressive to have an aide d'camp at parade rest.

I don't recommend trying to meet and greet everyone before the event. This could drain you of crucial energy. I try to simply be visible, look important but friendly. The fewer distractions before you go on the better. If you find yourself cornered by an overly talkative guest before the seminar, arrange a code that will alert your assistant to come over and bail you out.

They're always watching you

The audience is watching you and forming opinions of you from the first second they arrive. You need to be aware of this and exhibit a calm, cool command of the event. Start by controlling your own emotions. If some unforeseen problem arises — your assistant's car broke down leaving you to sign people in, the air-conditioner went belly-up two hours ago and your room is a sauna, whatever — you need to handle it calmly and professionally.

I once saw a horrible scene that drove this point home to me quite forcefully. Here was this advisor...some Senior V.P. for a major wirehouse. The coffee was cold and this guy was angry...no not angry...he was on fire!

He grabbed the house phone to call the front desk and went off like a volcano! Not more than two minutes later, a waiter arrives with fresh coffee and this advisor attacks him like a pit bull. "I'm not paying for this coffee...you can't run this hotel...you people are idiots...we ordered this coffee for 8 AM...blah blah blah!" It was unbelievable!

He was totally unaware of the crowd that had come to complete silence while watching this embarrassing scene. It was so bad, that one couple sitting next to me got up and WALKED OUT in disgust before the seminar even started!

> *This advisor will forever wonder why no one took his follow-up phone calls.*

As people arrive, I want to exude quiet command of the situation. No last minute running around, shouting in confusion. It helps to have all the details taken care of long before anyone arrives and have a top assistant to handle last-minute snafus.

To ensure calmness in the beginning, plan to arrive well before any guests might show up. That means at least 90 minutes before the scheduled start of the event. Not only will this enable you and your staff to solve any last minute problems, but also it will avoid the problem created when Ma & Pa Kettle show up early and you're not there. I promise you this happens all the time. Someone always wants to be the first. They walk in and you're not there...the room's not set up...there's no coffee. What's going through their minds? *"Hey what fools we are. We care more about this seminar than he does."* Not good.

Always use tables

The more comfortable people are...the more they like you. A table immediately triples the comfort level by giving people seventeen extra seating positions and a place they can rest their coffee, notepad or handouts. Also, on a subconscious level, the table acts as a protective barrier and people feel more secure...so they're more likely to relax and open up.

Tables also add an element of professionalism to the event. You can pre-arrange customized note paper with the name of the seminar, your name and address on it. You can provide water and those little hard candies. These small touches enhance your stature and message.

So if you have control of the room set-up...no matter what...use tables! If you are a guest speaker, it may not be your decision, but I would tell the program people I wanted tables, particularly if you plan to speak for over thirty minutes. If your seminars are so large that you can't fit tables in the room...find a new location or split the event in two. Tables are that important!

> *On a dramatic note, tables also allow for physical flourishes like the "Table Slammer." This is where you literally pound the table to punctuate a critical point. If you're going to use the Table Slammer be careful. I did this once and hit the edge of a dinner fork which went flipping through the air...very funny, but painful!*

Seating arrangements

There are three basic kinds of room set-ups: classroom, half-round or "crescent" and "U-shaped." Each has certain pros and cons. You should visit the site before your event and determine how best to plan the room. Talk to the facility staff and make sure they understand what you want. You do not want to be re-arranging chairs 30 minutes before curtain.

Here are a few examples of the kinds of seating you will find at most seminars.

Basic Classroom Style Seminar Setting

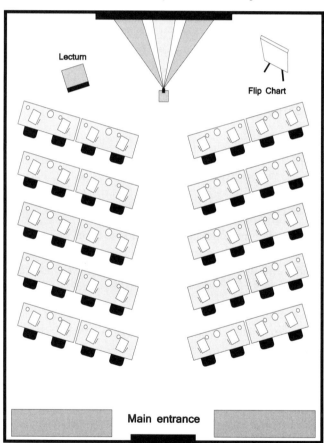

This is a typical seminar room set-up. The focus of attention is the front of the room and the screen. It's not great for audience interaction, but it gives you total control. Notice how the tables are slanted toward the middle. This is a nice touch but it's not mandatory.

I would generally use this for a training meeting where a full-course meal is not part of the program. This is common for hotels, but you're probably not ever going to see this at a restaurant.

Three-row Classroom Seating

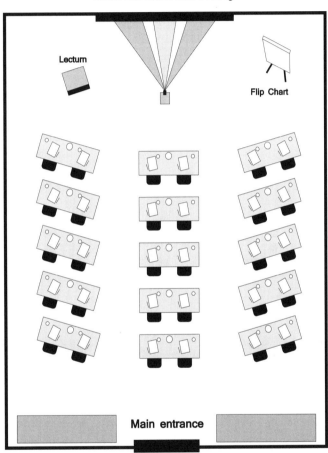

This is a nice variation of classroom that gives everyone an aisle seat like in first class on a large airliner. Try not to crowd three seats behind each table. That's tight for most American-sized audiences. The two-seat format gives people plenty of room to spread out and relax.

Half-Round Seating

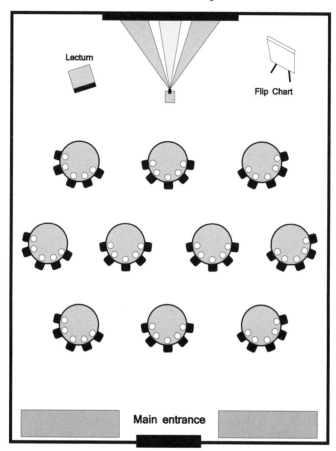

Half-rounds or crescent seating is typical for most restaurants and hotels that use the big ten-person tables for weddings and other events. Set the side facing you so that no one has to turn their chair around to see you and everyone has at least part of a table in front of them for refreshments note taking. Try to leave plenty of room between the tables for walking because you are probably going to be moving around and don't want to bump into people.

Also, note that each table is set for five. You will probably know in advance if you have all couples or any singles so you might set a few tables for six to allow for pairs to sit together.

For larger groups, you might want to consider having two screens like this.

Double-Screen Half-Rounds

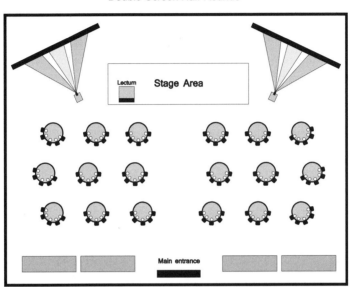

Double-screen is common for large crowds, but it's not my favorite set-up because it forces people to split their focus from me in the center stage area to the screens on the sides. But if you are getting such huge crowds you're doing something right, so it's worth the risk. I tend to do a lot of walking in an event like this.

If you ever find yourself doing a large keynote, you may be on video screens as well. Now you have a real challenge because any movements you might want to use in a stage show will be magnified by video. Talk to the camera crew beforehand and tell them to keep a wide shot. You're not going to run into too many gigs like this but they're fun and if you have one, and you want some extra help to prepare, please contact me at **frank@frankmaselli.com.**

U-Shaped or "Horseshoe" Seating

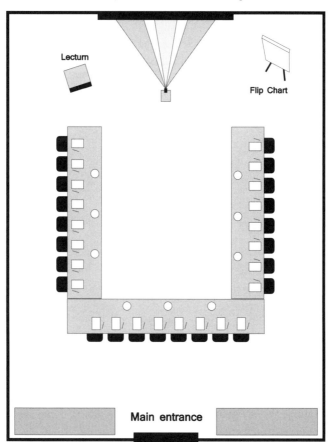

U-shaped or "horseshoe" seating is particularly effective when you want to encourage audience interaction. They can clearly see each other in this arrangement and you should work it like theater in the round making certain to include all sides in the discussion.

But beware – having people look at each other is not always a good thing. It removes the anonymity of reactions which tends to reduce the positive group dynamic. And it encourages snipers because they have a visible audience. I use this when I am facilitating a team discussion…not for general seminars.

If you have a lot of people you might be tempted to set the inner ring of the of the horseshoe…but don't do it. Now you're back to that exposed front and those people will be uncomfortable. Instead consider setting a double-U with a second layer of seats.

Double-U Seating

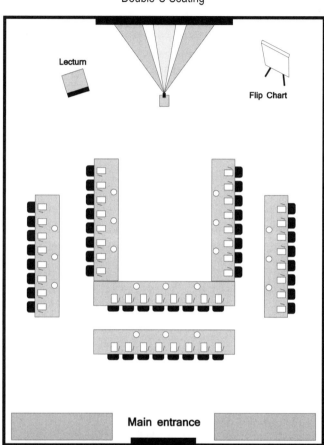

Table allow the use of props

Props, or "properties" in theater, are physical objects like coffee cups, pens, paper, whatever is lying on the table. They can be any tangible object and you can use them to make key points throughout the talk.

You can come up with dozens of clever uses for props to illustrate all kinds of investment concepts like diversification, risk, and correlation. They provide good visual humor and nearly always lighten things up a bit. It's a great way to make emotional contact with the crowd.

Treat them like gold

Getting people to like you isn't hard for most professionals in a people business like ours, but every little touch of charm, warmth and class that makes the event more pleasant for your guests will go a long way toward helping this process. So find your own style and treat these people like gold. They have come to hear you speak and in doing so have bestowed a singular honor upon you. Honor them in return with everything you and your team can do, within reason and budget, to make this the best event they've ever attended.

What about humor?

You're probably wondering, *"How can you get people to like you unless you use some humor in your presentation? Why aren't you talking about humor? AAGGHH!!"*

Take it easy. Humor is absolutely vital to the LIKE process. In fact, it's so important that it has its own chapter…so keep your shirt on.

Chapter 7

UNDERSTANDING

"We are an intelligent species and the use of our intelligence quite properly gives us pleasure. In this respect the brain is like a muscle. When it is in use we feel very good. Understanding is joyous."

Carl Sagan

The thrill that comes from teaching, from helping people understand their world a little better is a powerful enticement to do seminars.

When you see the look on someone's face as they come up after the seminar and say *"I understand!"* you'll know just how emotional a process it is for them and the feeling you get will be that reciprocal.

People are scared to death about money. They are bombarded with conflicting and confusing information every day by the media and other investment advisors and they don't know what or whom to trust. But because they fear being taken advantage of, they will often pretend they understand and this pretension hurts them in a very real, financial way.

When I do a seminar, my mission is to help the audience understand and take better control of their money. I know that many financial professionals will warn, *"Don't educate them too much or they won't come to you for help."* Quite the contrary. The smarter they are about money and investing, the more they will realize they need your professional guidance. Ultimately, the smarter the investor, (in real terms — not Money Magazine smart), the much more likely it is that our relationship can develop toward a higher level of trust. That's an ideal goal for any financial advisor.

The Hourglass Format

Understanding starts with the construction of your presentation. You need to have a clearly-defined structure into which you place all your ideas, support material, motivational themes and action steps. Too many seminars simply flow out of the speaker's mouth with no organization. These "stream-of-consciousness" talks are not likely to produce results for you or for the audience.

The basic structure you can use for most presentations is like an hourglass. You begin with broad concepts, work your way into detailed sub-concepts, facts and support items...then finish with a big picture and a review of the broad concepts. Even in the middle of your talk, when you're discussing topics in great detail, you need to come back to the broad theme. Always try to connect the details to the big picture.

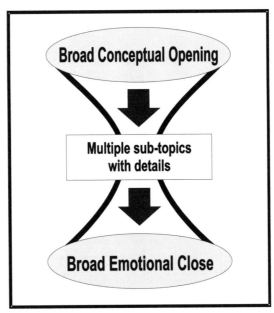

There are many variations on seminar format and you have to find what works best for you, but I have found a simple bullet-point structure centered around a main theme works best.

Here's a brief outline for a possible one-hour seminar on global investing. Obviously the subject of global investing is less controversial today than it was fifteen years ago. Most investors realize that they need to place some assets overseas...so I'm not saying I would recommend this exact seminar today. I just want you to see how I would structure a talk. You will see that the basic hourglass structure remains intact.

Global Investing in the New World Economy

1. Introduction

2. Power opening

3. The Challenge: Why are we here today?

What is the big problem we are trying and solve tonight? What are the unique challenges and benefits involved in global investing? I define two main issues here: first, the opportunity to participate in the tremendous growth and income potential of foreign markets relative to weak U.S. performance. Second, the need to properly diversify a strong long-term investment portfolio.

4. Overview: What are we going to talk about tonight?

This is a quick look at the agenda for the evening and any ground-rules about questions.

5. Main Seminar Body

- Sub-Topic #1: Why should you invest globally?

What's the potential upside? How can a proper global strategy potentially improve your performance and reduce your overall portfolio risk?

1. Greater selection of securities
2. Faster growth with a direct link to growth sectors
3. Higher income and the potential for currency gains
4. Non-correlated diversification reduces risk (maybe)
5. Movement of capital flows favors foreign markets

- Sub-Topic #2: What are the risks of investing globally?

A discussion of the risks and downside potential of global investments.

1. Normal investment risks typical of an all-US portfolio
2. Extra risks of global investing
3. How have these risk levels changed over the years

- Sub-Topic #3: How can you invest globally?

A discussion of various investment formats typically used for global investing and a look at the pros and cons of each one.

1. Individual foreign securities
2. Mutual funds or managed portfolios
3. ETFs (exchange-traded funds)
4. American Depository Receipts (ADRs)
5. U.S. companies with foreign exposure
6. Core and satellite strategy

- Sub-Topic #4: What themes should you consider today?

What are the forces and trends at work in the current marketplace and how can you take advantage of them in various investment strategies?

1. Infra-structure and development
2. Energy and commodities
3. Demographic trends
4. Country or regional expectations

6. Recap & Summary

What did we talk about? A quick look back at the major sub-topics.

7. Questions & Answers

8. Conclusion

9. Call to Action

10. Appointment close

11. Emotional close

This format gives you a basic framework within which to organize your thoughts. The body of the seminar may take different forms depending on the actual information you are presenting.

In this example, the main theme (Global Investing) is supported by four major Sub-Topics (why, what are the risks, how to invest, and themes to consider). Four is the most I will generally use. There's just not enough time to go beyond that and still leave room for the other segments of the talk like the Q&A or the Appointment Close.

Each Sub-Topic is covered by five to ten slides depending on the depth of the details. I never worry about the number of slides in a presentation. It's how you use them that matters. Sometimes, I spend several minutes on a single visual and at other times, I will race through a few slides in seconds. I will often include slides that I know I may have to skip for time purposes. That's OK...the pacing is usually determined by how well I think the people are understanding the material as I'm presenting it. This is another reason you have to pay close attention to the audience during your talk.

Basic seminar design

Logical flow

Regardless of your topic, the structure of your presentation should follow a logical path and have a clear goal. If you wander around aimlessly or go too deep into the details of any one Sub-Topic, the audience may get lost. Remember they do not know what you know. You must ease them into your world or they will walk away from your talk more confused than when they came in. By presenting your ideas in an organized manner and connecting each detail back to the big picture, you are truly helping people.

> *Talk about poor logical flow — I was doing a global investing seminar for a young FA in New York City. He was new at public seminars but was very eager to try his hand. He came to me a day before the event and said that all he wanted to do was to open the seminar by making some simple welcoming remarks and then to introduce me. I told him that this wouldn't be the ideal seminar structure for his own credibility, but he insisted and I agreed since this seemed to be all that he could handle.*
>
> *Instead of sticking to the game-plan, he got up, said "Hello & thanks for coming." and dove into a detailed discussion of currency hedging! I was stunned. I thought I was in a time warp. The audience was sitting there in shock wondering if they were in the right room.*
>
> *It took me a good ten minutes just to repair the confusion and get everyone back onto the main road. He must have focused on my credibility comment and became overly anxious to show everyone how much he knew, so he jumped into a very complex topic with no preparation.*

There's nothing wrong with wanting to look smart, except this over eagerness caused him to short-circuit the logical format of the discussion and thus risk the entire event

The exact same sub-topic or any complex discussion placed later in the seminar would have worked just fine. The audience would have had a chance to mentally warm up and his talk would have been much better received and understood. The way he did it, right at the opening introduction, it was absurd and very damaging.

The audience was immediately Lost in Space with Will, Penny and Dr. Smith never to be found again.

Whenever you have a big or complicated subject to discuss, always remember the elephant analogy. The question: *"How do you eat an elephant?"* The answer: *"One bite at a time."* If you break your talk down into small chunks and take it in logical step-by-step precision, even nuclear physics is easy to grasp.

The Six-P Presentation

If you ever need to explain managed money to a client, (i.e., mutual funds, separate accounts or wrap programs) then you need to learn this structure. I've used it for years and it has always worked for me. It's called *The Six P's* and it's brutally simple. It's been around our industry for a long time, so I'm not sure who should get the credit. Whoever did this first…nice work!

What makes it extremely neat is that it is both a framework for *presenting* managed money to a client as well as for *understanding* it yourself. In this way it simplifies your life on two levels. To get you started, the six P's are:

- **People:** *Who are these money managers; what's their background and what makes them special?*

- **Philosophy:** *Why do they manage money in this specific way? What led them to that approach?*

- **Process:** *Specifically how do they execute their investment strategy?*

- **Performance:** *How have they done over various time periods and relative to market and peers?*

- **Price:** *What do they charge and how competitive are their fees with comparable managers?*

- **Portfolio:** *How can I expect this manager to fit in with my client's overall portfolio? What will it do for the total picture in different environments?*

Many of you may already be familiar with this but if you would like to learn more, I have written a piece that should help you. You can download this from my website at frankmaselli.com.

Make it real and help them feel

Every speaker has learned the old maxim: Tell them what you're going to tell them. Tell them. Tell them what you told them. That's a little simplistic, but the basic truth of this advice is sound. For maximum seminar results, add two important sentences to that maxim:

Tell them why it's important to them.

Tell them how they should feel about it.

Everything you say should have some emotional meaning to the audience. Often, the meaning is obvious, but sometimes it's necessary to show them the meaning in very specific terms. For example, we know that diversification is important. We understand the relationship between interest rates and inflation. To us, this stuff is elementary because we live, eat, sleep and breathe it every day. To them it's like brain surgery. Investing scares the Hell out of the public and they will vapor lock easily if you don't make your talk relevant to them on a very simple level.

When the situation calls for it, go ahead and be very direct with them. If you want to be sure that they are going to understand your presentation, you might insert a brief commentary like this:

"Folks...much of what we're going to talk about tonight may seem complicated or difficult to understand. Some of it may even seem rather esoteric or meaningless to you at first. Let me just stop here for a second because this is critical."

"Everything we are going to discuss here tonight is very important to you in a real way — it all affects your money — and your money affects your life. And none of this...absolutely *nothing* we will talk about here is beyond your understanding. I will do my very best to be certain that you all are completely comfortable with everything we've got to cover. And if there comes a point in the seminar when you're 'a might bewildered' as Daniel Boone used to say...just stop me...and we'll get you back on board."

"When you leave here tonight, you will all have a better, clearer and more confident grasp of the important trends affecting your financial future. So much so, in fact, that I want each of you to go out and buy one of these flip charts and do this exact seminar at your next dinner party. You can amaze and astound your neighbors! You know...just clear the table...get out your multi-colored magic markers and go!"

This kind of a discussion may seem strange to you, but it's an example of something called *"pre-emptive emotional control."* You want the audience to feel something, so you tell them very specifically what you want them to feel...and they will start feeling it.

In the example above, you want to evoke the emotion of understanding, so you're going to plant the seed early in the seminar by telling them they WILL understand your talk. Give them a clear visual picture of the way they will feel and act after they leave the event. For this you use the zany (and very physical) image of the dinner party home seminar to cement this feeling of understanding.

Create the dragon

I like to begin the seminar by defining the problem or the *"conflict"* that brought the people out in the first place. Why are they here? What are they looking for? Are they suffering from low interest rates? Are they missing an exciting growth opportunity? Are they being buried alive in taxes? Are they trying to recover from massive stock market losses in their retirement portfolio? There had to be some emotional reason they got off their butts and came to see you . . . what was it? First, find it and then, re-define the reason for **them in your own words.**

> "Do you want to know why you're here tonight? What was it that moved you away from the TV and motivated you to take valuable time to drive here and listen to me? I'll tell you why you're here..."

Define a broad-based problem that hits a common emotional chord in all of them. This is the great thing about doing your own seminars — you get to define all the problems and the solutions in your own words. What more could anyone want?

> "Folks, you're here tonight because you a lot more time left than money! Millions of Americans are struggling with this same problem. Some of them are already retired and living on fixed income in a world where costs keep rising. Others are still trying grow a nestegg but may have endured terrible setbacks. It doesn't matter who you are or how much money you have...we are all affected by the same economic environment and the same problems. (PAUSE) Tonight, we're going to find some answers!"

Try to include every group you see in the audience. You want them all to see the same dragon so they will be simultaneously awed when you slay it right before their eyes. The good news is that you get to pick the dragon!

Unify the emotional state

The other benefit of this re-defining process takes us back to the previous chapter on LIKE. Remember we talked about audience synergy, the group dynamic of shared emotional response. When you successfully define a broad investment problem in emotional terms that everyone can understand and feel, you will have psychologically locked the audience together.

This is essential early in the seminar and should be constantly reinforced throughout the event. By bringing them together emotionally, you can use this connection to enhance and strengthen the intensity of their response to you. They will resonate as a nearly unified entity. Once this happens, you can really deliver a powerful message that will motivate nearly all of them to action.

This, by the way is one of the critical keys to the high closing rates you can experience as a result of your seminars. I'm talking about 75% or 85% closing within 90 days! That's how positive and exciting a tool this can be if you master these techniques.

Some of the most important moments in human history happen when a speaker brings a group together emotionally, and then, taking advantage of the group dynamic, leads them to action. From Marc Antony to FDR, Ronald Reagan and Barak Obama — the best public speakers have understood and used this process...and so can you. Now we can all think of negative examples as well...but I'm hoping you use your power for good, not evil.

Teach them well and they will love you

Teaching financial concepts can be easy and fun. Even the most complex subject can be broken down into understandable elements, and the process of understanding is fun because it has a direct impact on people's lives.

Teaching an investment concept to your audience can be exciting...like a mystery novel slowly revealed. Let me give you an example by looking at how I teach one such topic in my seminars. You might like it...you might not. Your style is what's important, so don't think you have to do it my way. You also might disagree with my facts or statistics. Don't get bogged down in that trivia. I'm only using this as a example of a process.

Non-correlated diversification

This is told as part of that global investing seminar. It would also work with any discussion of Modern Portfolio Theory. It's a great example of a *"visual build."*

This is a technique of combining your words with a visual aid that you draw slowly, in stages, only revealing parts of the drawing as you teach the concept.

"Folks, so far tonight, I've given you a few reasons for considering global investments in your portfolio...but now I want to show you the key to the whole thing. This is the one that gets me the most excited and I want to spend a minute on it because if you understand this...you will be a long way toward understanding how money works and how you can succeed in reaching all your financial goals."

Notice how we hit a few emotions here and how we worked back up to the major benefits of understanding how money works and reaching financial goals. I want them to see this segment as a critical part of the evening and I want to get their juices flowing.

"Let's say that you have all your money right now in the U.S. One hundred percent of your portfolio is U.S. based...either stocks or bonds or a combination...it doesn't matter. Let's draw this on the board because when you see it, the whole idea will be a lot easier to understand."

"By the way...the first person who ever drew what I'm about to show you...won the Nobel Prize in Economics...so I'm not making this up. We're going to have a graph with two lines."

Draw the vertical line, write RETURN with the arrow and pause.

"The vertical line measures the annual rate of return on your portfolio measured in percentage terms. Everyone pays a lot of attention to this line. In fact, we pay far too much attention to this line and far too little attention to this next line, but it's this next line that's most critical to your success as an investor. This next line is something no advisor likes to talk about, but it happens to be my specialty. This line...(draw the horizontal line) measures RISK!"

Now draw the horizontal line, write the word risk with the arrow. You can explain standard deviation if you wish.

"Remember we said that your portfolio is 100% in the US. For our example, let's assume you are in an index fund that matches the performance of the S&P 500...OK? Now, for any portfolio, there is a certain historical rate of return and a certain level of risk. So we can actually place a dot at the exact point on this graph that will represent your portfolio because we know these numbers very well."

Draw the dot and write 100% USA.

"Remember we said earlier that the foreign markets, over time, have outperformed the US market by a substantial margin. We can also put a dot on the graph to represent the foreign markets because we have all those risk and return numbers as well."

Draw the EAFE dot and write 100% foreign. Explain the EAFE Index and stress that it is a diversified index of several countries, not just a single foreign market. Chances are you will get questions about specific country funds or regions and this concept of a diversified overseas portfolio will become important.

"You will notice that I drew this dot further out along the risk line? Why is that? Well we all know that the greater return you want, the greater risk you must be willing to take...right? So if you took 100% of your money and invested it overseas...you would get a better annual return...but you would also be taking a lot more risk. (PAUSE) Does this make sense so far? OK...now we get to the interesting part."

"There is a line between these two points that actually shows the return and risk for any possible combination of foreign and US portfolios. This line shows what will happen as you begin to add foreign stocks to a US portfolio. The results are very interesting. In fact...it is this line connecting the points that won the Nobel Prize!"

"As we move overseas, what do you think happens to the risk and return? What does the line that connects these two points look like? Doesn't it look like this?

Draw the dashed line connecting the two points.

"This is common sense right? What happens as you reach for higher and higher return? You take greater and greater risk...right?"
PAUSE

"Well, that's what we've always been taught and that's what common sense tells us but guess what...that's wrong! Here's why this fellow won the Nobel Prize! By the way, his name was Professor Harry Markowitz from New Jersey. So some good things do come out of New Jersey."

The attempt at mild humor breaks the tension I'm obviously trying to create here. Just enough tension to get them excited and ready for the grand finale. Do not take any questions or brook any interruptions at this point. You should complete the thought in one continuous flow if it's to have the impact you desire.

"The actual line that connects these two points IS NOT a straight line...instead it curves like this."

Draw the curved, boomerang line.

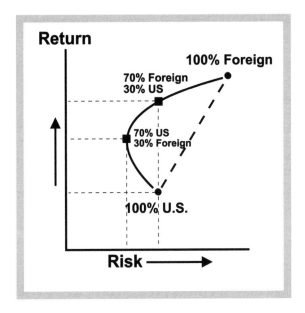

"Folks, this little curve is the key to Modern Portfolio Theory and it is the basis for proper asset allocation. In fact, it's the entire key to a secure retirement portfolio...so please follow me here."

"As we move from a 100% US portfolio slowly adding money to a foreign portfolio our rate of return goes up..."

Trace your finger along the curve.

"and what happens to our risk...our risk goes down! Until you reach a point on the curve right here where the risk is lowest, (the first square). Right at this point, the mixture in your portfolio is 70% US and 30% foreign! Taking thirty percent of your portfolio and moving it into diversified foreign investments actually gives you the lowest possible risk in a given portfolio."

Draw vertical line from point A down to the RISK Axis.

"But there's another critical point on this curve. Maybe you've already noticed it. Start right here at your 100% US portfolio and draw a straight line up to this point (second square) and you now have a portfolio that is giving you the exact same risk as a 100% domestic portfolio...BUT look what's happened to your annual return!"

Draw a horizontal line from point B to the RETURN axis.

"You have dramatically increased you annual return and taken the exact same risk you're taking right now in a 100% US portfolio."

"A lot more return for the same amount of risk...or a little added return for a lot less risk...it's your choice. But THIS is the beauty of going global and THIS is why we are here tonight."

"This phenomenon has a very technical term. We call it non-correlated diversification. It is the key to good portfolio design and understanding how it works will make a tremendous difference in your life. It is, in fact, the basis of all the work we do. And when we do it today, we're considering not just two asset classes....but fifteen. We take all these variable and we "optimize" your portfolio by giving you the best rate of return for the least risk. Not bad huh?"

Only an example

Don't panic! I know some of my facts and the shape of my curve might not be perfectly in line with your numbers. This is simply an illustration of a value-added teaching point and they right way to present a complex concept at a seminar. You can see how this discussion is easy-to-understand. Everyone in the room will be able to follow is and they will feel tremendously empowered by the knowledge.

The key is to draw the chart slowly, allowing them time to digest the spoken words while they see the corresponding picture. In most seminars, a complex visual like this would be done in one detailed slide. This forces you to explain your way through a maze of lines and dots and it makes the whole explanation very confusing to the audience. By using *visual builds*, you can take the time needed to reveal a concept slowly, one element at a time.

This style works with nearly every investment concept you might want to discuss in a seminar. Many in the audience will feel as though they understand money for the first time...and they will have you to thank for that understanding!

Use jargon carefully

Some people will caution you to *"avoid jargon!"* But we work in a jargon-rich profession, it's very difficult to avoid. Plus...jargon sets you apart as an expert with a unique language. As long as you remember that you're not talking to a room of investment bankers or CFAs, it's OK to drop an occasional industry-specific word or phrase, but you must explain it.

Today's audiences like to think of themselves as very sophisticated and knowledgeable, but they're not! Whenever you use an unexplained piece of techno-babble you create a mental fork in the road. Some people will simply lose the path and not catch up for many minutes if at all. Take the time to explain key phrases they NEED to understand to make them better, smarter investors.

Beyond the exotic-sounding *"alpha, beta, r-squared and Sortino Ratio"* some words that cause confusion include very common ones like *"equities," "the long-bond," "index," "NAV," "ETF," "yield curve," "discount or premium," "annuity"* and my favorite, the ubiquitous *"basis point."*

Most clients have no idea what a basis point is and when you say "basis point" their minds immediately race to the only other time in their lives when they heard the word point which was when they bought their home. When you buy a home, a point is a bad thing. Their minds make a primitive, limbic connection, "Points bad!" And you didn't say one or two points. You said "200 basis points!" AAAAGGGHH…they've panicked and you've lost them for a good five minutes.

The Teaching Take-away

This is the one exception to the rule of explaining jargon — a powerful technique we will discuss in the chapter on Confidence. It involves a small misdirection through the tactical withholding of certain technical information You should use this when you want to impress them with the depth of your knowledge and send a subliminal message that says, *"I am the expert and you are the public. As smart as you think you are, you can't possibly match my level of understanding."*

Check the map

If there was one thing that marked a top quality speaker from an ordinary one it would be what I call the *"audience mind-meld."* This is your ability to get into the heads of your audience and experience the presentation from their perspective WHILE YOU'RE SPEAKING! You can begin to develop this advanced skill by learning how to watch for certain clues that will tell you whether or not they're following you.

To mind-meld with the group, you have to focus on them, not on your presentation. It helps to know your material so well that you can do it without even looking at notes or slides. That's not always easy, but it's worth doing. This is one reason you should stick with the same basic seminar. By the hundredth time, you will know it cold and an be able to watch the audience almost entirely.

Be on guard for any fidgeting, whispering, yawning or looks of bewilderment. The first sign of these should cause you to check their progress or change the pace and delivery of the presentation. Positive signs like head nodding, note-taking, intense eye-contact and timely laughter tell you that you're on the right track.

One traditional technique is to listen for coughing or throat clearing. Both are a pretty sure sign that the audience is getting bored. This can be misleading, however, depending on the refreshments you've served prior to the seminar. Often, dairy foods like cheese or chocolates will cause excess moisture in the throat and lead to a spate of post snack throat clearing. If you served no refreshments and they're still gagging and sputtering, you might want to pick up the pace a bit.

In the absence of these obvious clues, It can't hurt to ask

> "Folks, is this clear to you so far? Is this concept beginning to make sense? Are we together on that?"

Don't do it every other sentence or it will become annoying, but do it at any critical juncture before moving on to the next waypoint. Often, in the middle of a detailed sub-theme of my major thesis, I will pause, take a breath (literally) and check the map (so to speak) to remind them of where I'm going with this thought.

> "OK, (PAUSE) we are looking at the relationship between inflation and interest rates. What I've just shown you is the history of inflation during the past seventy five years, so now, let's tie that into the movement of long-term bond rates. What you're going to see is an incredible connection here. This is one very important reason that we are so bullish on the coming market environment — because low inflation means continued low interest rates and low rates are great for the stock market. It has been throughout history and it will continue for some time!"

In this way, we round up all the stragglers and get everyone back onto the broad theme.

Never forget the ultimate goal

Your ultimate goal in conducting this seminar is NOT to turn the public into investment experts. It's to get them to take some kind of action — in most cases, that means an appointment. But, they're not going to do a damn thing unless they understand you.

It's OK if they don't ALWAYS understand everything you say or do. In truth, they're paying you to know this stuff so that they don't have to, and ultimately they just want to know that **YOU** understand it, but in a public seminar, where they've given their time to come hear your message, they expect you to go out of your way to be understandable.

This is not easy. In fact, many of the top industry gurus who regularly present to the public on behalf of major securities firms or mutual fund houses regularly forget this concept. I saw one well-known and brilliant expert do a public presentation recently, and it was terrible.

He stood motionless behind a large lectern in the dark to the side of a huge projection screen. His entire presentation consisted of one slide after another of these complex charts and graphs. If it wasn't for the occasional question from the audience you would have thought you were listening to an audio tape.

The audience was no smarter than when they walked in. Judging by the commentary I heard in the crowd during and after the event, they were more confused after he finished. It would have been a thousand times better if he simply talked to the audience. He had a great message but was so wrapped up in the high-brow intellectualism of his presentation, that he wasted everyone's time.

Use visuals and graphics

Visuals definitely make your presentations more understandable. People learn in many ways, but the visual reference frame may be the most important. We love to see images, watch videos and use our eyes, so I strongly recommend you use visuals of some kind.

I know some advisors who say they just like to talk through the presentation as if it were a conversation between them and the audience. That sounds very Mayberry folksy and it might be OK for a small group talk or a very short program, but I believe it's a big mistake in a seminar.

You simply need to have slides or a flip chart of some kind if you want your audience to understand your message and if you want to achieve the kind of success levels we are talking about.

The question becomes, which type of visual aid works best and how should you use them? The industry seems to have reached a comfortable and effective plateau with Microsoft PowerPoint and some of the other computer-generated shows. Overall, however, there are four basic formats for visuals in a typical seminar:

- *A PowerPoint slide show (or some other software)*
- *A flip chart or white board*

- **A paper handout**

- **A combination of the above**

Whatever you choose, here are a few things to keep in mind.

1. Don't overload the audience on visuals

Instead, use them sparingly. A good rule of thumb is to have one visual for every three minutes of presentation and to present one major point per visual. Crowding the visual with too much data makes it hard to read and forces you to deal with every subject on the slide without the benefit of controlled transitions to set up your next point and build drama.

2. Keep the graphics simple and big

It's so tempting today to use the four-dimensional floating bar charts and the rotating scattergrams. Personally, I'd scrap them all. I prefer big, bold, easy-to-see shapes like circles for pie charts and rectangles and lines. Hey, Einstein taught General Relativity on a chalkboard!

3. Keep your text bullets short

People hate bullet points that are really paragraphs in disguise. Bullet means just that — POW! No more than five words in a sentence fragment. And don't use 20 bullets on each slide. The size of the typeface must be clearly visible in the back of the room. The general rule is 24 points for every 10 feet of viewing distance. This usually limits you to six bullet points per slide.

I want to laugh at people who come in with visuals of detailed, typewritten pages of text. What are they smoking? Do they think that anyone is even *looking* at their material? Seeing a presentation like this makes me immediately vote against whatever they are asking me to do! If they can be so ignorant of basic presentation techniques…then they can't be skilled at much else either…is my thought.

4. Clear the visual before you discuss it

Whenever you pop a visual up on the screen the audience scrambles to understand what they're looking at. This creates a moment when you no longer have control of the audience...the screen does. Instead, tell them exactly what they're seeing.

For bullet points, do the same thing. Quickly read each of the bullets, top to bottom, and then go back up to the first bullet to begin your expanded discussion. If you don't do this, and instead start talking in detail about the first bullet point, the audience will begin to read down the list and not concentrate on what you're saying.

By clearing the visual, you keep them with you and you control the movement of their attention on the slide. And remember, take your time. If a visual is important enough to include in your presentation, it's important enough to handle correctly.

5. Use "visual builds" to create drama

A visual build prevents the *"read-ahead"* problem and is an excellent way to display information. With a build, each bullet point comes up one-at-a-time. Using software, you have a choice to then dim the previous bullet while you bring up the next one so when bullet #2 pops up bold and bright, bullet #1 fades to gray or some other color of lesser importance. This forces the audience to concentrate on the current bullet and stay with you, which increases their understanding.

> *Computer presentations allow builds as well as various "effects" for slides transitions and moving text or graphics. You can fly things in and out, bounce and rotate your words to create dramatic slides. Most of these effects are very distracting so I usually avoid anything more than a simple fly-in for a text build or zoom for a graphic build.*

Learning how to use builds to present information in a dramatic fashion is a very important skill and can greatly enhance the quality and impact of your presentation. Let's say you're a wholesaler presenting a money management discipline to a room full of FAs. You click to the performance slide and BAM...up comes a confused table of a thousand numbers and disclaimers so small that nobody can read it. Weak and useless! Instead, take your time and set the stage with a build.

> "OK...let's take a look at the fund's performance relative to its peers and its benchmark index. We're using the S&P 500 and the Lipper Growth & Income Average for comparison."

Good performance numbers can be a critical part of your story and a major selling point. Therefore, your discussion of those numbers should unfold in a dramatic fashion that builds excitement and helps people remember. If performance is bad, I would probably not highlight them in this way.

Here's a sample, three-slide performance build:

XYZ Super Fund Performance

	1YR	*3YR*	*5YR*
S&P 500	**14%**	**16%**	**20%**
Lipper Average	**17%**	**19%**	**22%**

Note that on Slide 1 we are only showing the stats for the S&P and the Lipper average. This is just a stage setter. Take your time explaining what they are seeing and why these numbers are important.

Now click on Slide 2 of the build:

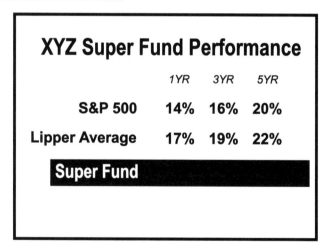

XYZ Super Fund Performance

	1YR	*3YR*	*5YR*
S&P 500	**14%**	**16%**	**20%**
Lipper Average	**17%**	**19%**	**22%**
Super Fund			

This simply brings up the fund name in highlighted background for visibility and prepares their eyes to see the numbers as they appear in that box.

Slide 3, 4 and 5 of the build brings up each performance number in sequence. The specific sequence depends on which points you want to highlight and what you're planning to say.

In the case of this fund, I want to show the one-year number first, then the three-year then finally the five-year number because that's the most revealing. It leads me into a story about the incredible consistency of management.

XYZ Super Fund Performance

	1YR	3YR	5YR
S&P 500	**14%**	**16%**	**20%**
Lipper Average	**17%**	**19%**	**22%**
Super Fund	**22%**	**31%**	**27%**

In some cases it might be better to start with the five-year number and work forward in time. Certainly longer-term performance is more important than the most recent numbers, but it's all a question of drama. You could choose to save your most dazzling statistic for the end.

Whenever you have performance or statistics to discuss that will enhance your story or help make your case, you must learn how to "reveal" them in the most dramatic fashion. It's a skill that will help you in every facet of your career. Try this visual build and note the impact it has on the audience. You will be amazed by the results.

By the way, please note how we eliminated the decimal points and kept the numbers simple and easy to read. Unless the decimal is critical to your story…don't use it. Human beings don't think in tenths of a percent. Also, there's nothing wrong with keeping the disclaimers small on the performance slide and having a full disclaimer slide later in the presentation. This un-clutters the visual.

6. Master the transitions

A transition is the presentation connector between two visuals. It's what you say after you're done with the points on the current visual in preparation for the next visual. It could be as short as a few seconds when you're using the slide projector, or much longer when you're creating the visuals with a flip chart. When using slides, the transition is as important as the slide itself.

The transitions prepare the audience to receive visual information and are very valuable as a way to increase your credibility with the audience. For those of you who are using slides and sticking to the script exclusively, the transition may be the only time when you are speaking your own words rather than merely regurgitating what marketing prepared for you. You should give much thought to the design of intelligent transition commentary and focus on the delivery using all the emotional techniques you're reading about in this book.

I recommend you avoid being a "parrot" but I also know that's where most financial professionals get their start in the world of public presentations. The sooner you can develop your own content and supplement what marketing gives you with your own words...the better you're going to do with seminars. For now, the transitions may be your only outlet, so use them well.

7. Check your visuals

Be sure that all your visuals can be seen from all points in the room. Sit down when you're testing, because the audience will be seated as well. If you need to raise the height of the projected image, you might need to do a keystone correction on the projector.

Also, check your presentation under real world conditions — using a projector in a brightly lit conference room. Sophisticated and subtle colors, shapes, images and backgrounds could cause you to lose sight of the content. Your Marketing department may be very skilled at designing evocative brochures and materials for the printed page, but those color palettes don't work on slides. There's nothing worse than a presentation that the audience can't see!

8. Proofread everything

I am hardly the poster boy for proof-reading, but carefully review all your visual material. A misspelled word or a poorly aligned graphic can detract from an otherwise excellent presentation. Don't assume that someone in headquarters has done this. If you're giving the talk…it's your job to be sure of quality control.

9. Make visuals attractive

Use colors that compliment and support your theme. People trust blue. Green calms them. They fear red and orange. Use yellow and black for bold statements. Pictures and patterns for slides and overheads are fun, but should not clutter the story.

Great visuals will indeed help the process of understanding, but you should not allow yourself to be upstaged by overly complex or flashy imagery. You are the star of the show and they are the supporting characters. Keep them in their place.

10. Use pictures carefully

Pictures are subjective elements in a presentation. They evoke different feelings in each person and their impact cannot always be accurately predicted by the presenter. The old saying is that a picture is worth a thousand words may be true. But the problem is the thousand words you *hear* when you see my picture may not be the same thousand words I *want* you to hear.

When I use pictures I stick to simple images that I can be pretty sure will evoke the message I am trying to send. For example, if I'm talking about global investing I might have a picture of the Earth from space or one of multiple country flags like at the Olympics.

11. Use video but be careful

Video is fairly common in presentations today and it can be fun. I've seen it used with great success, especially as comic relief from a dry topic. A good friend of mine is an ex-FBI agent named Jeff Lanza who gives talks nationwide on identity theft and crisis management (jefflanzaseminars.com). He uses several videos in his show and one hysterical clip is from the old Tonight Show with Johnny Carson. The famous "Copper Clapper" sketch with Johnny and Jack Webb never fails to get huge laughs.

I've also seen video over-used and the result is loss of connection between the speaker and the audience. The clips break up the flow of the discussion and cause the group to lose their place in the talk. You can actually see people wondering, *"Why are we watching this?"*

So if you are going to use videos, I'd recommend keeping them short and using them sparingly. Let's not even get into the legal issues of rights. Suffice to say that it's a complex area and you should do your homework first.

Pass around physical aids or props

These are "physical" because they are three-dimensional, real things that you have on hand as illustrative teaching tools. Two of my favorites are the magic shrinking dollar bill and the money stacks. I've seen several speakers do this but I think it originated with the brilliant industry guru, Don Connelly!

For a discussion of inflation, he pulls out a dollar bill. Then he asks the audience to give him a reasonable inflation rate expectation for the next twenty years. The number ends up to around four percent. He then unfolds another dollar bill that's attached to the first one — except this one is four percent small than the original dollar.

"Now that doesn't look too bad. But here's another four percent...and another four percent and another and another..."

Each time he unfolds another, slightly smaller bill until he gets down to twenty years worth of inflation and a tiny little dollar. This is a blast. It's so simple and yet so effective in front of a room. Immediately, they understand the effect inflation has on their money.

Turn the stack around and you've got a great way to show people how much income they're going to need in twenty years.

Another, even more dramatic example is the way he shows an audience the relative returns from inflation, T-bonds, blue-chip stocks and small-cap growth stocks. For each asset class he pulls out a stack of bills.

"What would your dollar have grown to if you had invested in Treasury bonds back in 1926? Anyone have an idea? Well...here it is. Your dollar would be worth thirty four dollars today."

He pulls out a wrapped stack of 34 dollar bills.

"What about in blue-chip stocks, like the S&P 500? Well, one dollar would be worth $1,540!"

He starts to pull out stack after stack of dollar bills piling them up right next to the puny stack of 34 dollars. There is a lot of room for improvisation during this process and you can have a ball with the audience while you're doing this.

"Well if those are blue chips, what about small-cap companies. I'll see your $1,540 and I'll raise you one...two...three...four...five thousand dollars."

Now, he's got a monster stack of bills...and the audience's complete attention. These are marvelous ways to drive home certain points in your seminar.

Physical aids can also include stock certificates, newspaper articles, foreign currency or actual products made by the companies you may be discussing in your presentation. Often, the simpler...the better.. Postage stamps work perfectly for Nick Murray, the legendary author, speaker and financial industry strategist. On the back of his business card he laminates two first class postage stamps — one from 25 years ago (13 cents) and one from today (42 cents). His clients are able to immediately see the effect of inflation on their everyday life.

When I do global investing seminars, I buy several dozen common items made by foreign companies that the typical person would be very likely to find around the house. I arrange these on a table in the front of the room and refer to them throughout the event. Afterwards, I give them out as fun little prizes.

This little display costs me $50, but by showing people that the products they use every day are made by foreign companies, I help them realize that global investing is not an arcane strategy.

One of my favorite physical items is a die-cast model of a Hummer which I use this to illustrate the concept of a multi-disciplined, diversified portfolio.

"Folks, I'm passing around a little toy model of a very interesting car…the Hummer! This has a lot to do with investing in today's markets and I'd like to share an idea with you for a minute."

"These are very popular vehicles today, not because everyone is going off-roading, but because people like the strength, safety, capability and protection these SUVs provide."

"That's the exact idea of a well-diversified portfolio! Take the Hummer for example. This is the top of the line SUV. It costs over $100,000 and has some amazing abilities."

"So let's carry this metaphor a little farther. Can a Hum Vee go as fast as a Ferrari? No! Is it as comfortable as a Mercedes S600? No. Can it carry as much as a pickup truck? No. Does it get the same gas mileage as a Toyota Hybrid? No. But what it *does* is combine elements of all four of those vehicles into one"

"If you're an investor today, your money is on the road 24 hours a day 7 days a week. You can't hide it under a mattress. It has to get out there and work. But by doing so, it's exposed to all kinds of risks and uncertainties. We never know what the weather or the road conditions will be like. Sure, we've seen a great Bull market, but we've also seen that markets can change with very little warning…like the weather!"

"When investment conditions get icy it's nice to know that one or two of your wheels are still gripping the road. If you hit a pothole or get a flat, your four-wheel drive independent suspension keeps you in control. I want an investment vehicle that can get me safely through to my goals no matter what happens to the markets."

This may sound goofy, but that Hummer model helps everyone understand the point with near perfect clarity.

Reinforce your message with handouts

Handouts are great for two reasons: they can be used during the seminar to keep the audience mentally involved with your talk and they act as memory aids after the seminar or a segment of the seminar is completed.

Use customized handouts as notes relieving your audience of the need to write too much during the presentation. Control the distribution of these handouts very carefully because you don't want them to read ahead of you. Give them out after you complete a discussion segment and then quickly review the handout noting key points. This works great and it allows them to stay focused on you.

In addition to note-type handouts you might include some or all of the following items:

- **Customized note paper (see Appendix)**
- **Prospectuses for any of your investment ideas**
- **Your own newsletter**
- **Company research reports**
- **Copies of pertinent third-party articles**
- **A bio sheet on you**
- **A bibliography of reading material on your topic**

For special audiences where you really want to generate involvement and deep understanding, use a story board workbook (see Appendix). This is a booklet in which you've got miniature pictures of the actual slides you're using with space at the right of each slide for them to take notes. The storyboard workbook allows the audience to follow your presentation in detail from point to point. In the PowerPoint print menu, select "Handouts" and it will print these for you.

The benefit of this kind of approach is grounded in psychological research that says, when you really want someone to learn something, get them to write it down. The process of transferring knowledge from right to left brain increases retention by upwards of 90%.

Admittedly, this is not for every seminar, but if you're making a detailed presentation to a board of directors pitching for a $500 million pension plan, and you know you're only going to get one shot at helping them understand your message, this level of sophistication may be warranted and very valuable.

Audio CDs & video DVDs

Offering an audio CD or a DVD of your presentation to attendees is a great way to reinforce your message long after they've gone home...and it can be a super source of referral business. This is standard practice at all the major conventions and trade shows.

Video is more difficult and expensive, because you're going to need two cameras at least if you're doing the shoot correctly. One will be a master shot on you. The other will capture special shots of you and of audience reactions while you're talking. For those of you at the top of your craft, I strongly recommend this as a powerful differentiation tool.

Record your seminar

When people notice that you are being video or audio-taped, they assume that you are important. Simply by wearing a lav mike or having a recorder in the room, you have elevated the perception of quality and respect in the minds of the audience. The implication that your words might have impact beyond that room and that one event lends an air of power to your presentation.

The final benefit to taping yourself is for training purposes. Every great athlete and performer watches or listens to themselves on tape. You are no different. If you feel the need to improve your skills, you should be taping everything, including phone conversations. Self-improvement begins with self-understanding.

Technology makes recording yourself so easy that there are no excuses. For audio, get yourself a small digital recorder – Olympus , Sony, Panasonic & Marantz all make a device that will record CD-quality sound and still fit in your pocket. The biggest issue is sound quality. Do not place the recorder on a table facing front and hope to pick up good sound. You end up with a lot of room noise and it's virtually useless as a review tool. Instead, get a good wired or wireless mike and attach it to the center-line of your body on your tie or shirt about six inches down from your chin. You may need to experiment to get the best result.

Video is the best analytical tool for seminars, but it's harder to implement. If you are really serious I offer a seminar evaluation program where I will analyze and critique you in excruciating detail. It's not cheap but it can cut about ten years off a trial-and-error learning curve.

Chapter 8

RESPECT

"If you want to be respected...you must first respect yourself."

Spanish Proverb

Respect is the critical foundation of every great relationship.

In a seminar, you want to convey an image of importance, power and knowledge. You want the audience to respect your abilities and professional judgment. You want them to feel fortunate and special to be at your event and ultimately to be your client. But you want to do all this WITHOUT coming across as a pompous, blowhard with an overbearing ego!

In nearly all cases, the amount of respect you generate in any given audience is directly proportional to the quality and emotional impact of your presentation. In short, the better your seminar, the more they will respect you as an investment professional...and the more they respect you, the better your results will be.

This rule doesn't apply to all financial professionals. For example, portfolio managers and technical experts are often judged on an inverse scale of speaking ability. Some clients actually like this "Nerd Factor" – believing that the worse they are as communicators, the better they must be as managers. Overly polished or excessively outgoing PMs sometimes come across as slick and may warrant caution. It's a strange world.

Why respect?

Part of my thinking for this approach is admittedly philosophical. I don't believe a meaningful business relationship can ever develop unless the clients respect you and your professional abilities. But in today's competitive world, we face tremendous forces that tear away at the respect for our profession.

The media consistently feeds the "don't trust anyone" mentality and erodes faith in professional advice. At times, we've done a pretty good job ourselves of undermining credibility in our own profession. The net result is that many investors who need your help do not seek it or accept it when it's offered. You may even find that your advice and recommendations are being questioned more frequently by many of your top clients.

Thus, in a seminar environment, and in business itself on a broader scale, you cannot expect to command respect by your mere presence. Instead, your actions, words, delivery and emotional effectiveness must earn respect over time.

The good news is that the audience WANTS to respect you. So you're already halfway there. And then there are several specific techniques that will build a climate of respect and significantly increase the likelihood of turning your audience into life-long clients.

Start with a good introduction

An introduction seems too basic a concept to warrant much discussion but, in fact, it's an important theatrical device for setting the tone of respect for the entire seminar. No speaker of substance or authority would ever jump up on stage without a proper introduction, so don't you do it either.

The introduction has a physical benefit as well as a psychological one. It acts as a buffer during the often noisy transition phase at the beginning of the meeting. People are talking, eating, moving around. Dishes may be rattling as the wait staff is busy clearing tables. The Star of The Show should not try to talk over that activity. In musical theater it's called the overture — something to let everyone settle into the proper mood for the spectacle to follow. You're the spectacle here, so be introduced.

The introduction may also be the place to make any administrative announcements such as parking validation, bathroom locations, or the use of recording devices. Don't be the person making "housekeeping" comments.

Who does it and what do they say?

Ideally, the introducer would be someone of prestige like your manager, a fellow advisor or someone known to the group, but it can be anyone with some "stage presence" and an audible voice. You may have a very capable assistant or you might consider partnering up with a colleague to handle introductions at each other's seminars. You can also ask a client or friend in the audience to do your intro. Assuming they don't throw you under the bus, that can be an effective endorsement. I've seen it work very well.

In any case, practice the introduction just as you would any other part of the seminar...it's that important. It should be smooth and energetic and less than one minute. A well-done intro should also build a sense of anticipation and excitement in the audience. Something like this:

"Ladies & Gentlemen, "Thank you all for coming tonight. (PAUSE) This is a very exciting and confusing time in the world of investing. Today, many people are facing some of the most important financial decisions of their lives — and they're asking questions. (PAUSE) Tonight, we'll try to give you some answers and clear up some of the confusion."

(This is a transition. Smile and deliver this casually but with enthusiasm.)

"You are in for a very EXCITING and ENJOYABLE evening."

(speak slowly)

"Our guest speaker tonight is a (title) with XYZ Incorporated. He brings with him some very impressive credentials and experience."

(Two or three bullets on who you are and your more important credentials.)

Don't worry. Even if you never graduated high-school, or just passed the Series 7 last week, you can find one or two credentials or worthwhile items of experience to mention VERY briefly. Or, go with #2 below.

"He brings with him a unique and dynamic perspective to our profession and we're very excited to have him here tonight!"

Yeah, the perspective of someone who has no clients yet...but they don't know that!

"Please welcome (pause) Joe Tentpeg!"   or

"It's my pleasure to introduce (pause) Mr. Joe Tentpeg!"

Now that's nice! You've set the audience up for your entrance with the appropriate amount of enthusiasm and prepared them for a very enjoyable session. Have you gone overboard? I don't think so. None of what we said was too obnoxious or distasteful. Isn't it better to be introduced like this than how I was once introduced at a Lion's Club meeting back in my early days. I'll never forget it!

"OK...listen up everyone. We've got a guest speaker here tonight. His name is Frank Mizooli...Frank Marsachi...some guinea name like that!

No kidding! It gets worse...

"He's gonna' talk about the markets or the economy or something like that. He's a stockbroker...so you better watch your wallets cause he's probably gonna' try to sell you something!"

"And after he's done we've got the ladies auxiliary with the cookies in the back and the fifty-fifty raffle. So let me turn it over to him...and maybe he can hurry it up!

Wow...doesn't that get you pumped up?

Always end on your name

The professional introduction always ends on your name. *"Please welcome...Joe Tentpeg!"* This is much more dramatic than leaking the name early in the introduction. You want the name to ring in their ears while you move to your place.

At your own seminar, the introduction should be memorized. It's less effective if the introducer has to read your credentials from a note card, especially if they're supposed to know you. They should also avoid tired phrases like *"let me turn the meeting over to..."* In Toast Masters, we had to pay a $5.00 fine if we ever said those words.

Use an introduction card for groups

If you are the guest speaker at a club or banquet, the introducer may not know you nor have had time to do much research. Give them a 3x5 card with bullet points of what to say. I will suggest that they are not limited to what's on the card so if they want to say something nice on their own...that's fine. But they will appreciate the card...I promise you. Bring two or three introduction cards with you. Often, the person doing your introduction may change at the last minute and you want to have another card ready for them.

Sample Introduction Card

Introduction Card for

Joe Tentpeg

- **Senior Vice President with Blowhard & Boggle**
- **25 years experience as a Certified Financial Planner**
- **A specialist in Retirement Planning and the author of numerous articles on investing**
- **Member of the ICFP, IMCA, NASD, NSA, CIA and FBI**
- **One of the leading experts in _____**

For those of you who might be wondering about that last bullet, let me pound the table for a second. Don't ever hesitate to say that you are an expert. To the public, and particularly to your audience, you damn well better be a specialist in the topic or you shouldn't be there speaking in the first place. And to carry that a step further — what the heck are you doing in the investment business at all if you're not an expert?

I know it's popular to be humble and to downplay your knowledge, but that's the first thing you've got to stop if you plan to be successful with seminars. I'm NOT saying that you should exaggerate, boast or overdo any of this. You don't need to. Compared with 99.99% of the U.S. population, you ARE an expert in this field, so be proud and use it to your advantage. Your self-confidence in your own abilities will evoke respect in others. No matter how casual, comfortable and down to Earth this audience may appear, they want to hear expertise, not rambling opinions from some "civilian" no smarter than themselves.

Find a connection to the audience

It's always nice to uncover something you have in common with your audience. If you are doing a seminar for a club or other organization you might insert a line into the introduction that will help bond you to the group or lead you into an opening. Years back, I was doing a seminar at a local sportsman's club. In my introduction I added that I was *"a member of the Amateur Trapshooting Association."* This was a true statement that allowed me to connect to the crowd and open in a relaxed mode.

Use a title

If you have a title, now is the time to use it. Titles sound impressive and may also highlight your qualifications. The introducer should speak your title slowly and with appropriate awe. Don't skimp on the verbal emphasis here. Words like "First Vice President," "Member of the prestigious Chairman's Circle" and all the other grand attachments that accompany your name must be enunciated with energy.

Perhaps you're the Retirement Plans Coordinator or a club-level producer, whatever. Use them...they work. You should orchestrate the mixture of titles in your introduction to end on the most impressive sounding one. Play with this and have some fun.

If you don't have a title, get one. Become a product coordinator or office specialist or something. Get your CFP or CFA or CLU or whatever you can that adds professional value to your career. Not only will you have something powerful to say in your introduction, but more importantly, you and your clients will benefit from the knowledge gained.

The introduction fulfills their expectation

I know that I'm beating this introduction stuff into the ground, but remember, the seminar is an emotional process. Every audience has certain expectations when they attend an event. From experience, they know that the more important the speaker, the more polished the introduction.

They expect this. Do less and you're cheating them of this emotional fulfillment and diminishes your stature, not disastrously, but a little bit. I'm not suggesting you play "Hail to the Chief," but I can't over-emphasize the power of subtle and subliminal processes like this.

Remember, it's not the introducer's job to OPEN the presentation; just to tell the audience a little about you and to set you up for YOUR opening. The introduction starts the emotional train moving, it gets them excited about YOU and makes them feel glad that they came to your seminar.

Sometimes, a good introducer will be able to say things that you wouldn't want to say about yourself...BUT that you would like the audience to know. I often work with one wholesaler who introduces me at meetings. He does a fantastic job and always mentions my MENSA membership in the intro. Now MENSA is no big deal, but the way he delivers it with a blend of humor and seriousness has everyone ready to hear from "the only certified genius in the industry!" It's fun, it enhances my credibility...and it sets me up for my DENSA joke.

The opening minute

Beyond the introduction, the first minute or two of your seminar is a very important time for generating respect. You should focus on these key points when you craft and deliver your opening.

A dramatic moment

The introduction has ended and you begin to move to center stage. Now pause for FOUR SECONDS and don't say anything! This immediately creates a sense of anticipation and drama. This four-second pause will do more to gain control of the room than any words you could say at this point. Also, the first impression is definitely a visual one and you've got to give the audience a chance to look you over. What are they looking for?

Height and posture

Sister Campanelli used to smack me daily for slouching. She said that posture is important and she was dead right. When you take the stage, stand straight, don't slump or slouch. People respect height and a sharp bearing.

If you're already tall, that's fine. If not, don't be afraid to use a riser. This is a heavy-duty plywood platform usually four feet wide, by eight feet long and ten inches high. It's often covered by a noise-dampening carpet. You can use one riser at the podium or create an entire stage effect with multiple risers in the front of your room.

I love risers. They make me feel majestic. One problem I've encountered with them, however, is noise — they have a tendency to squeak and wobble when you walk on them. I recommend that if your planning to use risers, check them out before starting the seminar. A shaky platform will distract the audience for the entire event.

Dress for success

Look like a successful business professional. How's that for vague advice? We could spend a day discussing this, but I will pay you the courtesy of assuming that you are polished and presentable in your appearance.

As for clothes, one school of thought says you should dress on par with your audience to make them see you as one of them. Others say you should dress to the nines to set yourself apart from the crowd. I have a simple rule for dressing the part — be neat, be clean and be yourself. A pressed suit is the standard dress uniform for both men and women in a public seminar. Beyond that, it becomes a matter of taste.

Maybe you're one of those "roll-up-your-sleeves" kind of speakers. That's fine and you will see politicians do this all the time. Remember, it's better to start out looking formal and get more casual as the drama of the meeting unfolds. Unbuttoning your jacket, even loosening your tie are excellent tools for dramatic effect if used properly. You can't go the other way — starting casual and dressing up as you go.

If the goal is RESPECT, just ask yourself, *"What does the ideal, textbook investment professional look like?"* Allowing for wide variance in body-type, always look professional, clean and crisp…enough said.

The Power Opening

The first words out of your mouth are critical for gaining emotional momentum with an audience. Choose these words with care and master the delivery of the opener because at no other time will the audience be as open to impression as they are right now. Slow down, take your time, be in control yourself and you will quickly gather control of the room.

There are many ways to open the meeting. Some like using humor, others prefer a dramatic "let's get right into it" kind of approach. I will very often use a "shocker" or a dramatic paragraph that sets a very exciting tone. It lets them know that they're in for a fun ride and I've got a firm hand on the tiller.

Depending on the mood you want to create you can start boldly or more relaxed. But whatever you do, be decisive and MEMORIZE the opening. Eye contact is critical. We can debate the merits of speakers who use notes vs. no notes. It doesn't matter if you are planning to read to the crowd from the phone book, the opening must be smooth, controlled and you should deliver it with direct, non-scanning contact.

A "scanner" is someone whose head constantly swivels while talking. They're looking in the general direction of the audience, and it may seem like eye contact, but their eyes are "watering the lawn" with glances that don't linger long enough on any one person for contact to actually be made.

Instead, find a pair of eyes, slow down, focus and deliver an entire thought to that one person. The power is enormous. Not only will that person feel a direct bond with you but people in the immediate vicinity will think you're talking right to them and the effect spreads.

Avoid the boring opener

Skip the common, obvious, trite or tiresome opener. Leave those to your competition. Let the first words out of your mouth carry lots of power and impact. For example, instead of saying,

> "Thanks for coming Ladies & Gentlemen. I'm here tonight to discuss retirement planning..."

Try something like this:

> "There are fifty people in this room right now. Twenty years from tonight...forty-six of you will be financially dependent on the government, flat broke, living on food stamps or worse yet...living with your children. Only two of you will be completely independent financially. Who is it going to be?"

That gets the blood pounding in their ears.

Here is one of my standard openings for a generic seminar called "Investing in the New Millennium" as an example. It starts cold...these are literally the first words that come out of my mouth after I have moved into position and let the audience look me over in silence for a four count.

The words themselves are spoken with a slow and deliberate pace...almost as if I'm searching for them individually. The emotional content is evident. Also, if you're nervous...the opening is where it will show. Slowing down the pace is not only a very dramatic technique, it helps keep my own nerves under control.

> "The vast majority of people today (PAUSE) are confused and troubled (PAUSE) about this economy. (PAUSE) They feel bombarded by the media, bullied by sales people and bewildered by the million things they need to know to survive in this financial jungle."

Nice...bombarded, bullied and bewildered. That's called alliteration and I'm way too fond of it. Now the pace picks up a bit and the volume rises...a bit more strident delivery.

> "Over the past few years investors have seen all their beliefs about money and investing fly right out the window. They know they can't live much longer on 2% rates and yet they're scared, and hesitant to make crucial decisions. And, to make it worse, right now...90 million

Americans are faced with the most critical investment challenges of their lives!"

Pause...let all that sink in for a minute. Make a mini-transition here.

"Tonight, we are going to shed some light on this darkness. We are going to break this problem down and analyze it carefully. (pause) And when you leave here (pause), you're going to have a very clear view of the choices open to you. You're going to feel much more confident and prepared to meet all the financial goals you have."

"Above all, you're going to be a little smarter than when you came in. You're going to understand WHY things happen in the financial world and specifically what you can do about them — and we're going to have a little fun in the process. That's a lot to accomplish...so let's get right to it."

Notice all the emotional hot buttons we hit — we said people are scared, confused, troubled and hesitant. Then we led them toward confidence, "smart-ness," understanding and fun. This is the whole seminar in a nutshell. In fact, that opening is a microcosm of their entire relationship with you.

Practice your opening until it's smooth and can be delivered with proper emphasis and dramatic flair. If you're going to be monotone and boring, please wait until the body of the presentation. Make the opening powerful!

The Shocker

The shocker is a surprise or unexpected opening. It's not easy to pull off with flair but when you nail it you can really set an exciting tone for the entire evening. Here's a simple shocker you can use in nearly any seminar:

Walk up to the podium and don't say a word. Once again, pause for a full four seconds. Now, reach into your wallet and pull out a $20 bill.

"Who can tell me where the market closed today?"

Hands will go up, people will laugh. You're giving someone a chance to show off. They assume you're going to give the twenty to the person with the correct answer, but wait.

"Anybody?"

Someone will invariably throw out a number very close or right on the market close. Start walking over to that person, very slowly.

"OK...now who can honestly say they have no idea where the market closed? Be honest."

More relaxing laughter and someone may raise their hand.

"Excellent!"

Stop...move quickly to that person and give THEM the twenty!

"I bet you all thought I was going to give the twenty to *him*."

Point to the person who guessed the close correctly.

"Folks, I've got some news for you...the winners in the world of investing are the people who know and obey the First Rule of the Serious Investor — Get your head out of the day-to-day and THINK LONG TERM! If you are glued to CNBC, worrying about how your stocks are trading or where the Dow closed on any given day YOU ARE DOOMED! That's the first exploded myth of the evening...we'll blow up a few more before the night is out!

Then move into your basic opening.

This kind of opening says the speaker is a fun, exciting, dynamic and creative person. If you're in the audience, you're wide awake and ready to have a great time and learn some stuff you never thought you would in your typical boring investment seminar.

There are many forms of the Shocker opening. Another dramatic opener involves the use of props. I love to use money in my opener because it reminds people of exactly why they are there.

Without saying a word, take a dollar bill out of your pocket. Hold it up for the mandatory four-second pause and then begin...

"Do you know what this is?"

Allow five or ten seconds of drama to build. Move ahead slowly.

"You may THINK it's a dollar bill...but it's not. (PAUSE) It's your entire retirement nestegg! All the money you've saved up until the moment you stop working. Here it is! Your IRAs, your 401k, your investments, your pension, Social Security, the equity in your home...everything!"

You've got their attention now.

"At some point in your life...this is what you're going to be living on and the chances are that you want to do everything in your power to protect this money. But let me show you what's happening to this money while you're not looking."

Take out a pair of scissors or just rip the bill as follows:

"Every year the nest egg is eroding. Piece by piece."

Snip off a small corner, then another and another.

"The government wants its piece."

Snip off one third of the bill.

"Inflation wants its piece!"

Snip off one half of what's left.

"The kids move home...and they want their piece."

Cut the remaining segment in half.

"Then the market craters...and millions of Americans are left with no margin of safety and a pack of trouble. This is why we are here tonight. To show you how you can stop the bleeding. Let's get started."

Visual, dramatic, powerful and fun. You have also used very physical concepts in the opening. In fact, what you've done without realizing it is connected with the visual, auditory and kinesthetic sensory reference frames all at once. This is like a three front attack on their minds. With an opening like this, there's no way they can ignore you even if they wanted to. You've got their attention. They're excited and under your control.

In short...to create a feeling of respect, do something different, exciting and something that shows an audience that they are about to embark on a stimulating and enlightening ride. Find a way that fits your style to open a presentation using some of the techniques we've discussed. You will see immediate results.

Respect is ultimately a mental attitude

Before you can become a truly effective public seminar presenter you've got to firmly *believe* in your own value — that you are an expert who can truly help solve people's most important financial problems. I recall many times doing seminars with young advisors. They would be nervous and jumpy and all giggly. They couldn't wait to get out there and prove to everyone how young and inexperienced they were.

I wanted to grab them by the collar and shake them. Stay focused...you're not some goofy college kid anymore. These people have come to hear you speak about their money. This is the time to demonstrate some presence and assume the role of a professional.

An audience wants to respect you. You're the speaker and for an hour or more, their leader! We are conditioned from childhood to respect the person in front of the room, so you're starting with a built-in advantage. All too often, however, we allow our own lack of confidence to show through and this damages the presentation and along with it, your chances for any follow-up.

I'm not saying that you can't be human and natural out there. All I suggest is that your moment in front of an audience must be wrapped in a self-assured, professional demeanor. This is the time to shine. Expect greatness and it will come. Expect failure and guess what?

Lord knows none of us would be in this business if we didn't have a pretty high degree of self-confidence already, but speaking in front of an audience has a way of making you doubt yourself. There's no way around it except to reach down deep inside and draw on those feelings of pride and confidence that got you here. They will not let you down.

Speak as an authority

Being seen as an authority figure has a tremendous impact on both Respect & Confidence. Some of you are going to disagree with my advice. All I can suggest is that you try it and see the results for yourself.

When you stand in front of a room and give a presentation, you may have a lot of people behind you who are not seen by the audience. I'm referring to people like your firm's economist, market strategist, portfolio managers, experts and geniuses who make the big calls.

Their insights may be very valuable in the creation of your presentation — BUT — in a seminar, always remember that it's YOU they've come to see. Every thought out of your mouth should be YOURS. Unless you are specifically referencing another professional's work, you should take ownership of all the opinions, theories, advise...everything.

Your goal is to get the audience to buy YOU...not the rocket scientists back in New York or the market gurus who give YOU advice. Those experts are not here doing the seminar. They are not the ones who will have to take the concerned phone calls when the market drops, hold the client's hand through tough times or convince a reluctant client to take action that's clearly in their best interest.

Sure, if you are part of a large company, you want the audience to know that you have a team of experts on your staff backing you up in case you need help. But YOU are the cog in this wheel and everything revolves around you.

It all comes down to a very subtle shift in the way you say certain things. Let me give you a simple example of what I'm talking about. Here are two ways to say the same thing. How do you feel about them?

1. "My firm believes that inflation is not likely to be a problem over the next four to six years. Our Chief Economist, Dr. I. C. Dimly is calling for two percent through the end of the decade."

2. "Everything I've seen and the work that I have done indicates to me that inflation is going to be roughly two percent over the next several years. Economist consensus bears this out and all the data shows that inflation is well under control."

The difference in the words is slight, but it leads to a major difference in how you are perceived by the audience.

Version #1 alludes to a Chief Economist and "your firm." Your role in this inflation analysis is that of a reporter, not an independent thinker. With #2, you are in the center of the process. The "everything" you may have seen and the "work you've done" is the exact same report from the Chief Economist, but the way you're saying it now implies that YOU understand and can reason through complex economic analysis. It creates a whole different picture — one that yields very powerful results when it comes to building relationships and your overall business.

You have a right and an **obligation** to impress the audience with your knowledge and ability. I'm absolutely NOT saying that you should claim credit for the ideas and effort of others. But we live in a great big universe of information. In our industry, reality is fleeting and truths change every day. In the midst of this confusion, the audience must believe that you are much more than just a spokesperson or an observer. You are an independent thinker with your own set of beliefs and analytical tools.

You may find, as I have over the years, that the bond between a client and an advisor is more valuable and longer lasting than that between an advisor and the firm they represent. I hate to put this so bluntly, but the company name on the door may change a dozen times in your career and there is very little corporate loyalty anymore. The connection you make with your clients – the one that is going to start right at this seminar tonight – must transcend any temporary corporate affiliation. So speak for yourself.

Using guest speakers

Many advisors do seminars with guest speakers like annuity or mutual fund wholesalers or portfolio managers. I have no problem with this...I've done hundreds of them myself and they can enhance your image as a "connected" professional if you do them right. But too many advisors simply stand up and say *"Hi everyone, thanks for coming. Here's Joe Expert."* And then they sit around a month later swearing that seminars don't work.

Bracket the speaker

No matter how important or dynamic your guest speaker may be — YOU must be in control of the seminar if you expect to do any business from the event. You should position the guest speaker a specialist or expert who works for you. They are part of the team backing you up. This is a process I call **"bracketing the speaker."** It goes like this:

1. Someone introduces you to the audience.

2. You do a power opening and as much of the body of the seminar as appropriate.

3. You transition to the guest and introduce him.

4. The guest speaks.

5. You come back up toward the end of the guest's presentation, (at a pre-arranged moment) and begin the Q&A session.

6. You run the Q&A session directing questions to the guest and answering those you can handle. You rephrase the questions as needed and steer the guest in the direction you want them to go.

7. You dismiss the guest with a very warm thank you.

8. You do the appointment close, the power close and end the seminar.

You want people to think that you are the center of a solar system of experts and specialists and that you have the power to deliver these experts to your clients. In fact, the only way they can access these experts is through you.

Open, close & Q&A

You can vary the bracketing process a bit, but you must deliver the opening and closing segments of the seminar. Discuss this with your guest. They know you need to establish audience control and they might suggest a powerful opener or close that meshes well with their talk. Avoid repeating part of your guest's message or stealing his opener. That could throw him off track if he is not prepared.

There are two ways to conduct a Q&A session with a guest speaker. You can become an active participant answering questions side by side with your guest or you can be a facilitator for the process.

If the presentation involves complex subjects and you have positioned the guest as the expert, you probably don't want to jump in with your two cents on every question. Let them do their job while you simply make sure the process goes smoothly.

If the questions are on less technical issues where you could be expected to have some knowledge, then it's OK to jump in, but avoid the tendency to give long answers. You may feel, *"Hey, this is a question I can answer...now it's my turn to show everyone how much I know."* This is a sure sign of insecurity.

Make the host look good

If you are a wholesaler, or another type of guest speaker at a seminar hosted by someone else, I think you have an obligation to make that person look as good as possible. As brilliant as you may be, the person who makes it all come together for the client is that advisor and you need to enhance their credibility with that audience. This isn't always easy, but to do less will diminish the business results of the event.

When I was a wholesaler, I frequently found myself in the uncomfortable position of doing a great seminar for an advisor and then having people in the audience come up to me afterwards wanting me to handle their account. It's not a good feeling knowing that these prospects are never going to do business with the advisor who hosted the event because the advisor didn't sell himself to the audience in any way.

Work with the advisor in advance and decide how much or how little of the event they want to handle. Encourage them to use the bracketing techniques I've detailed above. Help them craft a powerful opening and close. Talk about potential questions in which they can participate. And above all...always remember your role as a guest speaker is to help them...not to self-aggrandize. That might mean knowing when to say "Thanks," shut up and sit down!

I witnessed a train wreck seminar where the host advisor and the guest speaker actually got into an argument in front of the audience about some arcane piece of investment trivia. Each *one kept trying to outdo the other and I felt like jumping up and shouting... **"Stop fighting you jerks! You're losing everyone in the room and you both look like idiots!"** Needless to say, the advisor did no business from the event and the guest speaker was black-listed from the firm as a result. Worst of all the audience left dazed, confused and in worse shape than when they walked in.*

One positive thing you can do for the host is to set them up with a great third-party endorsement. As a guest speaker, you can toot their horn a bit and say something good about them to the audience. Don't go too far on this or you look like a shill, but a little something positive can work wonders. I used to say stuff like this:

"Folks, before I wrap up my segment of the talk tonight...I just wanted to say something nice about Bob Jones who put this evening together. He would never blow his own horn so I just wanted to blow it for him for a minute."

"My company is a very large money management firm. We have over a three million clients and we work with tens of thousands of financial advisors all over the country. (PAUSE) But we don't often get to do events like this because there are very few advisors like Bob. He really takes the time to explain to his people what's going on and he tries harder than anyone I know to make sure his clients understand and are totally comfortable with the strategies he helps them implement."

"Whether you end up working with my firm or not is immaterial. What's important...what's critical to your long-term success... is that you have found a rare breed of advisor in Bob. I don't think you could be in better hands and I want to thank him for the great work he does with his people and for putting this event together tonight."

Obviously this has to fit your style and you could tweak the content any way you like. I didn't say anything that would violate compliance rules or that could be construed as promissory in any way. So if you are a guest...think about something like this and talk it over in advance with the host. Your effort will probably be appreciated.

Chapter 9

CONFIDENCE

"Confidence is the hinge on the door to success."

Mary O'Hare Dumas

There are two kinds of confidence you need to generate during a seminar.

First, is confidence in YOU. You want the audience to trust your judgment and expertise. On a fundamental level, they need to know that you have the professional tools that can help solve their problems. On a deeper level, you want to give them confidence in you personally as someone who knows the ins and outs of your industry better than other advisors.

You also want them to develop more confidence in themselves. You want them to trust their own judgment just enough to feel good about coming to you and about accepting high quality advice. You may be the best financial advisor in the nation but what good is that if your clients can't recognize it or appreciate it due to their own lack of investment confidence.

If you generate confidence only in *your* ability and judgment, there's a good chance that they may not have sufficient trust in themselves to even set an appointment with you. They may think they need to learn more about the markets or wait until they have more money before they can seek your help. They may even fear placing too much confidence in any one advisor and stay away entirely.

Helping them become more confident investors makes them better, happier clients. They will feel more secure in their own judgment and better about themselves with you as their partner. That's the ideal situation.

Let's start with you. You generate confidence in yourself essentially by what you say and how you say it. Through these elements, you display a depth of knowledge about your profession, understanding about the implications of investment actions and an empathy for their real life concerns.

Start with knowledge

The basis of the entire seminar process is the fact that you KNOW SOMETHING. You are an expert in investing, maybe with a specialty in some particular branch, it doesn't matter. All that matters for our purposes, is that you have something intelligent to say — a message of some importance and insight. Otherwise, why are you doing seminars at all?

By the way, I would never presume to tell you what to say. You have your own philosophy about investing, the economy and what to do about it. The message you choose to send to an audience must be based on the kind of business you do and on what YOU believe is best for your clients.

The content of your seminar is entirely up to you, but assuming that you *do* have a message, there are two things that will make your seminar different and more powerful than those of other financial professionals:

- The organization of your thoughts leading to action

- The style of your delivery leading to trust

The way you structure and present your ideas is every bit as important as the ideas themselves. It may even be MORE important. We talked about organization of the seminar in the chapter on UNDERSTANDING. Now you need to realize that the better organized you are, the more confidence you will generate in the minds of the audience.

To the degree that you can present a logical flow of ideas leading to a viable conclusion, the audience is much more likely to believe you. If you jump around from thought to thought without establishing a firm foundation, the audience will reject your conclusions and lose confidence in your abilities.

As for delivery, there are certain techniques you can use to enhance the message being delivered. This will also raise the audience's confidence in you. Use them, and you will be more believable — it's that simple.

Build a confident presentation

There are five main construction materials you have available when you're building a seminar. These are:

- Opinions
- Facts & Factoids

- **Statistics**
- **Stories**
- **Quotes**

The basic way you put these together goes like this:

You start with OPINIONS:

"There is a coming retirement crisis in America! Millions of people are facing the toughest financial decisions of their lives and they are not prepared."

Backed up by FACTS:

"There are over 79 million Baby Boomers who will be facing retirement starting in the year 2010. Imagine this...the largest demographic group in U.S. history all drawing Social Security at the same time."

Enhanced by STATISTICS:

"According to the Bureau of Labor Statistics, when Social Security began, there were 35 workers supporting each retiree. By the time the Baby Boomers are all over 65, that number will be down to two workers for each retiree."

Dramatized by QUOTES:

"Richard Darman, the controversial and far-thinking director of the Office of Management & Budget under President George H. W. Bush, described this situation in very dramatic terms — 'The retirement crisis this nation faces in the next decade will change forever the way Americans think about investing and saving. It will have an economic and emotional impact on this nation far deeper than the Great Depression of the 1930's.'"

Personalized by STORIES:

"I just began working with a new client about a month ago. We'll call him Bob. He's fifty years old with a wife and three kids. He's worked for the same company for twenty years and he's begun to think about retirement. So, he came in one evening and we did a complete analysis of his financial situation...including projected costs for college and the possibility that he'd have to take care of an elderly parent. (Which are expenses faced by over 60% of Baby Boomers.) Let me give you an idea of the numbers we came up with."

"To generate an annual income of $90,000 which is only 70% of his current income, Bob would have to put away over $3,800 a month for the next 15 years! That includes his company pension AND social security and presumes his kids go to a state college. God forbid they get into Harvard or Princeton...his monthly number jumps up to $6,300 a month!"

I offer this segment as an illustration of the logical underpinnings of a theme. If you accept the fact that everyone has an opinion, that leaves you with four basic "knowledge tools" that you can use to generate confidence in any public presentation — facts, statistics, quotes and stories. The audience expects you, as an expert in your field and someone to whom they will entrust their assets, to demonstrate your knowledge and ability with some compelling combination of these tools.

Facts & statistics

Accurate, pertinent and carefully articulated facts form the base of your discussion. They are the meat, the bricks and mortar of the seminar. They are what will appeal to the audience's logical side, and even though you are focused on emotion, you cannot ignore their logical side.

People today like to think of themselves as logical investors. Whether that is true or not is open for debate. But I promise that if you walk into a seminar armed only with weakly supported opinions and expect to sway the crowd on the force of your presence alone, you're crazy. It will not work. They want hard facts...numbers and "proof."

The good news is that you can find facts and statistics to prove just about anything you want. Wall Street suffers from data overload. I guarantee that you can find support for any opinion you may have, given a little legwork.

Frame the statistics

Facts, data and statistics by themselves are dry, unemotional things. Used in an ordinary fashion, they are low impact items that often clutter and confuse a presentation. Most speakers deliver them in a very boring style. Instead, make them come alive by framing or packaging them with an introduction and a meaningful interpretation.

Facts and statistics are only valuable when they illustrate a powerful emotional message. It's the emotional impact of the data that you must highlight. For example, let's say you're about to quote a fact and a supporting statistic. You can simply blurt it out and let it hang there or you can deliver it properly like this:

Part 1: The Fact:

"The best performing investment throughout history (PAUSE) has been stocks."

Part 2: The Frame:

"That may surprise some of you considering this past decade of weak performance, but let me give you some data to support that fact. This statistic comes from Ibbottson. They are the resource data bank that all of Wall Street turns to for statistical information."

Part 3. The Statistic:

"According to Ibbotson, the average return on the S&P 500 over the past 65 years has been 9.2% per year. That includes the past ten years!"

Part 4: Repeat and Re-state

"Nine point two percent per year compounded since 1928...eighty one years of nearly double digit growth! Nothing else even comes close. And that's the S&P 500, not a select group of aggressive growth stocks or an actively managed portfolio. The S&P is just a broad index of big companies — some very good others not so good."

Part 5: Why is this important?

"Think about what this means. It's a simple statistic but it forms the base for our entire talk tonight. No other investment you can find will help you grow your assets faster or more consistently that stocks."

Part 6: Connection & Transition

"Now that's all just fine in a vacuum, but we don't invest in a vacuum. How does that performance compare to other investments you might make — bonds, for example? I said stocks were number one performing asset class and that nothing else comes close." (PAUSE)

Part 3 Again: The Connecting Statistic

"Bonds, during that same period of time, were #2 but with an average of only 4.5%! That's less than half the annual return on stocks."

Using a powerful statistic without a proper frame leaves the audience alone to find the meaning. A seminar isn't a mystery novel...TELL them the meaning in plain, emotional language. Tell them where the statistic comes from and how respectable Ibbotson is in our industry. Quote it in a semi-dramatic fashion with proper delivery and emphasis. Repeat it and add a new interpretation. Relate it to them in real dollar terms and finally connect it to the next point in your discussion.

You have created life from lifelessness

If you have several facts and stats to use in one segment of your presentation, it's not necessary to frame and repeat each one. Instead, let them build to a natural climax and then summarize them with an emotional interpretation. For example:

> "You've now seen the demographic chart that shows Americans are living longer than at any other time in history. You saw the numbers on Social Security and the savings rate and I showed you the statistics on the average investor's returns. All of this adds up to a powerful message — if we keep going the way we're headed, none of us will not be able to afford retirement!"

This approach to facts and statistics takes them out of the realm of the ordinary and places them into the exciting position they deserve. And with this approach, you don't need a lot of them.

I said facts and stats were the "meat" of the seminar. Carry this food analogy further. If you think of a seminar as a meal, to overload them on facts and stats is like serving six courses of steak and beef and chicken and sausage. All that "meat" will make them sick. Too many facts and stats will bloat their brains and they'll slip quickly into a mental digestive coma.

You've seen this a hundred times. Your firm's Chief Brainiac gets up in front of a room and does a core dump of every arcane techno-tidbit he's uncovered in the past six months. The audience is lost somewhere after the third scattergram. Mission failure!

The best seminars I've given or seen were based on one main theme supported by a small handful of facts and solid statistics. Even allowing for the fact that the public has gotten smarter, this is still all you need to create a seminar that will knock their socks off and have them calling you for an appointment.

Too many facts and statistics can even make an audience angry after a while. They will shut down mentally and begin to resent you for NOT creating an emotional argument as to why all of this is important to them. Meanwhile, you're up there diagramming the history of the Universe thinking you're doing a fantastic seminar, and they're looking for the nearest exit.

Tell them a story

Humans have used stories to convey important emotional messages since the dawn of time. We like stories on a conscious and sub-conscious level. They fit into our reality in a way which facts and statistics cannot.

There are three basic stories you should use in a seminar: the horror story, the docu-drama and the celebrity expose.

The horror story illustrates what happened to someone who didn't follow your advice or who made a decision based on an assessment of the facts that conflicted with yours.

> "Folks, I'm not the smartest guy in the world, but I can spot trouble a mile away. When I was a financial advisor back in Baltimore in 1983, I had a client named Dorothy. One day she called me and told me to liquidate her account. I asked 'Why? What happened?' She had a solid portfolio of blue chip companies, nothing too exciting, but a good portfolio."

> "She said she was going to put all her money in CDs at the local savings and loan. 'The rates are fantastic!' she said. I told her, 'Dorothy, no one can offer you 13% on a government guaranteed investment...it's just not possible!'"

> "She insisted, so I let her go. (PAUSE) You all know what happened to Savings & Loans back in the 80s. She is still waiting for her principal from those CDs."

> "The moral of that story is simple — there are no guarantees."

Is this too transparent? Well, maybe. But it plays very well in front of a crowd of people who are likely to think that banks are the safest place to stash their money.

The docu-drama

This is like a re-enactment designed to give them an inside look at some great moment in financial history. It simultaneously adds weight to your theme and illustrates that you have taken the time to study your craft (something that far too few financial professionals ever do).

My favorite docu-drama stars Lyndon Johnson, Jimmy Hoffa & Ronald Reagan. I use it to show how labor cost affects inflation. You can dispute the conclusions, but you cannot dispute the powerful effect this story has on an audience. They love it!

"Let me set the scene. The year is 1968. A conference room in the White House. At one end of the table, President Lyndon Johnson. At the other end of the table, (PAUSE) Jimmy Hoffa!"

"Now who was Jimmy Hoffa in 1968? (PAUSE) President of the Teamsters Union. Arguably the most powerful union leader in the nation. Hoffa had a feud with Johnson that dated back into Kennedy's administration. He pounded the table..."

(pound the table)

and said, 'Mr. Johnson, I'm going to close this country down in three days!'."

"Well, Hoffa had the power. He controlled the Teamsters and unions (PAUSE) UNIONS controlled 37% of the labor force in 1968. If he said 'strike' he COULD have closed the country down! Johnson had to back down."

(Pause and take your time for the story to sink in. The crowd is loving this. It's history come alive. By the way, did you notice that factoid I threw in there? Very casually, as if I was born knowing detailed labor market statistics.)

"Now, come forward in time to 1981. The same room in the White House. At this end of the table, (PAUSE) President Ronald Reagan. And at the other end...President of the Air Traffic Controller Union - PATCO! Does this ring any bells?"

(Some people will see where you're headed with this story and the excitement will start to build.)

"The PATCO President tried to do his best Jimmy Hoffa impersonation. He pounded the table and said, 'Mr. Reagan, we are going to close this country's airports down in 24 hours! We're going on strike!"

(PAUSE — people will remember this event and you'll see the spark of recognition in their eyes. They're really getting into it – which is exactly what you want!)

"Ronald Reagan said 'No! You can't go on strike. If you go on strike, you're fired!' Well that was a hollow threat. How could anyone fire the Air Traffic Controllers? These aren't truck drivers. There were only 18,000 of them. It takes three years to BECOME an Air Traffic Controller."

"So, they went on strike (PAUSE) and what did Ronald Reagan do? (PAUSE) He fired them! Not only did he fire them but he LOCKED THEM OUT! If you were an Air Traffic Controller who went on strike you could never be an Air Traffic Controller again!"

"Why is this important? Well, Ronald Reagan sent a powerful message to organized labor in this country. He ushered in the most anti-labor administration in the history of the U.S. Union representation declined from 37% of the workforce to BELOW 13%. Today, in a globally competitive market, when a union goes to the bargaining table they have virtually no ability to argue for (PAUSE — slow and soft) higher wages."

"Why is this important to YOU? Sixty five percent of inflation is labor cost. If you can keep labor costs under control you can whip inflation. Keep inflation down and you can keep interest rates low, the economy growing and the markets will soar."

You can carry this story forward to the recent congressional bailout hearing for the auto industry where auto labor unions had to give massive concessions just to keep their companies afloat.

Delivered well, a story like this ignites a fire of confidence in them that nothing can extinguish. You tied several historical events together in such a way as to illustrate a major global economic trend. For the first time, many of them will understand the big picture — all because of you!

If you can't find a story from your own life experience that fits your theme — get one from someplace else and make it yours. Take a story from a magazine or newspaper. I pick them up from every source imaginable. One of my best seminar stories came from an article about global oil and natural gas supplies in National Geographic Magazine. I used it for two years in all my presentations and it provided a very good proof source and visual aid to help add weight to my low inflation scenario.

Horror stories

Horror stories tell of tragedies that befell investors who did not take your advice. You probably have a million of them yourself or have heard several from other advisors during the course of your career. Whether they happened to you or not is immaterial. Tell them with passion and fervor and the audience will feel the effect.

Never underestimate the power of a good horror story...especially with older clients like those in the Ike and WWII generation. They are motivated more by fear than greed and are eager to learn of ways to "avoid" financial disasters. After all…they grew up in very uncertain times and probably still carry deep psychic scars from the Great Depression.

The "missed opportunity" story

This is a slight variation on the horror story where you are trying to teach the audience about the potential risk of doing nothing with their money. lost to inertia. Sometimes in this business, information is only good for a short lifespan. You must act decisively or you may miss out. I'm guessing you have a few of these stories as well.

The success story

People love a winner and these kinds of stories highlight a client who *did* take some critical piece of timely advice and is now doing very well. This is an example of what psychologist call "toward motivation" and it is particularly effective for Baby Boomers.

The values and attitudes the Boomers formed during their teens and early twenties make them more likely to respond to a great success story than to a horror story. It's not greed that drives them — it's achievement! Also, remember that success for a Boomer today may mean simple security and peace-of-mind, so you don't need examples of conspicuous wealth.

The celebrity expose

The celebrity expose is a simple story designed to link you with a mover and a shaker in the financial industry. Use these carefully because they can easily be perceived as mere name dropping if they don't fit your theme or are delivered in too grand a fashion. I almost prefer them as a "throw-away" or "aside."

Stories that link you directly or indirectly with top portfolio managers and regional business leaders all lend energy to your aura. Usually it's best to simplify and boil down such stories to their essence.

A few years back, during the big oil boom in the U.S., I attended a huge luncheon at which the guest speaker was T. Boone Pickens. Now there were well over a thousand people at this luncheon, but for years after that, whenever the subject of oil or gas came up in a seminar or in any conversation, my story would begin with,

"There I was…having lunch with T. Boone Pickens…"

It was completely true. He was there…I was there. We were both eating lunch. I saw no reason to go further.

Quotes

Quotes give legitimacy and strength to your theme that other knowledge tools can't match. They can add the credibility of a third party to your own and can reflect current mainstream thinking on a particular subject.

I like to quote two types of sources — the well-known and the unknown. I will quote big names like Warren Buffet or Ben Bernanke or from articles appearing in the Wall Street Journal, The Times, Business Week, Forbes and the like. These are people and publications that your audience knows and EXPECTS you to know too.

It adds power to be able to whip out a copy of the article or headline right in front of them. This "media surfing" can be a lot of fun particularly when you want to illustrate the foibles of the popular press.

Then come right back with the Chairman of the District Federal Reserve Bank, a corporate CEO, a foreign government official or a Wall Street analyst. I'll mention things I saw in The Economist, Lancet, Harvard Business Review and Institutional Investor — someone the audience has never heard of or a publication they are not likely to read. *"Why quote someone they never heard of or something they've never seen. What good is that?"*

This is important...your clients and prospects want to think that you are connected. They want their financial advisor to be part of "the game," a real "insider." It gives them a thrill to tell their friends, *"My advisor had dinner with Warren Buffett. (or lunch with T. Boone Pickens) Oh he knows everybody!"* It makes them feel important too.

They are really impressed when you can move beyond the celebrities and drop names of the real power insiders. The President of Ecuador or the Director of the Congressional Budget Office or the CEO of British Petroleum are not known by the average investor. You have now jumped two notches in their minds. And you've found an ideal factoid to support your message.

There is another huge advantage to referencing semi-obscure individuals or studies. If you think about it for a minute it will come to you! If not - just answer this question. A few pages ago I quoted Dick Darman, President Bush The First's brilliant Budget Director. Now you've been in the business for 20 years or so, you probably have heard of Dick Darman. But if I used the same words without quoting someone like Darman, would it have carried the same weight?

These kinds of "semi-obscure" quotes and factoids can be a compelling tool, especially in a world like ours, where every opinion is equally meaningful or meaningless and facts are fleeting, wispy things. Find the ones that support your story and that make sense to you and use them to add spice to your overall presentation.

Factoids are small but powerful

Unlike facts, stories, quotes and statistics which form the basis of the entire presentation, factoids are little bits of information that you can sprinkle throughout your presentation. They're intelligent "bursts of precision" that support your emotional message and give the audience the impression that you are extremely comfortable with the main and related topics. To find them, you can reference surveys, research reports, articles, or any of the thousand data sources we have at our disposal.

Use them in a relaxed style. Try to make them almost a subliminal tool rather than an overt one. For example, you'll be talking about growth in foreign markets and inject a factoid about Indonesia being the fourth largest country in the world with three hundred million people. This off-hand manner is what actor's call a "throw-away." You want them to believe that you're so conversant about Indonesia that this kind of stuff comes out of your mouth all day long. Scatter these gems throughout the body of your presentation and use them in your Teaching Take-Aways, which we will discuss later.

Always tell the truth

The simplest technique I've ever seen for developing a sense of confidence from a group of total strangers is an advanced concept called the TRUTH!

I find that even today, many presenters avoid touchy subjects and try to tap-dance around certain issues they would rather not discuss with an audience. This very often involves things like RISK and FEES. These are two great concerns of every investor, yet many advisors try to ignore them or sweep them under a rug.

I suggest you do the opposite — highlight them!

Look, you're not going to tell them anything they don't already know. Every investment has risk and every investment has some sort of fee or else we wouldn't be here. Why hide from it? Instead, hit it right on the head very openly and honestly.

Clients know from experience that many advisors and financial advisors are not eager to talk about sensitive subjects like risk, commissions or fees. And they're right! Is it any surprise that risk and fees are nearly always the unspoken objection in the investment sales process. Why we're afraid to talk about it is beyond my understanding, so I use this incredulity to my advantage.

"Folks, I want to talk about something that I suspect is very important to you — the fees for investing. All these great strategies I've outlined for you — what will they cost to implement? How do commissions work? What are your options and which method may actually be more expensive in both the long- and short-term?"

"I've found that many people don't really know how they pay for professional advice or how much the fees are on various programs. I suppose this shouldn't surprise me since most financial advisors would rather take out their own appendix with a rusty spoon than talk about fees, but I'd like to touch on this briefly, is this of interest to anyone?"

After thousands of seminars, I've never heard "NO."

In my experience, risk and fees are the two most trust-generating thing you can talk about. I've found that investors simply do not know what they're paying for various investment programs or what the real downside is in an investment. The only source of fee or risk information they have is the media, which publishes exaggerated numbers to make us look bad. You can't allow your worst enemy (the media) to control the thoughts of your clients…so be as pro-active as possible on these subjects.

Whereas commissions can be a topic all to themselves, risk can be weaved into every phase of a discussion of investment ideas. Focus very directly on risk issues because you want them to know that you don't hide from bad news and that you understand how important their money is. Also, you want them to believe that you're better, smarter, more honest and have a deeper understanding of risk than the typical financial advisor.

When you're talking about risk, remember, the average investor thinks risk means loss of principal. They need to understand that it also means loss of purchasing power. This is the erosion of the value of their assets through inflation over time. I recommend you devote a lot of energy to this subject.

I like to teach a concept called Personal Inflation Rate or PIR. This is based on the fact that as we get older, we spend a greater proportion of our income on things that go up much faster than core inflation – most notably, health care. I try to get people to understand that even though CPI inflation is only 3%, their PIR may be more like 6% or 7%. Obviously, that has to be factored into their financial planning process.

The second potential benefit of discussing risk and fees is that you reduce the threat of the unknown. You shine a light on the demon and often, it just goes away.

Neither risk nor fees are often as bad as the public thinks, so by bringing up the subject first, you have the chance to disarm the objection.

Take care here, however. You don't want to initiate your discussion of fees or risk by saying *"They're not as bad as you think."* That will only serve to make them defensive and galvanize their opposition. Also, you don't really know what they think yet. Instead, lead them into the discussion professionally and seriously, displaying as much concern as they would...even more! Then, move them slowly toward an enlightened understanding of the topic.

The Listerine Sell

I learned this concept from Dr. Marty Cohen, and it goes like this:

If you tell someone a negative thing about yourself they will nearly always believe you. If you follow it up with something positive — they will believe that too!

Listerine mouthwash used to have an ad campaign that said,

> "TASTES TERRIBLE...but it works!"

This is a valuable tool to use in a seminar, and here's an example:

> "I've got to tell you (PAUSE) I couldn't pick a good stock if it came up and bit me on the nose. But I do know how to find the best money managers in the world."

No one does everything well and HNW investors appreciate a person who is honest about their strengths and weaknesses. Make this work for you. You can't be all things to all people, so pick something they don't need, (i.e., commodities or technical analysis) and make that your "weakness."

Don't use it too often in one seminar or it will become obvious. Instead, I'll save it up for a point of critical discussion, or as a "bonder" in a moment of self-revelation.

Feynman on physics

Confidence goes hand in hand with understanding. These two emotional states blend very well together and lift you to a higher plane in the mind of the audience.

I think of myself as the Wall Street version of Richard Feynman. He was one of the world's top physicists and worked on the Manhattan Project, but the major reason he was considered to be the best is because he made the complex and truly arcane world of advanced physics fun and understandable to the average Joe with a sixth grade education.

It's great to know a lot about our business. But it's even better to be able to translate our business into understandable language for the common man. In front of the public, you can be the expert who demystifies the investment process — who makes the most difficult concepts seem almost mundane. The proper intensity of this style will leave your audience feeling that you are what I call "friendly-smart" — that is an extremely bright individual who doesn't condescend or make others feel like a fool.

A smart person is someone who can make you believe that they are really smart. A brilliant person is someone who can make you believe that YOU are really smart! There's a world of difference.

Give them confidence in themselves

One way to give them self-confidence is to teach them something that will make them better investors WITHOUT using an advisor. In this way you make them feel good about their own abilities to meet their financial goals. You empower them just enough to take control of their financial future, but not so much that they think they can go it alone.

Clearly, you don't want to go too far here, because the main purpose of the seminar is to get them to come to you. But the fascinating thing about empowerment is that the more you give them the more they think you have.

When you can make people feel good about themselves and their abilities in a certain area, you not only bond to them, but you actually increase the perception of your own abilities. To drive this point home clearly, I recommend a little technique called the **"Teaching Take-Away."**

Step One is the teaching part. Here is where you actually teach them a skill set or a piece of knowledge they could use completely on their own (if they had to) to make better decisions about their money. We discussed teaching techniques in the chapter on Understanding.

Step Two is the Take-Away. Having given them a taste of this godly knowledge you must now snatch it back from them and by doing so reinforce the feeling that *"You are the expert — they need your help!"*

You execute the "take-away" by combining a basic teaching point with one or two unexplained factoids, a piece of jargon or a specific situation that's too complex for them to grasp.

For example: I may be talking about the yield curve and describing how rates have declined over the past several years. As a throw-away factoid I may say something like

> "This all works just fine with a normal, positively sloped curve but if we slip into an inversion...all bets are off."

What did you say? You used a phrase that fits your yield curve discussion and makes sense to an investment pro but has virtually no meaning to them. By sprinkling one or two of these kinds of phrases at the end of a teaching point you leave them with just a little confusion and awe, enough to get them thinking...

"Wow, just when I though I understood everything he was saying he proves that he knows a whole lot more than I ever will. I need expert advice!"

Another favorite I used in my global seminars had virtually no meaning but sounded great and made me look like I knew some inside secret of which they were not aware. I said...

> "If I see Soros doing any short covering, I'm going long Deutsch Marks just for some protection...at least until the hedges are busted."

OK...George Soros is a little dated and the Euro is now Germany's currency...but it served its purpose at the time. Look, I know most of you are too forthright to use techniques like this but let me use a sports analogy to illustrate this point.

Imagine that you are Tiger Woods and you're playing an exhibition pro-am match with some business people. Tell the truth...don't you drive a couple of 400 yard par fours just for fun? Absolutely! Sure, you might take it easy and flub a shot here and there just to get a few laughs, but at the end of the day, you are Tiger and the crowd expects you to be amazing.

The "Teaching Take-Away" may sound complex or too contrived, but with practice, you can deliver it with ease. In so doing, you're simultaneously giving them tremendous value, high quality content and you're reinforcing their confidence in you.

Use written materials

We talked earlier about handouts. One of the most powerful confidence builders you can use is to give them articles and other materials written by you. These could also be newsletters, white papers, reprints of interviews or any other document that came out of your head.

By the way, what do you think is the number one method used by financial professionals for getting new accounts? Give up?

Write a book!

If you've got the expertise, the writing ability and the time...do it. There may be no better thing you could do for your business that sets you apart from the crowd as an unassailable expert. It's a bit harder than you might think, but not impossible at all if you stick with something you know really well. You might even be surprised to realize how much fun it can be.

And no one says you've got to have a book done by tomorrow. This is a project that you can take years to complete. It's taken me over twenty-five years to get this book to the point you see it today...and it's still not done. There will always be more information in your head than you can put onto paper. You will forever be coming up with new and exciting ways of explaining things. Getting your book into the hands of your potential client base can lead to tremendous success on local and even national levels.

Master the Q & A session

One of the best ways to instill confidence in an audience is by skillfully handling the question and answer session. This is a very important process with a dynamic all its own and we'll cover it in complete detail in Chapter 16.

Chapter 10

HAPPINESS

"There is no happiness where there is no wisdom."

Sophocles

"Happiness is having a large, loving, caring, close-knit family in another city."

George Burns

Human beings are obsessed by happiness.

We like to feel good…to enjoy ourselves and have fun. No crime there, but it does put an added burden on you. Nearly every audience wants to have a good time at the seminar!

Sure, they want to learn something about their money…but I promise you they don't want to work too hard to do it. They have too much on their minds to sit for an hour listening to some "expert" drone on and on. This is why I say that a good portion, upwards of 70%, of any seminar is…

Entertainment!

The good news is that you can provide lots of valuable content and STILL be very entertaining. In fact, learning and entertainment go together very well. People love to learn. Our very genes make us insatiably curious and we strive to gather knowledge throughout our lives. But if that knowledge comes attached to an evening of boring statistics delivered in an un-compelling and dry manner…it's no longer fun and it will have little impact on their lives. Worse yet, it will generate little business for you.

Seminars present investors with a dual-edged emotional dilemma when it comes to happiness. Side One goes like this:

> "I know I need to learn more about my money. Going to this seminar will provide me with knowledge that could have a direct impact on the quality of my life. It may make me richer or make my family more secure. It can make me seem really smart in the eyes of friends and colleagues at the office. It will give me an intellectual "ticket" to the "big game" where important people make important things happen. I can't wait to get there and I'm confident that this will be a great experience!"

Part Two is a little different.

> "I know I need to learn more about my money, but I could be home watching Dancing with the Stars or American Idol, or playing with my kids, or playing golf, or eating dinner or, or, or. So why would I want to drive twenty minutes to hear a boring lecture from some guy who's going to put me to sleep or try to sell me something I don't want or call me every week at dinner time for a whole year? Besides, Money Magazine said that I can double my money in three years and THAT will make me happy."

There you have the conflict in a nutshell. What will make me more happy, being at an investment seminar or being at home? And if I do go to the seminar, what will make me happy about being there and glad I came?" The audience's pursuit of happiness is the critical equation in the whole process. If you can make them happy, you will have accomplished a major mission in the war for their hearts and minds.

So how do you make an audience happy?   Two ways:

1. Give them the knowledge they are seeking.

2. Give it to them in a way that's fun and stimulating.

Easy to list but harder to do than would seem at first glance, so let me complicate this for you a bit.

Give them knowledge

This is the baseline minimum expectation for the event. You can assume that they responded to your seminar invitation because something in the title or discussion piqued their curiosity. They want information and their desire is fairly straightforward. If you're doing a seminar on annuities, they're not there to hear about stock option financing. So the basic knowledge part of a seminar is not too hard to figure out.

I like to deal with the knowledge issue right up front...very close to the introduction segment of the seminar. I don't want them wondering IF they're going to get the knowledge they came for.

> "Folks, I have three main goals for our discussion tonight. You may have some as well and I want to get those out on the table, but first let me tell you what I'd like to accomplish tonight. When you leave here tonight this is what you're going to know."

> "You're going to understand interest rates, what makes them move and the effect their movements have on the economy."

> "You're going to understand the major forces that are driving the stock market today AND tomorrow. Which industries are poised for growth and why."

> "And finally (remember, only three things) you're going to have a much clearer picture of what to do with your money. In the midst of all this confusion and noise, you're going to have a solid strategy...not a perfect one because nothing is perfect, but a strong game plan that will get you closer to your goals. How does that sound?"

> "Oh...and my own goal is to have some fun. You work too hard to sit and listen to a boring economics lecture for two hours, so we're going to do things a little differently than you may have seen in other seminars."

> "Now are there any things that I've missed that you would like to cover tonight?"

If you heard this how would you feel? You would probably be excited and filled with positive expectations. That makes people happy. It gets their juices flowing. They start to get happy about what they're going to learn and the fun their *going* to have before you hit one word of seminar content.

If they have issues they want you to cover, go ahead and include them as long as they don't stray too far from the topic. As you know, I stress audience control over participation, especially early in the event. So don't get too wrapped up in asking what they want to hear. Chances are you're going to cover everything and more.

Now go deeper

People love to peek behind the curtain…it's just a natural instinct. They want to learn the things that others don't usually get to learn. So, don't fight it. Give them a glimpse of the insider's world of money. Escort them behind the door into that back room where the wheelers and dealers play. Build specific items into your presentation that will give them this "secret" information. In fact, I'll bet if you did a seminar entitled:

"Secret Stuff That Has Been Known Only To A Handful of Super-Successful Investors And Has Been Kept Hidden From You Until Now!"

you would be turning people away at the door. I have my own version of this called

The Seven Secrets of Professional Investors

Same idea a little toned down for compliance purposes, but it's a great seminar!

The first way to do this is to truly give them a look behind the door by telling them things known only to financial professionals. One of my favorites is the infamous **CNBC Debunk**. I'll save it for a moment when I want to shift the tone of the event or give them a mental break. It goes like this:

> "Folks…let me just take a second for a little tirade here. We've been talking about sources of investment ideas…where to get them and who is reliable. We haven't talked about television…and for a very good reason. It may be the least reliable source of investment advice you have. How many of you watch CNBC or Bloomberg News or Fox Business channel?"

Several hands always go up.

> "That's fine…but let me give you a little unsolicited advice. Please…PLEASE remember one thing when you watch those TV shows. They are not in the business of giving valuable investment advice. They are in the business of selling air time to advertisers. And they do that by getting large numbers of people to tune in and stay tuned as long as possible."

> "Everything they do on those shows is geared toward those two objectives. They will tease you with half-complete headlines. They will scare you with innuendo and vague predictions of doom that

never come true. They will hook you with some upcoming tidbit of news that will keep you watching beyond the commercial break."

I break into my CNBC voice

"OK we've got Maria Bartiromo over at the NASDAQ. Intel earnings are coming out this morning. The street is nervous. They could be up…could be down…but get ready cause it's gonna' be big news…so stay tuned!"

"And at home the poor schmuck sitting in front of the screen goes,'*Oh my god! Honey…Intel earnings are coming out! I have to watch this!*'"

"Look I'm not saying that these shows are not good sources of information. Maybe, for the average investor, they are. But information is as cheap as dirt! No one ever suffers from a lack of information…it's everywhere and it's free for anyone who wants it. What's missing is the critical ingredient that you simply can't get from television – wisdom and insight. They don't have the time or the expertise to deliver that."

"And by the way…when you see those so-called professional investors on CNBC being interviewed, you know, one of those guru mutual fund managers, remember that they are also in the business of raising money for their fund. The typical mutual fund earns between one half and one percent on assets under management. So if Joe Jones goes on CNBC and brings in one hundred million dollars in new flows into the fund over the next few days, which is not impossible, that single appearance just earned them five hundred thousand to one million dollars in new annual fees! That's serious money folks."

By the way…that is absolutely true. I worked at a major money management company for many years and a CNBC appearance was good for some serious asset flow over the next few weeks. If you are an advisor you know what I mean. There is no easier sale than to put a client into something he has already seen on TV. It makes them feel safe. The sad truth is that the things you probably want to invest in today are not making it to the air until they are already hot…and by then it's too late. Look for the most out of favor industries, managers and ideas…the ones nobody wants to interview or talk about. There's your next superstar.

The audience goes wild over stuff like this! They feel as if someone, for the first time, is telling them the real story, and they're as happy as clams. There are hundreds of similar examples of things you can "uncover" to give them a look behind the curtain. I promise you this will make them smile.

Keep in mind, however, that stories like these are not major portions of the presentation, they are short inserts, humorous or poignant commercials designed to spice up a presentation. I wouldn't dwell on them for more than a minute or two at most. In fact they're best delivered casually, almost as asides.

One of my favorite stories to tell is of the great Wall Street analyst who saw his career go down in flames after a very bad lapse in professional credibility.

"Once upon a time, there was this famous Wall Street analyst. He was a highly respected professional who was also an Institutional Investor All-Star in a popular industry group. Whenever he spoke, individuals and institutions listened carefully and they usually did what he said."

"At the same time there was this big company in his industry that he covered. The analyst had a very low opinion of the stock and, for many years, he had told his firm's clients to avoid it like the plague."

"Then one day, this big company announced they were doing a major offering of new stock from a spin-off. This was going to be one of the largest equity IPO underwritings in history and the fees would be enormous for all the selling group participants."

"The analyst's firm badly wanted to participate in this underwriting and suddenly, lo and behold, the analyst changed his opinion on the company and their spin-off to an enthusiastic BUY!"

"Well, the firms was thrilled and so were the clients…and buy they did…because this analyst swung a big stick on the street. Billions of dollars poured into the new stock and as you might have guessed, it proceeded to head south immediately."

"It dropped so far south so fast that clients started to question the analyst's judgment. What made him suddenly change his mind on this company, they wondered to themselves and in major class action lawsuits…and how could he have been so disastrously wrong about a company he'd been so right about for years?"

"Well friends…you can guess what went wrong. Our analyst, as later revealed in a no contest plea, had violated a cardinal rule of his profession. He climbed into bed with the evil investment bankers and sold his soul for a few million bucks in underwriting fees."

"Thousands of investors lost hundreds of millions of dollars and the firm had to write some very big checks to keep people from rioting. The moral of the story is be careful where you get your advice."

How the "Big Boys" do it

The migration of ideas and investment practices in our industry seems to progress from large institutional money to small institutional money to large individual money to Mom & Pop. The managers of the General Motors pension plan were doing tactical asset allocation and quantitative portfolio construction long before it became popular for a $20,000 IRA.

As we on the retail side have become more sophisticated and as technology has enabled us to incorporate these strategies into our portfolios, we're actually doing the same types of analysis and portfolio construction that they were doing at the largest institutions 50 years ago.

Knowing that they have access to the techniques of the largest, most successful institutional or private investors makes your audience feel happy if they understand the benefits of them. So if you plan to talk about an investment technique or strategy that has its roots in a "higher level" of professional money management, you need to bring the benefits into sharp focus. It will help make a stronger case and elevate you in the eyes of your audience.

Knowledge is important...

But what counts is how you package it. Think back for a second to your college days. Did you ever have a professor who really made a subject come alive? One who dispensed knowledge with excitement and made the subject fun.

I had one such professor for Intro to Genetics (yes, I was a Biology major). Talk about a tough subject filled with facts and complex details...all I remember was that I loved going to class. He made every class fun and stimulating. We were learning, we were laughing, we were intrigued and made more curious by every bit of knowledge. Every day was a thrill. It still makes me smile. There is no doubt that we learned more having fun than we would have if the class had been boring. He realized that this was a great subject, filled with fascinating discoveries.

It's the same with investing. To most people, the world of investing is an arcane place filled with powerful people all doing mysterious things. Clients hear about our world every day from the media, and they know that everything has some impact on their lives, but they don't understand it at all.

Investors know they need help…they know they need knowledge and they're desperately seeking someone who can lead them out of confusion and into enlightenment. But at the same time, they can't devote a lot of energy to understanding our world. After all, they're busy with their own business or family.

So what do we do? We cram our seminars full of data and information to the point that we squeeze out all the fun. This is a major problem and it's a critical reason seminars don't work for so many advisors.

I believe that successful seminar presenters are able to share their valuable investment information in such a way that the audience is captivated and enthralled by the discussion. This leads to HAPPINESS and happiness is the key to understanding. The more they're enjoying your seminar…the more value you can give them and the more they will want to work with you.

The world of money is intensely fascinating and fun! Chances are the you feel that way too, or you wouldn't be here today. So why allow your seminars to be dull and boring? Let the audience feel your passion and joy.

Enjoy yourself

A happy presentation starts with *your* attitude. Is this seminar a fun event for YOU…or are you dragging your butt in after a tough day at the office all sloppy and tired just trying to get it over with?

If they feel your energy and enthusiasm…it will infect them and they will begin to get happy too. To this end I always try to keep a thought in my mind. I remember that these people gave of their own time to come see ME? Who the Hell am I? Some fat Italian kid from Staten Island with a slightly above average vocabulary and a Series 7?

Recalling my humble roots makes me feel thrilled that they showed up. This feeling comes through because I'm genuinely glad to see them and I love talking to people about investing. (The only thing I love more is talking to people about TALKING! Can you tell?)

I'm their ticket to the big game. I'm their connection to the world of finance and investing. It's a role you should cherish. It's richer than any Broadway character.

I'm overemphasizing this aspect of your attitude because most of you have been *under*-emphasizing it for far too long. I've been to hundreds of seminars all across this country and it's clear to me that very few investment professionals recognize the role they're being asked to play. **This business isn't about money — it's**

about psychology. This reality is only now starting to spread through the our industry.

When you make the decision to do investment seminars, I think you've got to get a little excited. If you're incapable of getting excited or so burdened by your day-to-day responsibilities that you perpetually wear what I call the "fiduciary frown," then why bother getting up in front of an audience. Stick to the telephones. You'll be much better off and your clients will too.

So that's #1 — be happy yourself. Get fired up about everything around you...the risks, the challenges, the rewards, the winning and losing. You're a starting player in the greatest game our society has ever invented. It's a game that powers every aspect of life on this planet. A seminar is your chance to share that feeling with the spectators...people who can only watch from the sidelines while things happen to their money out there on the playing field.

I have a favorite saying. It's LOVE THE JOURNEY! None of us is guaranteed the destination. All we get is the chance to take a trip.

If this role is too much for you and if seminars don't get you excited, why in God's name are you doing them...that's what I want to know.

Make them feel good about themselves

Let's say you're doing a 7 p.m. seminar. This audience worked a hard day, came home, wolfed down dinner, brushed off the kids, never changed clothes, got back into the car and drove to some hotel to sit for an hour or two to learn about money. In today's society, that ranks up there with Hercules mucking out the Stygian Stables.

I will often compliment them for taking the time to come and suggest, very directly, that they should feel happy or proud of themselves for making this effort. I don't recommend this at the opening, but maybe half- or two thirds of the way into the talk I'll give them a feel-good pep talk like this:

> "Look around. Do you see any of your neighbors here? Anyone from work or your club? Probably not. Folks, YOU are the ones who took the time to come here tonight. I know you're busy and there are a million things you would rather be doing, but you just made a wise investment in your future. This two hours will arm you with some very important knowledge that you need to reach your financial goals. I applaud you and I think you can tell that I'm trying to give you some real value for your time! Let's get back into it."

Now they're sitting there feeling delighted with themselves thinking, *"Hey, I AM a really good person for coming here tonight!"* They're also delighted with you for recognizing their effort.

HUMOR

Humor plays a major role in my seminars (as you may have guessed), but be warned that humor is also the most difficult speaking concept or skill to master and incorporate comfortably into a presentation. Ask any professional actor and they will tell you that comedy (making people laugh) is a hundred times harder than drama (making them cry). The good news is that you can improve very quickly with practice and experience.

The first piece of advice is to just relax and don't try to be funny. It's very hard for people to be humorous when they're thinking *"I've got to be funny now!"* Audiences can feel your stress and they will get tense themselves. So if you're going to use humor, make it natural low-effort.

Why use humor?

Because human beings love to laugh…that's why. Don't even *think* about doing a seminar without humor. It's not an option. I don't care how boring you are or how serious the topic may be…you've got to have some laughs or you will be violating such a fundamental principle that your seminars will likely have no positive impact.

A more enjoyable flow

Humor lubricates the emotional and logical processes of a public presentation better than any other mechanism. It also creates a sense of fun that permeates the entire seminar event and puts people in the right frame of mind to consider a relationship with you.

Humor keeps their attention

The audience is more likely to stay tuned into the presentation. The human attention span has shrunk dramatically over the past decade. I call it the *"Remote Control Syndrome."* As you're up in front of the room, notice if people's minds begin to wander? Is your audience staying focused throughout your presentation? Here you are, deep into your thorough analysis of second-level derivatives and their use in foreign stock option short-against-the-box inverse cross-hedging. The next sound you hear will be one gigantic CLICK as they simultaneously switch their brains off.

Humor keeps them interested. It keeps them awake and excited. It nurtures a sense of the unexpected making them feel that no matter how serious or technical you may get, or how their attention may temporarily wander — there is something stimulating and fun coming just around the corner.

Easier to digest complex subjects with humor

Humor can help you navigate through the seminar and move from one sub-topic to another. It gives the audience a chance to catch their breath and relax their minds for a moment. This greatly aids the digestion process. Remember, you're feeding them lots of important information about a very critical subject. You need to insert several mental rest periods into your presentation...like lemon sherbet breaks between courses in a meal. These will likely fall at the natural transitions in your seminar outline. A little levity can spice up the transition phase and prepare them mentally for the next concept.

Remember with a smile

Humor is one of the best memory aids known. If you have something you absolutely want them to remember, maybe a statistic or a fundamental investment concept — tie it to a humorous story, a funny anagram or even a funny physical gesture. Get them to laugh and smile and they are ten times more likely to recall whatever it is you want them to remember.

Just think about this book for example. I want you to remember the emotional hot-buttons and mind states of a seminar audience. I could have simply listed them in alphabetical order. But somehow, linking them up with the acronym LURCH FACE had a certain appeal. You may forget some of the words attached to the these letters, but the chances are that you will always see the face of Lurch, from The Addams Family and you'll remember something.

Humor is your Swiss Army knife

Even better, humor is the Leatherman Multi-Tool of public speaking. From time to time in your career you may find yourself in different presentation situations that might be awkward or uncomfortable. Maybe you've got a hostile room. Maybe you're locked in a tough Q&A session. Maybe the LCD projector or the microphone blew up in your hand. Being able to use appropriate humor at the right time can save the life of your presentation.

In the beginning, humor will be like a small multi-tool — the one with a tiny blade and a nail file. As you get more adept at using different types of humor and delivering it effectively, you will become more flexible and resilient as a presenter. No situation will unnerve you. It's like having one of those really big Leatherman with the chain saw and magnifying glass.

One more reason...

I've given you the tangible reasons for developing your skills with humor. Now there's one intangible reason which you can choose to accept or not. A sense of humor, in my opinion, is a sign of intelligence, maturity, sophistication and professionalism. People who are at the top of their profession are usually very comfortable with relaxed humor. The best public speakers certainly are. This is a big picture image thing, but I think I'm right about this. You be the judge. Whatever the case, it can't hurt to develop an understanding of humor and its use in a presentation.

Some of you may be thinking...

> "Hey...wait just a minute here! I'm a financial professional with a lot of important information about interest rates and stock market analysis and economic predictions. These people came to hear everything know about investments. I've been in this business twenty years and by God when they leave here they're going to know how smart I am. I don't have time for humor!"

All I can say is that the goal of a public seminar is NOT to show the world what you know...it's to position yourself as someone with whom they want to do business. You go a very long way toward starting or enhancing this relationship by making your seminars an enjoyable, enlightening and entertaining experience. Humor plays a major role in this process.

Humor is NOT comedy

When we say "humor" we're not talking about stand-up comedy. That's too far over the line. Always remember that you are an investment professional. If I was a potential client, I'd likely be fearful of someone who was too outlandish or too funny. In any public presentation, there is an appropriate use of humor.

The trick is to find the level and mixture that's right for you and your audience, and then to control the timing and distribution of humor to perfectly blend the entertainment with the information so that you enhance the overall impact of your presentation.

Keep it relaxed & comfortable

Comfortable is important. The object here is not to make people feel threatened by your use of humor. Uncomfortable humor may be derisive, insulting, confrontational, excessively sarcastic or neurotic. You've seen many comics use various types of uncomfortable humor with good success in comedy environments. It won't work in an investment seminar. So Howard Stern is out.

In a seminar, I think humor should be used to uplift and positively stimulate the audience, assuming that's the emotional essence of the message you're delivering. Unless you're very skilled, your use of humor should compliment and coincide with the main tone of your presentation. For advanced speakers, the controlled use of contra-stylistic humor including sarcasm, irony, satire and even some sardonic wit can also be a very powerful technique.

Humor is personal

Humor is also a very personal concept. What to you may seem like a real howl may be ho hum or bad taste to someone else. Rule #1 in using humor in a public presentation is AVOID OFFENDING ANYONE. The quickest way to lose an entire room is to be offensive or to use inappropriate humor. Even people who think you're hysterical will never dare laugh for fear of creating collateral offense.

If you think you have something funny to say and you think there's the slightest chance that someone might be offended — **DON'T SAY IT!** These days, the politically correct pendulum has swung nearly out of sight. Inappropriate or off-color humor in a public presentation could cost you your job or land you in court. So be careful and use good judgment. Carelessly spoken, a word becomes a weapon that cannot be withdrawn and could easily turn on its user. I've seen it happen with devastating effect.

And don't get suckered in by the crowd. I did a seminar one time and I had a video clip from a movie in my presentation. I thought the video made my point in a very funny way and I had it set up and ready to go, but I wasn't sure if I wanted to use it because it had some foul language in it and I just didn't know the mood of the room.

Well, we got toward the end of the presentation and there was the box with the video. I said… *"Let's skip this."* But the crowd started roaring… *"Play it..play it!"* I said. *"No it's a little vulgar and I don't want to offend anyone."* But they laughed and insisted… *"Go ahead...it's OK...play it!"*

The mood seemed right. Everyone was having fun. And so I figured what the hell, we're all adults here…so I played it.

Needless to say, my instincts were correct. That simple video clip turned out to be a monstrous mistake. The situation blew up like the Hindenburg and had a devastating impact on several innocent people. I won't bore you with the gory details but just believe me…when I tell you to be careful with edgy humor, I am speaking from painful personal experience.

Great, now I've scared you completely. Don't worry. That's a horror story that you will never experience. The humor you will be using is nowhere near the edge of the envelope…so you're safe. It's much more likely that you will suffer from too little humor than too much.

Mastering the basics of humor

Humor comes is several different formats: the joke, the story, the one-liner, the quip, the sight gag, (an expression, mannerism or other physical situation). Each of these has a fairly specific formula and may be used to greater or lesser effect depending on the circumstances.

Also, don't worry about being spontaneously humorous. Sure, everyone can be witty or hysterical at times and often it just leaps out with little forethought. But you can't do it consistently, under pressure and with positive emotional impact…so don't try.

Humor, even in professional circles, is rarely ad lib. There are probably only half-a-dozen performers in Hollywood or on TV who are allowed to go off-script. Being the office jokester doesn't get you into this club.

The majority of the humor we mere mortals use in a public seminar should be carefully planned and practiced. That's OK because good planning and rehearsal can make it seem as though everything is spontaneous, and the audience will THINK you're naturally funny. Remember, funny is part in the material itself and part in the delivery. They go together but are not equal partners. Great material can't save poor delivery, but great delivery can take weak material and make it hysterical. Great material and great delivery is what legends are made of.

What about jokes?

You've probably seen those books of Public Speaking Jokes. Professionals, toastmasters and lecture-circuit types have been using them for decades with great results. For the novice or intermediate-level seminar presenter these little quips and short humorous anecdotes can be an effective weapon — BUT they require practice so that they come out in a natural style. There's nothing worse than an inexperienced speaker, or someone who is not naturally funny, desperately trying to BE funny with a memorized joke. This is one of life's uniquely uncomfortable moments. In a strange way, with an experienced audience, it could actually be funny to try it. Hmmm…

For me, written jokes are never spontaneous enough. I prefer to develop my own quips and anecdotes tailor-made for the audience at the time. This is a skill that requires the ability to listen and observe an audience.

Should you feel the urge to tell an actual joke, try to make it as natural as possible. Make the transition from discussion to joke as seamless as you can. A simple two-beat pause will work well as the entry to a joke. You've seen speakers who telegraph a joke. It's like shouting *"OK here's a joke now!"* It doesn't work. Also, if the joke is the only fun and humorous thing you're going to say all night…don't use it. It will stand out like a sore thumb and draw attention to the fact that you are uncomfortable with humor.

Self-deprecating humor

The easiest way to get others smiling is to smile and laugh at yourself. Remember, you're having fun so go ahead and show it. Laughing at or making mild fun of yourself is called self-effacing or self-deprecating humor. It's a great tool which can be used as part of a very effective and relaxing opening.

"Before we get started, I have to warn you that I am Italian. That means I can get very excited and emotional when I talk, especially concerning a subject that I feel strongly about. "

"I'm going to try to stay calm, but today, we will be discussing some of the most fascinating and intriguing ideas in the entire investment business. These ideas can change your entire financial future…put your kids through school and guarantee you a comfortable retirement! And they're so simple that anyone can do them RIGHT NOW!"

"See I'm doing it already, aren't I? OK…if I get a little carried away…just throw a donut at me and I'll calm down. By the way, the people in the front row each get an extra cookie as a reward. Sitting so close to me can be hazardous."

Obviously, you can't use that specific opening, but why not build something similar about yourself?

I'm also someone who very obviously enjoys eating. I may say,

> "Folks, you'll have to pardon me if I lose my concentration tonight. On the way in I caught a glimpse of the cheesecake in the back and my mind may wander."

I may return to that image later in the night, especially if I actually should lose my train of thought.

> "I'm sorry, it's that cheesecake again!"

Try not to overdo the self-deprecating humor. There is a line beyond which you begin to lose respect and credibility. I will not make jokes about my investment expertise, industry knowledge and my firm. Most of my self-effacing quips are physical or personal, something that lets them laugh at my human side...NOT my professional side.

> "Ha...I couldn't pick a stock if you put a gun to my head!"

Not good.

I saw a woman doing a seminar and she was fantastic right up to the point when she said, "Oh I'm so scatter-brained and disorganized!" Not good. You could almost hear a switch go off in the audience's mind...CLICK!

Never make fun of your company either.

> "Oh...PaineWebber (they're gone now) What a pain in the butt it is to work for this company. Bureaucracy? Let me tell you...you don't know from bureaucracy!"

Not good.

Funny headlines

I knew a speaker who used to cut out quirky headlines from newspapers or magazines and hold them up as an opening. It was hysterical so I started doing it myself and audiences loved it!

> "This is a confusing time to be an investor. No wonder people have trouble making decisions. Look at the headlines in the newspapers."

And then begin to pull out headline clips from major papers...all taken on the same day. Naturally, these are carefully culled to illustrate a point...that the media has no idea what they're doing and the financial advice they give investors is contradictory to the point of being hysterical.

I love to add a headline from some tabloid...

Woman Marries Elvis on Alien Spacecraft

it sort of puts a capper on the theme.

Cartoons

I attended a seminar once where the speaker was as dry as a salt lick. He was terrible...not a funny bone in his body. Yet the audience was howling and having a ball. At the break they were all buzzing about how funny this guy was and I'm sitting there thinking, *"Are you watching the same seminar I'm watching."*

Then it dawned on me. His trick was that every fourth or fifth slide, he would flash up a cartoon that had nothing to do with the talk he was giving. They were funny and he was getting credit for being extremely humorous without doing anything himself. Brilliant!

Cartoons can help a lot, and you can find these in any number of places. I used to subscribe to the New Yorker Magazine just for the cartoons. Now you can go to **cartoonbank.com** to find anything you could want.

I heard of one guy who when he found a cartoon with a really funny picture that had nothing to do with his subject, would scan it into his computer and change the caption to be even funnier or more applicable to the seminar audience. I certainly do not recommend that, but I did hear of someone doing that...once or twice.

Make fun of them

It is also OK to poke a little fun at the audience. You want to wait until you've built up some rapport before roasting them, but they like to laugh at themselves too. A good example of this mild jesting can be seen in the story of inflation we told earlier. If the mood strikes me and I think the audience can handle it, I will pick members of the audience to play the various roles. Someone becomes Lyndon Johnson and Jimmy Hoffa and Ronald Reagan.

> "At one end of the table is President Lyndon Johnson. At the other end of the table is a man who is today the most famous corpse in America...Jimmy Hoffa."

Whoever you pick to play Hoffa will get a laugh. You can have some fun with this if you like...

> "He looks a little like Jimmy...not today of course."

There are many ways to poke mild fun at the audience, this is only one. You should find the humor in your talk and build specific segments into the presentation as possible "fun spots." If you sense the crowd is with you, go ahead and use them.

Keep it simple

Humor works best in small, balanced doses applied strategically throughout your presentation. Avoid long, drawn out stories or a continuous barrage of comedy. The main reason you're there is to help people with their future. Humor, as important as it is, cannot interfere with that goal. But if I've gone more than five minutes without a laugh…I get nervous.

I know an excellent public speaker who is funny, witty and very interesting. But just when the audience starts to get caught up in his presentation he transforms as if possessed by some comedy demon and he starts going wild. In acting parlance, he starts "chewing up the scenery."

He goes into these long ridiculous jokes with absurd foreign accents and facial mannerisms and obscure punch lines which leave the audience sitting there wondering, *"Can he possibly think he's being funny?"* This costs him significant credibility.

He's missed the point of humor. He force-feeds you a heavy side dish of unnatural humor instead of using a light dash to spice up his main presentation.

Tailor it to the event

Not all presentation formats are the same and you should structure your use of humor around the needs of the audience. The after-dinner speaker, for example, needs a whole different set of humorous inserts than the keynote speaker at a symposium.

If this is your event, the people are coming specifically to see you. Here, the use of humor can be more standardized as part of your normal presentation. But let's say you're the guest speaker at the local Lions Club or the Kiwanis or some other organization. Now you may need to inject more humor into your talk. Often, the program chairperson can give you some insights as to the group's expectations. Do they want a serious talk or are they looking forward to a very entertaining session? I will talk more about group presentations in a later chapter. They are a world all their own.

Opening with humor

The beginning of your presentation is a great time to use some light humor because it relaxes the audience and eases them into the event. The type of humor you use as an opener can vary widely giving you a broad selection from which to choose. For example, you might use a series of humorous quotations, a brief story or a humorous commentary about a headline in the local paper that relates to your topic or to the audience.

Risks of a funny opening

There are two main risks to opening with humor. First, you might blow the delivery. This causes a critical misstep right in the beginning of your presentation forcing you to regroup and lose a little early momentum.

The image of an amateur speaker stumbling through an opening with a planned joke has become such a cliché that you should avoid it — with one exception — where you have so fully mastered the delivery that you can actually top the cliché. Done well, a humorous opening makes a strong statement about your confidence as a speaker. But given today's tougher audiences, the risk is too great and the reward is too small for the average speaker.

Second, you might severely misread the emotional environment and the audience's personality or tolerance for humor.

A hysterical example of this was seen on the sitcom Frazier when he was asked to be the guest speaker at a fancy banquet dinner. Unknown to him, the city's Catholic Bishop, who was supposed to introduce him, was lost at sea in a freak boating accident a few hours earlier. This was announced to the audience while Frazier was out of the room. So unaware, Frazier proceeds to roast the Bishop for being late with a series of horrible jokes. It cracks me up every time.

I had my own horror story with a humorous opening gone way bad. It was in Decatur, Alabama doing a big public seminar for two wonderful advisors. I had never been in Alabama and having just read the book "Confederates in The Attic" I was uncertain about the kind of reception I would get as a northerner. As people came into the room, they looked so serious and sullen so I decided to get things moving and open by taking advantage of this perceived cultural difference and by poking some fun at it.

I racked my brain to come up with the most outlandish and unexpected opening I could…just to break the tension I perceived in the room. The advisor introduced me and I started with…

"Let's get one thing straight right now. I'm a Yankee from New York and we kicked your butts!"

Now I just thought that this was the most outrageous thing I could say and that they would immediately get the joke and we would all have a great laugh.

Crickets! They didn't make a sound...not a single SOUND!

As a speaker, you have two choices at this point. You can run away from the whole opening, start laughing yourself and hope they join in. Or, you can push harder and try to top the surreal level of outrageousness you just displayed.

Of course you know what I did. I pushed harder and harder all night trying to crack this room and break them into fits of laughter. For forty five minutes they stared at me politely and I swear they weren't even breathing...no signs of life whatsoever.

I finally wrapped up, made some excuse about having to catch an early plane and re-introduced the advisor who was going to close the event. As I made it to the back of the room, two men got up and walked out with me. Visions of Ned Beatty in Deliverance flashed into my head. One guy walked over to me and said softly but sternly..."Hey Yankee. The war ain't over!"

Still shaken the next morning by this miserable failure, I called the advisor to apologize for my massive screw up. I said "I am sooooo sorry about last night. I completely bombed. That was the worst seminar I've done in twenty years. I tried so hard to be funny but I didn't get a single laugh."

He said "Frank what are you talking about...that was the best seminar we've ever had. We all had a good laugh after you left!" That memory will stay with me forever.

A risky moment

The opening segment of a seminar is a dangerous moment for you AND the audience. They don't know what to expect any more than you do. After you get to know each other for a few minutes, the use of humor is much less risky.

Don't assume that because you know one or two people in the room and they are real cards or cut-ups who love a good joke that the rest of the audience will appreciate bawdy or cutting edge humor. Remember the group dynamic. People tend to react much more conservatively in groups than they would as individuals. Your friends could leave you twisting in the wind after a blown opener.

If you insist on opening with a canned joke...try this. First, practice the joke with all the timing and delivery nuances until you have it down cold. Do it in front of a mirror or with a video camera. Then try it on a group of friends. Practice until you can deliver it with total confidence. Commit to yourself that you will never fumble the opening kick-off.

Then...work on the drama of the moment. Remember that the opening few moments of your seminar are primarily a visual process. The audience hasn't gotten used to the sound of your voice yet, so they're mostly assimilating you through their eyes right now. To make them focus on your words, stand still and slow your hand movements while delivering the joke.

Often, I will begin my opening in a very serious tone. I will slowly and deliberately build into what looks like a serious opening. I want to catch them by surprise with the punch line. Never "telegraph the joke." Far better to keep them guessing right up until the end. The result of this style is often quite exciting and sets a vibrant tone for the rest of the event.

It is not necessary that you drop them to the ground in spasms with your opening joke. Mild laughter is plenty. At this point in the opening, they still don't know you or what to expect. You're not going for the big guffaw. Your goal is simple. You want to leave them thinking, *"Here's a guy who knows how to be funny in an intelligent way. This is going to be a great presentation."*

Here's a good, multi-purpose opener that can be tailored to nearly any group. I don't know who first told this but I've used it for years with good effect. Remember, delivery is crucial. This looks like it's too tedious, but it *tells* much better than it *reads*.

Albert Einstein was on a plane from New York to San Francisco. He turned to the man next to him and asked, *"Pardon me Sir, may I ask...what's your IQ?"*

The man said. *"I have an IQ of 145."* Einstein was thrilled. *"145...that's wonderful. What line of work are you in?" "I'm an Engineer,"* the man said. *"An engineer,"* Einstein smiled, *"That's great...I'd love to discuss physics and electronics with you. This certainly going to be an interesting trip."*

He then turned to the woman on the other side and asked, *"Madam, may I ask, what's your IQ?"* She replied, *"I have an IQ of 153." "153...that's simply remarkable! What line of work are you in? "I'm a astronomer." An astronomer!"* Einstein cried. *"How wonderful. I love astronomy. We can discuss the nature of time and space, new galaxies and quasars. Oh this is going to be fun."*

He then turned to a well dressed fellow sitting across the aisle and asked *"Sir, please may I ask what's your IQ?"* The man said proudly *"I have an IQ of 63."* Einstein paused...*"Hmmm...a sixty three IQ? How did the market close?"*

A little old, but it still works...maybe.

Humor must fit your style

Ultimately, what matters is your own personal style. Nearly every one of us is funny in a different way and what works well for someone like me may be disastrous for you.

In general, when all else fails, always remember that there is something funny and mildly laughable in everything around us. Simple reflection, more than concentrated effort to be funny, is often all you need to evoke happiness in an audience. I'm certain you're more than capable of finding humor in life or in a given situation. Let that side natural of you show through.

Your use of humor can bond you with the audience far more than content, and it's more memorable too. Over the years, I have had dozens of people come up to me at conferences and tell me what a fantastic presentation I did ten or fifteen years ago. Then they usually add, *"I remember you said _____ and I laughed my head off!"* The content alone might have been be forgotten, but the connection you make with humor lasts forever. Find your style and don't be afraid to use it. The audience will appreciate your effort and you will have succeeded in the larger goal of making them happy.

Chapter 11

FEAR

"To conquer fear is the beginning of wisdom."

Bertrand Russell

"Knowing what must be done does away with fear."

Rosa Parks

Your goal in a seminar is not to scare people…it is to help them identify, understand and overcome the fears they already have deep inside them!

Fear is a very powerful human emotion and a it can be a great motivator that causes people to take positive action. It can also be a dangerous tool if misused by a professional in a position of authority. It can paralyze people into depression and cause them to make very bad decisions. At its worst, fear is a true weapon of mass destruction that can cause nations to go to war!

You won't be dealing with that level of impact in your seminars I'm sure, but as a presenter, you will be faced with fear issues every time you speak. How you understand fear and deal with it can make a tremendous difference in the lives of your audience.

What are they feeling?

Every audience has certain fears that motivated them to come to your seminar. What exactly are those fears and how can you make them go away? The answer will be slightly different for each person but you need to make some intelligent assumptions and generalizations. Start by asking a few questions.

- How are people feeling today in general?

- What is going on in the world that may be causing them concern or anxiety on a broad level?

- What is happening in the world of money and investing that may be affecting their mood and their reaction to my topic?

- What has the media been saying about this topic and related issues?

- What am I hearing from my clients and other professionals?

By asking these questions, you are trying to assess the general tone of the group in broad terms and then work to a more focused understanding relative to my specific presentation. You are in constant touch with people every day and my guess is you won't have to work too hard to figure this out.

The good old "Tech Bubble"

During the late 1990s, seminar audiences were generally euphoric. It was a time of great dreams and aspirations. The markets were soaring and the media was filled with exciting stories about the latest dot-com success. The Billionaire's Club was on the cover of every magazine; we were talking about the Peace Dividend and how to share our budget surplus. It seems like a lifetime ago.

Seminars back then were actually very difficult because people didn't think they needed advice or help from a professional. Pleading with folks about sound asset-allocation and proper diversification was a waste of breath. All they wanted to hear about was the latest hot tech idea and how to retire early. In those seminars, you had to dig deep to uncover any fears. But it was necessary if you wanted to wake them up and realize that 35% returns were an anomaly and the great times weren't going to last forever.

The Lost Decade

Fast forward to today. People are terrified! We have been living through what the Wall Street Journal calls "The Lost Decade" — the first ten-year period in U.S. market history with negative equity performance. We are at war against terrorists. Energy and commodity prices have exploded. The housing market has collapsed and the "de-leveraging" of global markets has created a near-panic. Stock and bond market volatility is higher than anyone ever imagined. A recession economy has everyone in bunker mode and the entire mood of the country has shifted decidedly downward.

Anyone who walks into your seminar now is probably pretty scared already. They may be too catatonic to even understand or trust your message. You absolutely don't need to add to that feeling of panic. Instead, you need to substantially reduce their fear level before they will be able to process your message.

What's your goal with fear?

Your goal in a seminar is to clarify the fear the audience is feeling and make it real. You want to help people come to grips with it…to understand it and to get serious and focused on it. Then you can start to make the fears go away…or at least reduce them over the course of the seminar. Only when that fear is exposed and conquered, can you expect the audience to act.

Many people today have a vague, gnawing sense of uncertainty when it comes to their money. It's like seeing a shadow of something moving in a dark room. It is this hidden or misunderstood fear that can hurt them the most. Part of your job in a seminar is to show them how, with wisdom, professional insight and proper strategy, this fear can be conquered.

Why deal with fear at all?

Some advisors have told me that they avoid using fear in their seminars. Instead they stick to the facts and to a scientific presentation of the ideas and strategies.

I have nothing against facts and science, but that sounds like an awfully boring evening to me. Don't forget, fear can be fun! Used well, it will make your seminars much more exciting, informative and entertaining. And by making the fears go away…we are actually helping people…which is the entire reason we are in this profession in the first place.

Did he say *"entertaining?"* You bet. An audience looks forward to a speaker who can get their juices flowing and they are thrilled when you deliver a message with emotional impact. Fear is probably the most powerful emotion people feel when it comes to money…so in a seminar you can't ignore it.

The ethics of fear

Remember, you are not creating fear in a seminar! Fear already exists in the audience's mind. You are simply tapping into it, redefining it and focusing it. And then you're going to make it go away.

By itself, fear is neither good nor bad. It's how you use it that makes all the difference. Unfortunately some people are still using fear to mislead and exploit audiences. They try to scare already frightened and vulnerable people into some kind of product sale that may be better for the advisor than for the client. This has been going on for centuries and it's wrong! There is no place for this behavior in the new financial services industry.

Your purpose in a seminar is to use a controlled, intelligent exposure to fear to get people thinking and acting in their own best interests. By properly accessing an audience's fears, you can move them giant steps toward a positive solution. This is an extremely valuable service and it is totally ethical.

Intellectual vs. Emotional Fear

I define intellectual fear as a fact-based statement of the situation. Think Mr. Spock on Star Trek. Intellectual language is generally cold, logical and devoid of any feelings. It's often the way we tend to talk as advisors and it can also be the way some clients express their own concerns. That's because they want to seem like intelligent, sophisticated investors in your eyes. Here's a simple example:

> "Many investors today fear outliving their retirement income. Their current portfolio cannot sustain the lifestyle they've been accustomed to and they may be forced to re-evaluate their spending priorities or generate higher returns."

That's certainly an accurate statement...so what's wrong? Well it's simply not going to reach anyone on the emotional level needed to take action. For that you need to translate intellectual fear into emotional fear...maybe like this:

> "Folks, there are people in this room tonight who may actually be facing the unbelievable reality of moving back in with their children. How many of you have had that nightmare? Do they have a room for you? Where will your grandkids sleep? Are they ready for this financially? Are you really prepared to give up your personal freedom and become a burden to your own children?"

We are dealing here with two interpretations of the general fear known as "Outliving Your Retirement Income" which is shared by millions of Americans. The second paragraph was exactly the same fear but dealt with in simple, real-world emotional language. As you can see, the emotional fear makes the intellectual fear come alive. It cuts right to the heart of what keeps people awake at night. It's tactile, visceral and visual.

When you build your seminar, you need to think about the fears your audience has and how you want to focus them. You then can build elements into your presentation that make those fears come alive.

Talk about someone with a serious illness who is unable to afford hospital care. Hide someone behind the front door waiting for the mailman to arrive with the Social Security check so they can go and buy groceries. Sit a parent at the kitchen table with a child who wants to go to college but can't afford it. These are the mental pictures that give them goose bumps and will prompt them to action, not the dry dollars and percentages of an actuarial analysis.

Get them to understand exactly what it is they are really afraid of…and then show them exactly how to overcome those terrifying moments. Now you're doing some real good in front of that room!

There are others: an investor trying to grow his asset base may be coaxed into overly risky investments because he intellectually fears a below average rate of return. Emotionally, he fears looking stupid in the eyes of his colleagues who may have taunted him with stories of exaggerated returns and market prowess. He doesn't want to be seen as too conservative…not a *"player"* or missing out on a *"sure thing."*

In a bear market environment, someone might fear losing all their money in stocks that seem to keep spiraling downward. They may fall victim to dangerous market timing schemes and be stuck on the sidelines during the critical early stages of the recovery which follows.

If you ignore their fears and fail to address their emotional issues about money, they will not connect with your message or with you. Your goal is to tailor your emotional message so that you address these fears and by doing so, demonstrate that you understand their deepest concerns and are prepared to help them.

How do you tap into their fears?

The fear is there, just below the surface…so you don't need to dig too deep to bring it into the light. I like to tell stories, use quotes and anecdotes. But more than anything, I find it best to mix fear with humor.

There's a simple reason for this and you can see it illustrated on the following chart. When you hit their fears too hard, you quickly move up the motivation curve until you reach a point of maximum motivation. Pass that point, and their motivation begin to drop slowly until you reach VAPOR LOCK at which point it drops like a rock. They are now too scared and they've shut down to further emotional input.

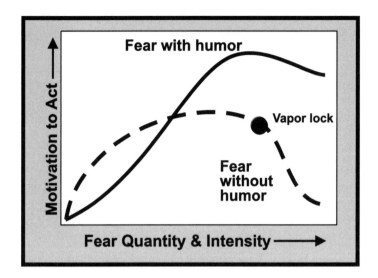

When you mix their fears with humor, their motivation curve rises more slowly, but stays at a higher peak longer. When it drops it falls more slowly and not nearly as far. You are tapping into their main emotional driver but you won't paralyze them into inaction.

Exposing an audience's fears is like a roller coaster ride and humor is the big safety bar. It reassures them that they are not going to fall out of the seat and plummet to their death, so they're more eager to take the dangerous yet exciting ride. Without the safety bar, virtually no one could stand the pain of seeing their fears so openly uncovered…especially in a public setting.

Also, to carry this analogy further, every roller coaster ride has a few flat sections. You wouldn't last long if you stayed in a sixty degree banking nose dive for the whole ride. In your seminar, you can use humor and varied delivery techniques to break their fears up into more comfortable exposures. The net result is much better message retention, higher overall motivation and substantially greater enjoyment.

Here's a simple example of this fear/humor mixture. It's a scene I call "The Dreaded Phone Call."

> "My parents are retired now and getting old. How many of you have parents who are sixty five or older. (PAUSE) Then you know what I'm going through."

> "Their concerns about money are very real and very painful, just like millions of Americans today who are in or getting close to retirement.

What they fear, what keeps them awake at night is the 'Dreaded Phone Call.' It goes something like this..."

Slow your pace and lower your voice. Watch how the room gets quiet with everyone focusing on you. They're getting into the emotions of the story.

"Son, remember how your Dad and I helped you with college. And we were there for you whenever you needed some money — your first car, your house. Well, we're getting old now and honestly, we just can't make it on our own anymore. (PAUSE) We were kind of hoping you and Rebecca had room for us because we may need to move in with you for a while."

You will see a very powerful reaction in the crowd. The fear has reached them on a deep, gut level, but because it's such an emotional fear, you can't let it sit there too long, so now you can break the tension with a little humor.

Still serious . . . very deadpan.

"Now I'm lucky. I'm a financial professional. I'm ready for this phone call. I've prepared. (PAUSE) Every six weeks I change my phone number and my parents will never reach me."

Everyone laughs. The emotional salvo has hit the target but you don't want them to perish, so you save them with a little humor and then move on.

"Ah, you laugh, but it's a very real fear. Many investors today are scared to death about outliving their income. They actually worry about living too long! Think about that! They're healthy, energetic and ready to enjoy life, but they've run out of money and they have to move in with their kids. What could be more frightening than that...not only for them...but for their children too!"

Now I can transition into my next point of discussion.

You can embellish or dramatize the Dreaded Phone Call story with as much emotion as you like. The point is that exposing their fears with some humor makes your entire message more enjoyable and meaningful to an audience.

Tell a scary story

Stories or anecdotes are a great way to uncover their hidden fears and still keep them safe from too much harm. A good story allows you to illustrate a very frightening scenario and allows the audience to maintain a comfortable emotional distance from the devastation. The CD story I told in an earlier chapter is a good example. It gets the point across but it's not so severe as to cause vapor lock.

Remember to tell them how the "victim" in your scary story felt. This leads them straight to the emotions you want them to feel.

Scary stories with happy endings are great too. Particularly if you were the cause of the happiness. Be careful not to overdo this. It could come off as too self-aggrandizing.

Scary quotes & headlines

If you want to talk about masters at using fear to motivate...look no further than the popular media. They know that bad news sells and they use it every chance they get. They will help you illustrate any fear-point you could want to make. You should have a file filled with great headlines like:

"Retirement An Impossible Dream for Most Boomers"

"Market Plunges on Credit Collapse"

"Bonds No Safe Haven for Weary Investors"

I love these kinds of attention-getters. If you want to have some fun, use a group of three or four real headlines in a row and then hit them with a headline from one of those tabloid papers. You know the kind...

"Woman Gives Birth to Bat Boy" or

"Brittany Spears Falls for Space Alien"

It's a great way to stir up some emotion and poke a little fun at the media at the same time. You want them to be a little scared but not to put too much blind faith in the press.

In addition to headlines, you can find some great quotes or statistics to help you tap into the fear they're feeling. These may need less framing since they're predisposed to believe bad news, so you can use several in a row to generate a good "dramatic build."

If I had the technical skills I would love to compile a short video taken from CNBC and the other major TV news sources and just splice together the times they use intense fear with words "plunge," "crash," or some other apocalyptic phrase. I think it would amaze people to see the subconscious way the media tries to scare them. It's insidious and does real financial damage.

Do more seminars when folks are scared

Many advisors cut back on the number of seminars they do during difficult economic times and that's exactly the wrong thing to do. Scary times are when people need you most. They need you on the bridge of that ship to help them navigate the storm. Hey, I'm sure that the Coast Guard would love to have all their rescue missions take place in calm, tropical waters…but that's not the way it works. It's when the sea is roiling and the wind is howling that they leap in to save lives.

It takes uncommon courage to face the danger head-on, but the rewards are worth the risk. So get started. Not only will you find highly receptive audiences but you will be doing a valuable service and earn a reputation as a professional who steps up to the plate when times are toughest.

Chapter 12

ACTION

"Action may not always bring happiness; but there is no happiness without action."

Benjamin Disraeli

"The great end of life is not knowledge but action."

Thomas Henry Huxley

Without audience action of some kind, seminars can be a costly waste of time and resources.

So what exactly do you want people to do as a result of your seminar? This is the focus of the critical Call-To-Action portion of your seminar and it's a more complex question than it may seem. In fact, you may want different people in the room to do different things, but we will get into details in a minute. First let's deal with the big picture.

I like to build my Call-To-Action in three parts. I give the audience three specific things I want them to do after they leave my event. Three seems to be a magic number that people can remember…so I rarely give more. The first two can vary depending on the topic and the audience, but the third one is nearly always the same action and, in my opinion, it's the single most important step anyone can take after the seminar.

Set an appointment to meet with me!

Let me show you how to build this Call-to-Action and then get into the specifics of the Appointment Close.

The Call-To-Action

This segment comes at a specific point in the seminar right after the Conclusion and before the Emotional ending. It looks like this:

Action Step 1: Topic-specific action

Action Step 2: Topic-specific action

Action Step 3: Meet with me

The first two steps will depend on my topic. If I were doing that global investing seminar we used in our prior example, Step 1 might be for everyone to do a broad portfolio review to list the international components of their holdings. This is probably something they can do on their own. It would require a little organization, but it's not a complex analysis.

Step 2 would be a more detailed global exposure analysis where we accurately measure the percentage of their holdings, earnings and returns they are getting from foreign markets. They probably could not do this without help. Even though we discussed it in the seminar, it requires careful examination of data that most individual investors would not have the time to find. It's obviously something for which I would want them to use me.

Step 3 is to set an appointment to come see me and this take me right into one of the most critical elements in the seminar.

The Appointment Close

One of the biggest questions I get from advisors is… *"What can I do during the seminar to get appointments with as many people as possible?"*

The appointment is the critical payoff for the entire seminar process. It is the single most important action the audience must take both to secure their own financial future and for you to build some new relationships from that event. A great seminar is largely defined by the number and quality of appointments set…so it makes sense to spend some time mastering this technique.

If you *have* done a great seminar – the emotional kind we have been teaching you to do in this book – you will have a very good chance of setting appointments with a majority of the people in the room. Here is something else you can do to boost those odds even higher.

The "Appointment Close" is a new concept that I have been developing for a few years. It's basically a five-minute addendum you attach to the Call-to-Action designed to increase the number and quality of appointments you get from the seminar. It works very well, especially with today's more intelligent, yet guarded audiences.

Before we get into the specific tactics, let me warn you that there is no perfect phrase, no magic bullet you can use at the end of the seminar to get people to come see you. Appointment setting is a holistic process. That means that every aspect of the seminar leads toward the appointment. Everything you do counts…including the invitation, the location, the room setting, the food, the factual content of your talk, the slides and visuals, your use of humor, and of course, most importantly, the emotional impact of your message. In reality, everything you do during the course of the seminar will help you or hurt you when it comes to the appointment. So before we can discuss the "closing techniques" we have to understand that **there is nothing you can say at the end of a seminar to make up for major failures during the event.**

On the plus side, if you did everything right and you hit the nine critical emotions as we are detailing in this book, there is almost no way you can miss. Let's assume therefore, that you already understand and have mastered the emotional dynamic. You have just done a fantastic seminar and you are ready to set some appointments…now what do you do?

3-Step Overview

There are three things you should do when encouraging attendees to set appointments.

1. Talk about the appointment.

Tell people exactly what the appointment will look like and what they can expect when they come to see you.

2. Give them something to look forward to at that meeting.

Something good is going to happen to them on this appointment. They are going to learn something new and valuable and maybe leave with a free report or analysis of some kind.

3. Make it as easy as possible for them to say yes to the appointment.

I want to remove all the possible obstacles that would keep them from making this commitment such as no calendar, check with spouse, etc. We are going to cover these three steps in detail but first let me answer an important question you may be asking…

Why do we need a specific appointment segment at a seminar?

Isn't it enough just to do a great seminar and tell them that you will be calling them in a few days to set up a personal meeting?

There are a couple of answers to this.

First, you can't wait a couple of days to follow-up after the seminar. People are very busy. In a day or two they will have almost completely forgotten you and the emotional impact of your message may have faded to a distant memory. You have to strike while the iron is red hot…and they will never be more eager or willing to set an appointment than right there at the event! So waiting is not an option in my opinion.

The second reason I do a specific appointment close is that people have a natural resistance to making this commitment. They are a little scared to sit down with an advisor. They have heard about the hard sell and they just don't want to go through that. So even if you've done a fantastic seminar…there's still going to be some innate fear and hesitation.

I hear from advisors all the time who tell me they get great feedback from the audience, but they set very few appointments, or the ones that do set, cancel for unknown reasons. This is very common. People will come up to you at the end and tell you what a wonderful time they had and how much they learned. Your comment sheets will be filled with glowing reviews. You will think you've hit a homerun only to find that very few individual meetings result from the seminar. Why is that?

Well it's normal human fear combined with apathy and procrastination and general inertia. Getting people to come see you one-on-one is a lot more difficult than getting them to a seminar…for a whole bunch of reasons the biggest one being they lose that audience anonymity…they are now face-to-face and can't hide.

My point is -- don't argue with the fear…it's natural. All you can do is try to make it go away…to get them to believe that the appointment is going to be a relaxing, fun, enjoyable and enlightening experience with no pressure or pain.

Final thought before we get into the three steps. The typical investment seminar I see out there today is a thinly disguised sales pitch. It's focused on some product…an annuity, a money manager or a specific program of some kind that you are pitching.

A heavy product sales seminar will drive your appointments right into the ground. There is virtually no chance that people are going to come see you after you've pitched them something for the last hour because you have totally convinced them that there will be sales pressure on that appointment.

Some of you may be OK with that. You may say, Hey Frank…I have a product that they really need and that's the whole reason I'm doing these seminars in the first place. Maybe you do reverse mortgage seminars and you are not there to conduct a complete financial plan. You want people to come see you who are ready to sign up immediately.

If that's the case…you're fine….pitch away! You are operating in a different space than the full-service financial advisor. The three-step appointment close will help you, but you already know you are thinning the herd down to ready buyers.

In the world of the financial advisor, a product seminar is the kiss of death. So please don't do it. Nothing you say at the end of the seminar can overcome a heavy-handed, used car sales presentation.

If your goal in doing seminars is to expand your client base and grow your overall business…then the kind of seminars you should be doing are generic, concept-driven, educational, upbeat and enlightening events with no product selling. In today's world, people are looking for wisdom, insight and for a professional they can trust who will take good care of them …not someone who has stuff to sell! I think you understand this and your seminars should reflect this caring and intelligent approach you use with your clients.

Step 1: Talk about the appointment

Step one of the appointment close is to explain what's going to happen on the appointment. I want to take the mystery out of the whole process and make it transparent and clean. Do this with actual presentation slides, by the way…not just off the cuff, so it takes some preparation. I say to the audience…

"You may have some questions about this appointment so let me anticipate some of these for you."

(Slide) Our First Appointment

(Bullet 1) "What's going to happen?"

"Well I am pretty flexible if you have some specific questions you would like addressed but my agenda our first meeting is simple. I am going to ask you four questions. The answers to these questions could dramatically improve your financial future…they are that important. That's it really …nothing too complicated. It's mostly just a chance for us to get to know each other a bit and for me to learn more about you."

The four questions can vary widely and we will get into that in a few pages, but the purpose behind saying, "…four questions" is to get them to realize the appointment is not going to be a massive financial physical. This removes some of the pressure from the meeting.

Sometimes, someone in the crowd will ask… *"So what are these four questions?"* At which point I will usually either laugh through it with something like, *"You have to come to the meeting to find out."* You can also say simply, *"I don't know…because the questions will be different for each of you. Your answers could lead our discussion in many different directions."*

My whole point is that this is not going to be a six-hour painful ordeal. It's going to be fun, easy and very valuable for you.

(Bullet 2) "What will I learn that's new?"

"You will probably learn quite a few things that we didn't have a chance to cover in tonight's seminar. You may learn how some of these concepts apply to your specific situation. You may learn a few things NOT to do…things that we just didn't have time to get to tonight. At the end of that meeting you will have a much clearer picture of your own goals and how you can reach them."

(Bullet 3) "How will I feel after the appointment?"

"Happy and smart! You're going to feel happy because you took a small, but important positive step toward securing your future. Smart because you will walk out with some ideas and strategies that will help you make better financial decisions going forward."

Happy and smart are two very powerful emotions. If I were talking to a Baby Boomer audience, I might also add "in greater control." You will feel more in command of the future. Boomers want their advisor to help them take greater control of their lives…so plant that impression in their heads.

(Bullet 4) "What should I bring?"

"Nothing! No tax documents, no brokerage statements…you don't even need a pencil! Just bring you. You and your spouse or your partner…the two of you just come to the meeting and let's take some time to talk."

"There will be plenty of time to do a complete financial analysis. That's not the purpose of this meeting. The main purpose is to get to know each other and to see if we have common ground for moving forward together."

I know advisors who will disagree with this. They insist that the prospect bring critical documents to the first appointment and some of them have even told me they make the person go home and they cancel the meeting if the prospect doesn't bring their paperwork! Frankly, I think this is pure insanity.

If you've told someone to bring documents to a meeting and they don't bring them…they're sending you a message. They may simply not be ready to open up yet. Don't make this first appointment about the numbers and the details. Make it about the people. Throughout my career, I have found that the person who comes to the *second* appointment is often radically different from the one who came to the first. They're much more relaxed and more open.

Now I'm not saying that you can't get into any details and ask specific money questions on the first appointment, but I would not want the focus of the meeting to be that ubiquitous financial physical. You may be rushing the relationship too quickly into the realm of performance, numbers and statistics.

(Bullet 5) "Will you try to sell me anything?"

"Absolutely not. That's not how we operate at the Maselli Group. I think… I *hope* I've shown you here tonight that we are a little different from most advisors out there. What would you like me to sell you….I have no idea what you need. The days of the heavy-handed sales pitch from a financial professional are over…and if you are not experiencing that difference yet, you've just been working with the wrong advisors. So the answer is no selling at all. Just talking and getting to know each other a bit."

(Bullet 6) "Where will we do the meeting?"

"Anywhere that's convenient for you. My office, your home, your office…whatever works best for you."

There are many reasons for this. An appointment in the prospect's home or office can yield massive amounts of information that will help you understand and bond with those folks faster than any other location. It will show you what's important to them and what makes them tick. I try to get into the client's world as soon as they are comfortable and I've found that when I've visited them in their habitat instead of mine, the relationship is much stronger and more fun.

Also…think about this. You're doing a meeting in a client's office. Chances are they are very proud of what they do. Let them talk about it. Ask them to show you around and take a tour of their shop. You are engaging with them in an emotional arena in which they have invested years of effort, energy and passion. In my opinion, there is no better place to do a meeting than in the client's work environment if it's feasible.

Doing the appointment in your office is more formal, and some might say, more professional…and I have no problem with that. I'm not saying you do every meeting off-site. In my plan, we will get back to my office shortly, but for the first meeting, I want you to be in the place that's most comfortable and easy for you.

(Bullet 7) "What happens after the appointment?"

"There are three possibilities."

"1 - We decide that we like each other and that we want to work together. At that point we will probably set a time to do a more thorough analysis and discovery process regarding your specific financial situation."

"2 - We decide that we like each other but the time is not right to work together for some reason, so we stay in touch and when you're ready…we move forward."

People are not always ready when you're ready. There may be some liquidity issues – a rollover that hasn't hit yet, something that prevents them from actually working with you. There may be relationships they have that they're not ready to eject from at this point. Whatever the reason…we still like each other and I'm going to stay in touch with you. By the way, I never let someone go who has come to one of my seminars. You are going to be on my prospect list forever…unless you tell me to drop dead…and maybe even after that.

I can't tell you how many times I've had someone come to a seminar and they were not ready to move for some reason…so we just stayed in loose contact – and then a year or two later they popped back up on the radar screen. *"Frank…my broker just left his company and I don't want to work with that new firm…so I thought I'd call you."* My seminar attendees are warm for life…I will eventually get you.

"Possibility three is that we decide we don't like each other. We call each other names and run screaming from the room. This is not likely, but it is possible. There should really be some kind of natural rapport with your advisor and maybe I'm just not your cup of tea. Or maybe you're not mine. It's possible!"

I mostly just put option three up there for a little humor at this point in the event. It usually loosens everyone up and sends the subliminal message that I am a confident, professional who is selective in my clientele. I don't work with everyone. In many ways, you have to qualify to be my client…and I think that's a great position to take.

OK…so that's how I talk about the appointment. I like the Q&A format because it's conversational, but you don't have to do it this way. Also, I've given you a lot to choose from here but you can edit this discussion any way you want. This is all very smooth and natural, and done with a spirit of fun and excitement. I want them to be enthusiastic about coming to see me. The energy and passion they felt at the seminar will carry through to the appointment…and that continuity and consistency of good feelings will generate tremendous results for you.

Step 2: Give them something to look forward to

Something good is going to happen to people who come in for an appointment. I tell them what they can expect.

> "At the appointment, you get a chance to talk. Obviously tonight I've done pretty much all the talking but when you come in, I want to sit down and listen to your story. I really look forward to listening to everything you have to say. The appointment is your chance to bring up the concerns that you have about your finances…and that's a very important thing that we cannot do at the seminar. You will also learn some new ideas…things that you can use completely on your own if you so choose."

Some advisors say, **"Don't give them strategies that they can use without you."** I think that's the old school. I'm not too worried about people taking my ideas and implementing them without me…so I try to give tremendous value both at the seminar and on the appointment. In reality, people don't have the time, expertise or energy to implement these plans without your help.

By giving them ideas that have no strings attached, I also think it demonstrates that you are a confident professional who really knows what you're doing.

> "If you come to my office, you'll get a chance to see where we work. It's where the magic happens. I'm very proud of the office and the team we've built. You will also meet the rest of my team. I have some great people that will be working with you when you become part of the Maselli Group and I'd love for you to meet them."

"You will get some valuable information as well. We will actually do a complete mutual fund analysis for you that will help you identify some strengths and potential weaknesses in your portfolio."

"Finally, you will have an experience unlike anything you've had with past advisors. You're going to feel something very different from our team. When you walk out of that appointment, you're going to have a tremendous sense of confidence in yourself and in us. You will have just taken a very powerful first step toward securing your family's financial future…and it's going to feel very good."

If you have any give-away items, like umbrellas, gym bags, golf balls, books, etc., this may be a fun time to insert those into the mix. I doubt that a little gift item is going to sway anyone who doesn't want to see you but the idea reinforces the feeling of fun and relaxation on the appointment.

Step 3: Make it easy for them to say YES

This may be the most important part of the whole process. You have to take away all the potential obstacles to people setting an appointment…anything that could get in the way of your meeting. I actually have a slide for each of these excuses or objections. For example, you are going to hear things like:

(Slide) "I can't set an appointment because…"

(Bullet) "I don't have my calendar."

"I know that most of you didn't bring your calendar or your BlackBerry…no problem. We can always change the date and the time of the appointment later. That's easy. It's the act of *setting* the appointment that's critical to your success. It says that you are willing to take a single, positive step in a potentially new direction for your future. And that is a very good decision."

On the appointment card, I give them room to enter three possible dates and times so this is easy to deal with.

(Bullet) "I want to think about everything I've heard tonight."

"I hope so! These are critical issues that could affect your family's entire financial future. The problem is that by tomorrow morning, you won't remember anything you heard. The appointment is a chance to reinforce what you just learned and to make it come alive for you personally – to see how all this theory can work for you specifically in real life."

(Bullet) "I already have an advisor."

This is a very common objection and there are two basic approaches to it: the logical and the emotional. Start with logical:

> "Of course you have an advisor. Everyone today has teams of advisors. You probably also have a doctor. But think about this...your MD, family practitioner wouldn't do your hip replacement or your heart bypass. I am a specialist in protecting your assets for a secure retirement. "

...or whatever other specialty might fit the discussion you've had tonight.

> "If that's what your getting from your current advisor then you're already doing all the things that we've suggested here tonight and you're OK. But if not...then you can see the difference between a specialist and a general practitioner."

Now, the emotional argument:

> "Everyone has an advisor. But if you're here tonight...you came for a reason whether you know it consciously or not. You're here because somewhere deep inside you sense that you should be doing better things with your money. I'm not saying that you're angry or even unhappy with your current advisor...I'm sure they're nice people. But there's something missing. You're looking for a higher level of care, of help, of guidance, of contact, of intelligence, of protection. That's what brought you out tonight. Take the next step!"

Now, a fun one!

(Bullet) "I'm scared!"

> "Some of you may still be feeling a little frightened by the idea of sitting down with me one-on-one. Oh sure the seminar was fun, and you picked up some info, but now you're thinking *'Oh no...this guy wants to meet with me!'* and you're scared. I understand that...believe me."

> "All I can say is relax! When you are ready to get some help...I will be here. There is no pressure. I've been doing this for nearly three decades and I've learned that people move at very different speeds. As good as our ideas and strategies may be...not everyone is ready to embrace change at the same pace. So take your time and just stay in touch with us. At the end of the day...there is no doubt that we can help you reach your goals and do it safely and intelligently.

But it can only happen on your terms when you are ready to be helped."

If you think of any other possible obstacles to setting an appointment you can include on the slide as well, but those are the big ones I have discovered. So with that done, I now hand out…

The Appointment Card

This is a very simple tool and I like it that way because I don't want anything getting in the way of the appointment setting process. You can pre-set them on the tables, place it in your seminar folder or hand it out after the main body of your talk. It looks like this:

Private Appointment Card

Name_____

Address_____

Daytime Phone_____ Evening Phone _____

E-mail _____

First Choice	Date _____ Time _____ Location _____
Second Choice	Date _____ Time _____ Location _____
Third Choice	Date _____ Time _____ Location _____

Please list in any order, the main issues you would like to discuss at our meeting. We are not limited to these, but they can be a good start.

_____

_____

_____

_____

_____

                                          Thanks!

Actions for different sub-audiences

In any one seminar, you may have several different sub-audiences and each one may require a slightly different action step. For example, you might have a mix of clients, prospects, centers-of-influence and total strangers at the event. The call to action is different for each group, so you need to be able to blend your action steps for the maximum effect.

Prospects & strangers

Action Step: Set an appointment

We just talked about this, but you should know that most seminars yield appointment ratios in the 20-30% range with the best coming in around 50%. For me, and now for you too, that's not good enough. The high quality of your seminars will merit an appointment ratio of 75% - 110%.

Wait...110%? How is that possible?

I want people to be so excited when they leave my seminar that they tell their friends the next morning and total strangers call me to set an appointment.

> "Frank, you don't know me, but my buddy George Smith attended your seminar last night and said you were the greatest thing since deep dish pizza. I'm getting ready to sell my company and was wondering if I could come to see you."

This can happen...believe me.

Existing Clients

Action Step: Change investment behavior

Getting a client to come in for an appointment is not a problem, so for them, my action step is more targeted. You may want them to do something specific inside their account or portfolio. This is where the specific investment or concept-related action steps come into play.

The body of your seminar has probably been a discussion of a several broad strategies and ideas that you want them to explore. Remember, we did NOT pitch a product, but rather we talked in general terms about themes, big-picture concepts and possible investment options. So keep your call-to-action centered around those themes for clients.

Centers-of-Influence (COIs)

Action Step: Invite me to future meetings

If you're talking to COIs, club members and company executives, you have a tremendous opportunity to expand your marketing reach...and you should take advantage of it. These people are not likely to set an individual appointment or to immediately change their behavior, but they can give you access to a larger group of people who will. That's your target!

Imagine, for example, that you've been asked to speak before the monthly meeting of the local Association of Human Resource Directors. This can be a potential diamond mine for you but you will completely blow it if you try to close them all on setting an appointment or doing some kind of business.

Your goal is to get them to invite you to come speak to their company, maybe to address their 401(k) participants, maybe to set up a monthly training program for pre-retirees, maybe to examine their retirement plan...a million possibilities the least of which is doing individual business with the people in the room. This is an example of the leverage power of seminars and you should be proactively targeting these kinds of COIs. See the Appendix for marketing ideas to use with clubs and organizations.

Working with COIs is tricky because they run a big risk by inviting you into their groups. If you do a bad job, they lose credibility. Your presentation to COIs must be carefully crafted in order to give them a taste of the excitement you bring, but without going too far overboard.

Once, I forgot my goal with a group of COIs and it cost me. I mistakenly shifted into "change behavior mode" when I should have stayed in "future meeting" mode. They saw the excitement and the passion alright...but it scared the heck out of some of them so I never got asked back. Bad move on my part!

Use action language

The call-to-action begins with your use of language. Your words should be visual and physical. Get them out of the intellectual and into the sensory reference frames of touch and sight. For example, of the two statements below, which makes you want to move?

> "Now is an opportune time to do some strategic investing and detailed financial planning. At our appointment, I will help you implement this course of action in your portfolio."

or

> "Right now, tonight when you get home...sit down, pull out your investment file. You know, the big folder with statements from 1986 — get a giant envelope and stuff everything in there. You might need a big Hefty bag if you can't fit everything in an envelope. Don't try to sort it or organize it. That will just drive you nuts. Bundle this whole thing up and throw it in the car and bring it all over here. We will sit down together, order some pizza and dig through this mess until we find some daylight."

Clearly #2 has more specificity and more tactile language. I want them to picture us sitting down going through their portfolio. I want them to imagine the action in their minds like a golfer creating the image of the perfect approach shot. By making the action come alive for them verbally and breaking it down into small simple movements, I can get them one step closer to actually DOING something.

Chapter 13

CHANGE

"Nothing endures but change."

Heraclitus

"Change is the law of life. And those who look only to the past or present are certain to miss the future."

John F. Kennedy

A seminar can be the catalyst for some major positive changes in a person's world.

But change of any kind is a very emotion-filled process often involving lots of psychological baggage, pain and distress that makes it very hard to implement. We are creatures of habit and we love our old routines…even if those routines are harmful to us.

Sometimes all the logical arguments in the world have no effect. Have you ever tried to convince someone else to do something that was clearly to their benefit and met with massive resistance? Then you probably know how difficult it is to get another person to change. You can preach till you run out of air and still they don't move. You can argue, illustrate, beg and still get nowhere. Stress levels may rise dramatically and often a relationship can come crashing down under the weight of the change process. So first, it helps to recognize that change is not easy…even if you've done a great seminar.

Overcome inertia

Isaac Newton said it best... ***"An object at rest tends to remain at rest unless acted upon by an external force."***

Most people have a high degree of inertia built into their portfolios and their existing financial relationships. This feeling of passivity and reluctance to move may exist despite poor performance, bad service and damaging advice. I can't tell you how many times I've met with people who was being decimated by their current advisor and STILL they refused to make a move!

Scale back your own expectations of the amount of change you're going to seek during the seminar process. All you want to do is give them a little shove to get that body in motion. You are not trying to accelerate them to Warp 7. Once they are moving, emotionally, you can increase the speed and alter the course of their motion as desired.

It's like pushing a stalled car. You're going to expend a lot of energy to start the car moving, but then, it becomes easier to steer and control the speed with much less effort. Save the steering and speed changes for the follow-up appointments. For now...just get them off their butts. Thus your goal during the seminar is to transmit two emotional messages:

1. Change is normal and good

2. Working with you will be fantastic

There is a third message where you convince them that changing relationships is not going to cost them lots of money, make them feel foolish or force them to confront their other advisors. This is too much for a seminar, so save it for the follow-up appointment.

Change is normal and good

We know that the investment world is based on constant change, yet to say this to a roomful of investors is scary. They fear change nearly as much as they fear losing money. I have found the best way to bring up the subject of change in a seminar is to start by highlighting the concepts that remain stable and to cover change as a casual occurrence within a more consistent big picture. Get them secure with an established base of timeless principles and then ease them into the new ideas. Here's an example of a discussion on change I've used to make the process feel more comfortable.

"Folks, the world of investing, as confusing as it seems sometimes, is built on several basic principles that have never and will never change. I'm talking about things like diversification, like owning high-quality companies with solid earnings and dividends, like investing for the long run rather than a short-term time horizon."

"Sure, there may be times when these rules seem to be outdated. And I'm not saying you shouldn't leave some room for new ideas that take advantage of short-term market disconnections and opportunities. Success means you have to be flexible at times and occasional course corrections are a normal part of any valid plan."

"I have a simple way of thinking about change that may provide you some comfort. Think of investing like taking a flight from New York to Los Angeles. You know where you are starting – New York, and you know where you want to go – LA. You have a general idea of how you're going to get there – by plane headed west. So far…so good. Those big picture elements represent your goals and the broad strategy of your financial plan."

"The pilots are highly skilled professionals and they have hundreds of air-traffic control experts and advanced technology to advise them along the route. Maybe we will have to divert around a thunderstorm in Kansas City. Maybe there's turbulence at 35,000 and we have to go up to 40,000 feet. Maybe we will hit a strong headwind over the Rockies and it might take a little more fuel. None of that really matters because at the end of the flight…I know I'm going to be in Los Angeles."

"The changes that occur during the flight are minimal. I doubt that anyone would want to force the pilots to fly through the thunderstorm or to stay at a bouncy altitude or to forego the extra fuel load for headwinds. These decisions and contingencies are a normal part of any journey. Flexibility and change is a prudent part of any investment strategy."

"Let's translate this into investment ideas for a minute. Maybe the old 'buy-and-hold-forever' mentality has been replaced by a more nimble 'buy-and-protect' strategy that uses covered calls or put options. Maybe instead of rising earnings we look for rising cash flow and dividends. Maybe we get better diversification with some things like commodities and Asian REITs than with the EAFE Index. These are minor course corrections in the big picture strategy."

The whole point here is to get people to recognize that change is built into our process and we make them seamlessly without major disruptions to the plan.

Working with you will be fantastic

The second part of the change process is to convince people that YOU are a good idea. There has to be some reason for doing business with you otherwise people will not make a move. So what makes you compelling? Why do I want to work with you? What is special and unique about you? What do you do really well? What can I rely on you to do for me? These questions are part of your story and you should have one before you start doing seminars!

Building your story

If you are successful in any way, you have probably already done this, but let me share a few thoughts that could help or augment your story development.

Go with unique

They say that differences sell, yet most advisors sound exactly the same. We say and do the same things and we explain our "value proposition" in almost identical language:

> "Here at the Smith Group we listen carefully to our client's needs. Then we use the most advanced financial solutions and the amazing team we have behind us to custom-design a strategy built specifically for you."

Blah…blah…blah! There is not a client out there who hasn't heard this a hundred times. Look, maybe it's working for you, so I don't want to capriciously trash your approach, but at a seminar, it can't hurt to be a little different…or at least to highlight the differences as well as the similarities.

Remember what we talked about in Chapter One? The only sale you have to make at a seminar is yourself. Now might be a good time to test out the success of that strategy.

> "Here at the Maselli Group we pretty much do everything every other advisor has ever told you. We have products, they have products. We have experts behind us…so do they. We listen to our clients and build customized solutions for their specific needs…and every top professional does the same exact thing! So why should you work with us?"

"The answer is me. When you work with the Maselli Group...you get me. There is no other financial team on the planet who has me!"

"Now some of you are probably thinking...thank God no one else has him! I couldn't take another fine minutes of this guy...please make him go away! And that's fine. I'm obnoxious, I'm opinionated and I probably come across to many of you as a egocentric know-it-all. And...as further proof...I possess a keen sense of self-awareness...which is also nice."

"If you honestly didn't enjoy tonight. If you didn't pick up something valuable from our hour together. If you're bored to death and you're walking out of here more confused and less confident than when you came in...then all I can do is apologize and wish you well. I am definitely not the right advisor for you."

"But if you have any sense that I know a little bit about this crazy business and that I truly have a passion for helping people...then maybe we have the basis for a good relationship. My team and I would love to help you in any way we can."

Obviously you can't say these exact things about yourself, but I think you get the tone and the objective of this segment. If you've done a great seminar, let that momentum carry you through the commercial. The audience will never be more ready to buy you than they are right now. Do not waste the energy and the good feelings you've built up in the room. Make the uniqueness about you and you may find this works wonders.

The other reason this is likely to work is the attitude investors have right now about Wall Street. Maybe by the time you read this it will have changed, but as I'm writing it, our industry is suffering from the worst public image we've ever had! The very words *"Wall Street"* evoke feelings in the public on par with *"The Black Plague"* back in the 14th century! You and I both know this is unfair and not true, but the damaged reputation outweighs the reality of the good we do for people...so don't fight it...at least not yet. I would try really hard in my seminars to detach myself and my process from anything that reeked of big Wall Street systems, procedures, products, people, etc. Over time I will be able to prove my individual merit and that will transcend the industry's image in the minds of my clients.

I'm not comfortable talking about me like this

OK...maybe this isn't your style. Maybe you think saying all this about yourself or making the focus of the commercial about you is distasteful in some way.

Personally, I can't understand why, but you can still need to answer the question: *Why should I work with you?*

So let's find another characteristic or set of traits that make you different. Is there something in your discovery process, for example? One of the things I've been preaching to top advisors is that they put all their key clients through the Kolbe A Index®. This adds a powerful and revealing scientific element to client profiling that can dramatically uptick your results.

> *If you do not know what I'm talking about or if you haven't taken the Kolbe yourself, stop reading right now, go to my website (frankmaselli.com) and take the test. It costs $50 and takes 20 minutes but it's the greatest investment you will make in your own success. If you take the test I will do a free Kolbe analysis for you and translate your scores into what it means for your performance in our profession. I've done thousands of these and I promise you it will help you tremendously.*

Are you an expert on some area of investing or do you specialize in some particular client group? If so, that's unique…so tell me in the commercial.

The bottom line is that this is your chance to get people excited about you. It's your Super Bowl ad and you have to make it count. You've earned the right to do a great commercial…so don't waste it by boring them to death.

Tailor the commercial to the audience

I can't tell you what to say in your commercial, but I strongly suggest that you incorporate generationally appropriate language and imagery into your story. The two age groups you are most likely to be talking to are Seniors and Baby Boomers. Each has different financial needs, but they are dramatically different in the things they need to hear from you.

This is a deep subject and we can spend a lot of time on it, but you need to understand that each generation has certain characteristics born out of their life experiences. If you build your commercial with an awareness of these messaging elements, you will hit the target much more frequently.

For example, seniors want to know that your company is stable, well established, and that they are part of a group of people like themselves. Any message should contain references to factors such as longevity, strength, size, consistency, teamwork and experience…like this:

> "Our company is one of the oldest and largest firms in the industry today. We have over ___ billion dollars in assets. We've been

around for over ___ years and we are our team has a combined experience of ___ years solving problems just like this."

"We have helped hundreds of clients in situations just like yours. You are not alone. We know exactly what needs to be done and we can do it for you."

"When you work with Blowhard and Boggle, you are part of a family that's committed to your success."

With a Baby Boomer audience, however, the focal points of the message need to be different. Boomers tend to respond well to companies and people that are innovative, creative, dynamic and forward thinking. They are less interested in old, large and established firms or with people who live by strict rules and procedures. I might tweak my message to something like:

"We broke the mold. At the Smith Group, we have succeeded by doing what everyone else in our industry said couldn't be done."

"We use a completely customized approach to investing. There is no rule book, no procedures manual. Everyone is different and special and we build solutions specifically around your needs."

"We are always growing, learning and expanding our capabilities for our clients."

"We find ways to get things done. We are always thinking of new strategies to better help you do the things you want to do."

"We are your coaches, your guides on the journey. The decisions are yours but we are here to help you make the best ones you can."

I know this may seem trivial, but it's not. I actually have an entire training program on generational communication. It's vital to your success as an advisor particularly if you are operating outside your own generational group. For example, you might be a 20 or 30-something advisor trying to build relationships with 50, 60 or 70-something clients. If you don't speak their language…you're doomed. The converse is also true. If you are a 60-something advisor trying to connect with the 20 or 30-something children of your top clients…you need an equal understanding of their world to succeed.

Run your commercial at the end

Most presenters make a dreadful mistake of placing their commercial right in front of the seminar like this…

"Good evening folks. Thanks very much for coming tonight. Before we get started on our seminar I'd like to tell you a little about the Smith Group and exactly what we do for our clients."

Please don't do this. First, almost everyone else does it so that's bad. Second, it violates our Power Opening concept and gains you no respect during that critical early phase of the event. Third, you simply haven't earned the right to do a commercial yet. You have given them no value, no inspiration, no laughter. It's like begging for a standing ovation before you've performed and it will annihilate your results.

No one cares about you or your incredible capabilities until you've proven by your efforts in the seminar itself that your different, smarter and better. AFTER the seminar, that's when you do the commercial. And after the kind of seminar you're going to be giving now, your commercial will hit with tremendous impact and produce wondrous results.

Can I just skip the commercial?

You can, but why would you want to?

You've just done a fantastic seminar. You've given the audience tremendous value, insight and wisdom and they've enjoyed your efforts tremendously. All of that is wonderful, but there is still a missing piece to the puzzle. Simply put…the real magic cannot happen until they become your clients.

If you believe that you can help them make positive changes in their financial lives, then you have a moral obligation to try. You can't help a single soul until they open an account or write some kind of check. Asking people to build a relationship with you is a professional act…it's all in how you ask.

A great seminar is probably the best start you can get, but you still need to do some business or else all this becomes an academic exercise. Work on your commercial, get it tight, keep it simple, don't tell me your life story from birth…just give me the critical things I need to understand about what makes you and your team different, special, and better. Then let the power of the event work on them. If you do everything we've taught you in here…the commercial will flow very naturally and be a welcomed part of the process because they will WANT to work with you.

Chapter 14

ENTHUSIASM

"Nothing great was ever achieved without enthusiasm."

Ralph Waldo Emerson

Long after the seminar is over…after they've forgotten all your slides, facts and statistics…they will remember you passion and enthusiasm.

Enthusiasm is a basic ingredient for every great presentation and a core attribute of every great speaker. The audience needs to feel your energy if you want them to get excited. For the next sixty minutes, you are the Energizer Bunny in that room and you are going to charge all their batteries. So make sure you feel it yourself and you know how to transmit it if you are going to make seminars a meaningful part of your profession.

I'm not saying Rah, Rah, cheerleader enthusiasm or some shot-out-of-a-cannon, Red Bull mania. That's not what they want and it could hurt you big time. I'm talking about professional energy and passion.

An exciting topic…I hope

Enthusiasm is hard to generate when you are bored by your own seminar, so let's assume for the sake of simplicity, that you really like your topic and that you think it's interesting, timely and valuable. I realize that this may not always be the case such as when the marketing department has built you a tepid, safe slide show with boring stats. But even the most deadly dull content contains isolated pockets of fun…so let's accept the topic as strong and go from there. Now, what specifically can you do to transmit excitement to the audience?

Delivery defined

Delivery is the whole presentation of an idea; the actual words you speak; the vocalization including inflection, pitch, pace and tone of your voice; your overall energy level; hand, eye and head gestures; body position and movement — basically everything...along with the subliminal content and meta-messages.

Everyone has a style of delivery. For amateurs, it's not something they can control, it just exists. For professionals, the goal is to craft and control the delivery of your thoughts so that you can evoke specific feelings and reactions in the audience.

You've heard the old saying, *"It's not what you say...it's how you say it."* That's delivery. Taking a phrase, a sentence or a word and giving it added meaning by packaging it in a certain style of delivery.

You control delivery by understanding the many variables involved in a presentation. For example: You can speak the exact same words and change one variable like **word emphasis** and see how the meaning of the sentence changes. Try it...

Here's a simple test. The sentence is: *"My fund is number one."* Try it with a different emphasis each time.

"*MY* fund is number one."　　(Not THEIR fund...MY fund!)

"My *FUND* is number one." (Not my whole portfolio...my FUND!)

"My fund *IS* number one."　　(Not last year... it's number one today!)

"My fund is *NUMBER ONE*."　　(Not just pretty good...number ONE!)

This seems strange or too basic, but note the different feeling and meaning of each sentence. That's just one variable in one simple four-word sentence. Imagine how many variables there are in an entire one-hour seminar. It staggers the mind. Yet that's what delivery is all about.

Curtain up...light the lights

Years ago, I used to do a lot of theater. Once, while I was in college, a famous Broadway producer named Joseph Papp spotted me and he actually offered me a role in a Broadway show. I turned it down out of sheer ignorance and Mr. Papp was so stunned by the stupidity of my decision that he was almost speechless! Except for one thing he said that stuck with me all these years. He said, *"You're smart kid. The only actors who make any money in New York are the stockbrokers."* I laugh at the irony.

Doing a seminar is so much like acting that it's scary. In fact, it's very much like a one-person play for which you are writer, director and star. The one difference I can think of is that in a seminar, you're trying to impart real knowledge — stuff that's going to help people retire, educate their kids and live a happier life. In that respect, the *content* of your seminar is more important than a Neil Simon comedy, but the *delivery* techniques are nearly identical.

Two acting elements have a tremendous impact on the energy and enthusiasm levels you transmit: Vocal variety and physical movement.

It starts with...your voice

Your voice is like your own personal information superhighway – your main transmitter of outgoing data. Throughout your entire life, the spoken word is the means by which you convey the majority of the information you want people to know. Yet as important as the voice is to your everyday existence — how many of you know anything about how it works or how to make it more effective?

I know that some of you are thinking: ***"Hey, my voice is my voice...there's nothing I can do about it."*** Or even better: ***"The quality of my ideas is what counts...not how I sound!"***

Wrong on both counts, Sparky! There are many things you can do to improve the quality of your voice. In computer jargon this is called *"bandwidth."* The greater the bandwidth the more information a data line can carry. By improving the quality and expressiveness of your voice you can convey more information more accurately and with greater impact.

As for the quality of your ideas...if they are so valuable (and I have no reason to doubt this) why are you transmitting them over inferior equipment? It's like broadcasting Pavarotti with two cans and a string! If you really have something valuable to say...then say it with maximum clarity, fidelity and accuracy. Whether you are doing seminars, talking over the phone or in a one-on-one meeting, improving the vocal delivery of ideas will enhance the receptivity of your message tenfold.

This isn't as hard as it seems. Don't worry. Even a slight improvement will be very noticeable and simply using one or two vocal variation techniques will greatly enhance your presentation.

Vocal exercises

Your vocal cords are very thin strips of flesh controlled by dozens of tiny muscles. They form a complex and elegant system capable of great subtlety and power, but they need to be warmed up, stretched, worked out and kept healthy just like any other muscle in your body if you expect them to perform when called upon.

Unfortunately, any description I can give you about vocal exercises would be weak compared to one hour with a voice coach. I found two great websites on voice training at **www.thevoicetrainingstudio.com** and **executivevoicecoaching.com.** The first one teaches something called Speech Level Singing and it's a new way of thinking and using your voice that's more natural and healthier than some of the old-school techniques. Obviously, you're not going to sing at a seminar, but the skills are universal. If you Google voice training…you will find a lot more info.

Hum a little tune

The simplest thing you can do immediately and safely is to warm up your voice with humming. Here is an effective exercise you can do just about anywhere, in the car, at your desk or in the shower.

Start with a tone. You know the song "Do Re Mi" from The Sound of Music. Just start with "Do," keep your lips closed but your jaw relaxed and the teeth apart. Do not take a deep breath, but rather breathe naturally and comfortably. Simply hold this tone for as long as your breath lasts. This should be somewhere between 5 and 12 seconds. Don't strain or push for volume…just let the air from your lungs flow freely through your vocal cords.

Now move one notch up the scale to "Re" and do it again. Work your way up until you begin to feel uncomfortable…then stop.

Don't try to overreach your range at this point. Now work your way back down the scale to the original "Do" tone. At this point, begin to work down the scale to that point of slight discomfort and stop.

Feeling OK? Now try this. Start with a middle-range "Do" and work up the scale with one breath. Go slowly, one beat every second.

"Do — Re — Mi — Fa — So — La — Ti — Do"

Now go down. Remember, you're not actually saying the words…you're humming the tones. Now move your starting tone up just a little bit so that your next "Do" sounds like "Re" did just a minute ago. Work up the scale again until you feel that slight strain…then go back down. Don't strain!

Now work down the scale from the middle "Do" note. Great! You've just taken a major step toward improving your voice. Do this for five minutes a day every day for two weeks and you will see a dramatic difference in how you sound.

"Do" to "Do" up or down the scale is one octave. Most professional singers have a range of two to three octaves. Ideally, you should work to develop a supported and sustainable range of one and a half to two octaves – plenty of room to express any emotion that might cross your path.

As a speaker, it's important that you work on vocal support and a natural, sustainable sound. You want to be able to speak clearly and project your voice without straining. The diaphragm which creates the air flow, can generate two-hundred watts of power while the vocal cords can only handle two! Push too hard and you will blow out your voice.

Professional voice training could be a smart investment. Four to six hours with a vocal coach ($50-75 per hour) will teach you much of what you need to know about your voice. Continued practice will give you the power and control you need to be a very effective and exciting speaker.

Vocal variety

I would estimate that the sound of your voice represents up to 60% of the total message you're trying to deliver in a seminar. The actual words you say are roughly 30% and your body/eye movements are the other 10%.

Thereisnothingworsethanaspeakerwhodroansonandoninononeneverendingsentencewithoutvaryingthetone,pace,pitchorenergyinhisvoice.

Wow, I'm hypnotized. The most timely and exciting topic can be rendered totally impotent by a monotone drone. To create some excitement in the presentation, you must learn how to use your voice and properly vary the five basic vocal elements:

- **Pitch (high or treble / low or bass)**
- **Pace or speed (fast / moderate / slow)**
- **Tone (strident through casual)**
- **Inflection (calm through explosive)**
- **Volume (shout through whisper)**

Words, by themselves will not move people to action. In fact, the words may never make it from their ears to their minds. It is the combination of these mechanical variables that empower the actual words and give them life. It is your delivery that causes them to pay attention, to focus on what you're saying, to listen critically and intelligently and ultimately say, *"Hey this guy really knows what he's talking about. Let's work with him!"*

There is no standard vocal formula for creating emotion. If you ever want proof of this — a fun thing to do is to attend the auditions of a local theater company. As each person is called to the stage to read the exact same passage you will hear a different delivery. Some speakers can convey excitement with high pitch, fast pace, flat inflection. Others do it with the opposite set of variables. Some have no clue at all and will really make you laugh.

You can hold "auditions" for your own seminar. For example, we said that the opening segment of your seminar was very important and should be completely memorized. During your rehearsal period, tape yourself delivering the opening with various delivery styles. Try an energetic, fast pace. Then try a slower, more deliberate style. Then mix it up all the variables and see what effect this has on the meaning of the words. You might be amazed to learn that a few minor changes in delivery can double the impact of your opening.

In an ideal world, you would do this with the entire seminar, or at least with all the critical passages in the program. This process can help with a new seminar that you've never given before as well as one that you've given hundreds of times. Often, we get into vocal ruts that we're not aware of. Taping is critical. I can't tell you how many times I've listened to myself on tape and said *"Geez...I was way too strong here or too weak here."* or *"There's a better way to say this,"* or *"I hope nobody heard that!"*

The key to vocal variety is to be natural and comfortable. Too much tinkering and overdone variety can be annoying to an audience and make you sound "affected" as if you're purposely trying to over-manipulate the delivery. I call this the "Game Show Host" presentation. It's too slick and too controlled and it's not your goal. Better to think of a natural one-on-one conversation with the audience and just keep the energy level and volume up

Natural takes practice

Think about acting for a minute. A movie actor has a camera two feet away and a microphone in his face. Every sound or facial gesture he makes is faithfully recorded to be played back on a 60 foot screen in Dolby Digital. This allows for a very wide range of vocalization — everything from a scream to the softest whisper can be used to convey emotion.

On stage, you must project emotion into the room. You need to fill the air with energy. It's much more difficult and to make it come out natural takes skill and practice.

You can use a microphone in your seminar and I encourage it...not to make you louder, but mainly to increase the variety of vocalizations you have available. Now you've got a blend of both worlds, the stage world of projected emotion and the movie world of intimate conversation. This can lead to some exciting results.

When you want to get big and bold, move the microphone away from your mouth and allow your volume to build naturally. When you want to bring them in close, emotionally, turn down the volume, bring the mike in close and whisper.

I know an excellent speaker who rehearses the entire presentation out loud several times. She practices and rehearses until the words and phrasings sound completely natural. When speaking without practice, or presenting "extemporaneously," she is terrible — very stilted, confused and hard to understand. But give her time to prepare and she'll knock your socks off. AND she'll make you think the whole presentation is spontaneous. Amazing!

I'm the opposite. I have a lot of trouble rehearsing a presentation. If I feel comfortable with my material, I prefer to just let the ideas flow out in a unrehearsed format. I love to base my presentation on my sense of the audience. My advice would be don't try it unless you're feeling very confident and you've mastered the basics.

Find your own style and make it more exciting by designing vocal variety into the presentation. Construct specific modules or segments that allow you to get excited. Create phrases that must be said slowly and deliberately with a soft voice. Create others that require a rising tone or a vocal *"build."*

Professional speakers use this emotional construction process all the time. Take politicians for example. They have speechwriters who know exactly how to deliver emotions in just the right dose at the right time. Ronald Reagan was an actor and his writers knew they could rely on him to convey complex messages in his voice and facial expressions so they gave him a chance to do it. By stark contrast, George W. Bush had severe limitations and I imagine his writers consumed cases of scotch in preparation for a major speech. I'm curious to see how Obama's writers overcome this Mr. Spock affect he seems to have. Oh, he's a gifted natural communicator, but emotion isn't his strongest suit.

The point is that you have strengths and limitations as well. So build your presentation with those in mind.

Insert a few dramatic techniques

In addition to the sound of your voice there are specific speaking techniques or tricks you can use to make your presentation more appealing to the ear and richer in emotional content. One of these is...

The Drip

It's like Chinese water torture only good for you. Think about it...one drop on your forehead is meaningless. You might not even feel it. Three straight days of dripping on your forehead will drive you insane.

We don't want to go that far, but the principle is similar. There are segments of your seminar that must be repeated for the message to sink in and have the impact you desire. If you want someone to remember something, tell them three times. If you want them to take action, tell them five times.

You can often use the "instant replay" where you say something, pause and say it again verbatim.

"Folks, fewer than 3% of 65-year-old retirees are financially self sufficient. LET ME REPEAT THAT. Fewer than 3% of 65 year-old retirees are financially self sufficient."

Then repeat it again using more descriptive language.

"Of the 35 people in the room right now only one of you will have enough money to maintain your lifestyle when you reach retirement age."

Now put it aside for a few minutes but be ready to come back to it later in the seminar and repeat it again.

"Why is growth important? Well, remember we said earlier that only 3% of retirees will be financially self-sufficient, so you've got to build your asset base and the only way to do that is with growth-oriented investments."

Without knowing why, many people will leave your seminar with that "three percent" statistic floating around in their heads. It will leave an impact.

Triads

These are a major tool of political speakers and have a strong emotional effect. A triad, like many speaking techniques, is a statement made in three parts. It has a very distinct delivery and it works because of some innate genetic affinity for things that come in three's, (which is why good jokes build on triad form). Here's an example:

"Stocks are the best source of growth."

"Stocks are the best source of rising income."

(PAUSE)

"Stocks are the best way to meet your financial goals!"

The words "Stocks are the best" form the base of the triad. Each statement is delivered with slightly different emphasis on the variable portion, in this case "growth, income and goals."

Try it again, only with a slight switch in structure.

"Keeping your money in the bank will not allow you to retire."

"Investing in bonds will not allow you to retire."

"Buying real estate will not allow you to retire."

"The only investment that will allow you to retire...is stocks!"

You can use this form several times in your presentation with great effect. It gets the message across nicely and adds a professional touch. By the way...I've never seen a seminar written like this. You won't get this from the company's slide show. You've got to put it in there yourself. By the way...the actual investment advice to own stocks may or may not be accurate...I'm only trying to illustrate a speaking device here.

Figures of speech & devices

Figures of speech, if not labored, add greatly to the color of your seminar. We all use figures of speech without even realizing what we're doing, so they will ring comfortably in the ears of your audience.

A *simile* is a comparison of one thing to another:

"His portfolio was like a carton of broken eggs."

An *analogy* goes a little deeper and usually offers one or two sentences of explanation.

"The market today is like a wild roller coaster. It goes up and down in hair-raising swings and the ride can get a little scary unless you have a seasoned professional sitting next to you to hold your hand.

A *metaphor* is a comparison in which one thing is described as if it were another:

"This bawdy casino called Wall Street."

Irony says one thing to convey another:

"In an attempt to make his portfolio grow...he buried it alive."

Hyperbole is the use of exaggeration for emphasis:

"He was the best portfolio manager in the entire solar system!"

Rhyme should be used sparingly.

Anaphora is the repetition of words at the beginning of successive clauses or sentences similar to our first example in triads..."*Stocks are best.*"

Assonance is the deliberate repetition of a vowel sound, but in combination with a different consonant, so that it is not what is normally thought of as rhyme: "old oak," "mad hat," top notch."

Consonance is the repetition of final consonant sounds, as in: "tip top," "knick knack," "ding dong."

Alliteration is the repetition of initial consonant sounds. It's one of my favorites.

"Deliberate, defined discipline!"

"Beaten, bombarded and bewildered!"

"Tried and true."

Cadence is rhythm combined with inflection, the melody or even musicality of the phrases:

"Give me liberty...or give me death!"

"Mr. Gorbachev...tear - down - this - wall!"

There is some overlapping among these categories and terms. The important thing is to grasp their function rather than to worry about what they're called.

Movement & gestures

Movement and gestures are often confusing to amateur speakers, but to a skilled seminar presenter, they can be tools of great precision and impact. When we talk about *movement*, we're referring to your entire body walking around the room. Gestures are more subtle uses of your hands and arms as well as facial expressions.

Movement helps you keep the audience's attention and can spice up a presentation. It allows you to emphasize or punctuate key points and convey a feeling of energy and excitement. It gives you a physical transition effect between major sections of your talk. It can also be used to regain audience control and disarm potentially dangerous situations if they arise. We will discuss the "Sniper" later, but movement is one of the critical ways to shut down a troublesome person in the crowd.

Some types of movements can be distracting and tiring. I've seen speakers who oscillate from one side of the room to the other at a steady rhythm. They're like a tennis ball caught in a slow-motion baseline rally. It can actually put people to sleep.

Before you move…ask yourself a few questions:

1. Where are you going? — Do you have a target or are you merely wandering? Wandering is not good. Better you had stayed home. Set a target point and go there.

2. Why are you going? — What's the reason for the move? Are you shifting pace or themes? Are you trying to connect a thought to a previous idea? Are you sensing that they are tired and you're simply trying to wake them up? The reason or "motivation" for the movement will help answer then next question.

3. How are you going to get there? — Are you going directly at a rapid pace or are you sauntering casually? Both will work depending on the message you're trying to convey. For example, you might start walking as you begin a new thought and time it so that you reach center stage at the precise moment of climax. You may want to signal a dramatic shift of mood by walking briskly to the back of the room. You might want to physically unite the crowd by starting a thought on the left side and running over to the right side to repeat the thought.

4. What are you going to do once you get there? — Once you arrive at your designated spot, what's next? Do you hold that ground and deliver a few thoughts from this new locale? Are you just stopping by on the way to an even more important position? Is this a good place to begin a new thought or segment?

As you can see, movement is not haphazard. It needs to support the content. That same principle applies to gestures.

In the world of gestures we are primarily dealing with more subtle motions of the arms, hands, eyes and face. Although not as dramatic and bold as full-body motion, gestures can be extremely powerful tools that will help you transmit many different meanings and messages.

"Interest rates have fallen…" show me fallen with your hands and arms. *"The opportunity is huge…"* How huge? Open your arms wide like you just caught a

BIG fish. *"Move 30% of your assets overseas."* Do it! Carve up an imaginary pie right in front of them and carry it across the room.

Gestures add a sense of drama to your words and they can often express tremendous emotion without words at all. We use hundreds of gestures and facial expressions in normal, every-day communication and each one has a certain meaning. For example, if I say something and then roll my eyes...that usually denotes sarcasm. My gesture actually "says" the exact opposite of the words I used.

Sizing your gestures correctly is important. Too small and you can't be seen by people in the back row or you may appear timid and unconvincing. Too large and you look like you're having a bad reaction to some medication. You should videotape your seminars and have someone you trust evaluate the emotional content of your movements — first with no sound and then with sound to verify a matching image projection.

Loosen up a bit

The vast majority of speakers I've coached over the years tend to understate their movements, so you can probably afford to let go a bit. As long as your movements and gestures support the emotional content of your message, movements can help a lot with very little downside.

If you're not comfortable with movement or gestures, you may first want to watch some professional public speakers or politicians. Learning from a television actor is less useful because TV gestures are totally different and much more subtle than stage movement.

One of the best sources for technique on movement and gestures is those television evangelist ministers. This has nothing to do with religion, so don't go getting offended here...OK?

My favorite was Jimmy Swaggart. For all his faults, the guy was truly an amazing speaker! He had such a range of delivery styles that you could watch him for an hour and not see the same technique twice. The hands, the eyes, the use of props, body movement, stage position, and microphone technique...all coordinated with his words and perfected to drive home his emotional message. He cried, he laughed, he shouted, whispered, pounded the podium, you name it and he did it...on stage I mean. Whew, what a workout...for him AND the audience.

Now I don't recommend that you mimic these styles completely. There is a difference between evangelical preaching and investment seminars, if not in content, then certainly in audience expectations. If, however, you ever get a chance to drop by one of these sermons...do it. From purely a delivery point of view, I guarantee you'll learn something.

Subtle touches

There is another category of gestures you can use with great impact in a seminar. These are dramatic elements designed to communicate a subliminal message. I'm giving away some secrets here but one good example comes at the end of a presentation.

I want the audience to believe that I'm physically *"drained."* I do this to convince them that I've given 200% during the seminar, which is a way of implying that I will give 200% as their financial advisor.

To convey this exhaustion I might take my glasses off and rub my tired eyes - take a deep breath to gather my strength between major thematic points - lean against the lectern, take off my jacket, un-button my tie, get a drink of water, gently mop my sweating brow.

There's a hundred of these little gestures and they can be customized to the situation. They can help you gain control, build empathy, stall for time while you're thinking, punctuate a phrase you want them to remember and loosen up a room.

Don't go crazy

The combination of vocal variety, movement and gestures definitely adds energy, excitement and enthusiasm to your seminar, but for a small percentage of you, there is a risk of going overboard. Too much excitement and you could lose credibility. If you're going to err, do so on the side of caution. Far better to have an audience walk away slightly bored than to have them thinking you're a nut job who can't stand still.

I realize that many of you will not feel comfortable with all this acting technique. That's OK. If you incorporate one or two simple ideas or use a little more vocal variety, I guarantee you're not going to hurt yourself and you WILL see an improvement in audience response.

The vast majority of people doing investment seminars across the nation today are not using any of these techniques. You now have an advantage that you can use at your discretion.

Chapter 15

THE RECAP

"Speak properly and is as few words as you can, but always plainly; for the end of speech is not ostentation, but to be understood."

Anonymous

Tell them what you told them.

You're done with the body of the talk and you're getting ready to move into Q&A. Before you do, take a minute to recap. Tell them what you told them and reinforce the logical manner in which you analyzed the problem. The recap is a vital transition element in a talk and it re-focuses everyone on the broad theme.

"OK…is everyone's head swimming now? Hey, I don't blame you…we've covered a lot of ground here tonight. We looked at the economy. We examined why inflation and interest rates are likely to remain low for the next few years and then we detailed three broad strategies you can use right away to best position your portfolio for the remainder of this decade."

Don't skip the recap. It only takes is 45-60 seconds, but it gives the audience a chance to take a breath and make the mental shift into the critical Questions & Answers (Q&A) segment. A good recap will allow them a moment to collect their thoughts and formulate questions. It will often remind them of ideas they may have had earlier in your presentation. A recap also signals that you are getting close to the end of the event…which is a good thing. They can begin to wind down and relax a bit. Used properly, a recap reinvigorates an audience – it gives them a second wind and an attention boost for the home stretch.

The recap also allows you to insert one or two quick *"factoids"* that you omitted from the body of your talk. These can reinforce the image in their minds of you as the expert. It can also be a good time for a humorous story or a little levity. This adds to the relaxation process.

By the way, when I say that anticipating the end of the event is a good thing, I don't mean that they're glad you're done because you were bad or they weren't having a good time. No matter how good you are, people can only sit and listen for so long. Their brains can't take more than sixty or max ninety minutes of content, even well-delivered, emotional content.

Have you ever been in a seminar kind of losing the focus, maybe drifting off mentally. Then when the moderator or speaker says *"OK only ten minutes until the break!"* you begin to perk up. *"Wow, only ten minutes...I can stay tuned in for ten minutes...then I get a break!"* Suddenly you're back into the talk.

Finally, I use the recap to send two important messages:

1. I am in charge here.

2. I just gave you a tremendous amount of value and information, but this is not as easy as I'm making it seem.

These are important concepts for a few reasons. First, you want to establish solid audience control before the dangerous Question & Answer session to follow. If you go into the Q&A with any sense of weakness or confusion, you run a greatly increased risk of enemy sniper fire.

The recap reinforces the main thematic elements of your talk. This sets up the Q&A "foul poles" — the boundaries beyond which you do not have to address issues or answer questions. These will be very important as you'll learn in a minute.

The second message is also a great one. You will find as you do more seminars that people will come to appreciate your ability to make the complex world of money seem simple and easy to understand. Concurrent with that appreciation, will be the unspoken understanding they have that it's NOT really as easy as you made it seem. They know that's true but the fact that you tried so hard to simplify it makes them like you and respect you even more. I might add something like this to the paragraph above:

> "Folks, please understand...and I think you do...that tonight was just a broad brush overview of what is, in practice, a fairly complex subject. In one hour, it's impossible to teach you everything you might need to know to make these kinds of decisions. My team and I have spent years learning these strategies. We work with them every

day and customize them for clients. Yet even with that experience, even WE need to rely on our experts for some answers."

"That customization process makes all the difference. At almost every one of my seminars, someone walks away feeling so excited by this discussion that they immediately try to implement some of the techniques we discussed as stand-alone strategies without taking into account the impact on other pieces of their portfolio. And that's great...we want you to be excited. These are exciting ideas!"

"Typically, they call me a week later and say '*Frank...you said I should buy XYZ or do such and such with my portfolio. I'm having trouble making that work.*'"

"This is totally understandable. You're smart people and you want to apply what you've learned. All I say is, be careful, use good judgment and balance the impact of the strategy with the portfolio as a whole."

"To use a sports analogy...investing can be like playing professional football. Tonight I gave each of you a pair of new shoulder pads and a shiny new helmet. That doesn't mean you're ready to play in the NFL."

Doing a recap like this is simple and the benefits are significant.

Chapter 16

MASTERING THE QUESTION & ANSWER SESSION

"A coward turns away but a brave man's choice is danger."

Euripides

"It is not every question that deserves an answer."

Publilius Syrus

The Q&A session is the most dangerous part of the seminar…it's also my favorite!

It exposes you to the crowd in a very direct and vulnerable position. In fact, the fear of Q&A is the single biggest reason many advisors hate seminars in the first place. If you screw up, you run the risk of destroying the emotional mood you've established for the past 45-90 minutes.

On the other hand, if you're good, you'll gain tremendous credibility and reinforce your messages. You will get a chance to highlight and embellish the key concepts you most want them to remember. The audience will see you as someone who can think on his feet and move beyond any prepared text or speech. That's a VERY good thing!

How to get the questions flowing

Make no mistake about it...you WANT questions. A presentation that generates questions is one that has prompted an audience to *think* not just listen. There are many things you can do throughout the seminar to assure that you get questions. You can even go so far as to plant the actual questions in their minds when a particularly tricky or controversial sub-topic is being discussed.

> "Now some of you are probably wondering...why our investment discipline forced us to wait until the stock had appreciated 30% before we bought it. That's a great question and we can cover that in the Q&A."

I will often pick out a friendly face in the crowd and give them the task of asking a specific question during the Q&A feigning that I don't want to get sidetracked at this point in the presentation. In reality, I want to use them to "shill" for me later in the event.

> "OK...it's your job to remember this and ask me later! You got it?"

The turn to the person next to them and joke...

> "And it's your job to remind him!"

People love being assigned jobs at the event. It makes them feel important and special.

If you've done your job, the questions will follow very naturally. Sometimes, however, you must prompt the audience to get the flow started. This is a very easy technique that I learned years ago and it rarely fails if you do it right. Learn it, practice it...it works!

When you're ready for questions, simply say, *"Are there any questions?"* and raise your hand like you do in school. Keep it there for AS LONG AS IT TAKES to get a question. Maybe three seconds, maybe thirty. Even the toughest crowd, filled with people who can't wait to get to the door, will respond after 10 seconds.

The key here is to NEVER break the silence or drop your hand down. Once you say *"Are there any questions?"* you must not speak or move again until you get a question!

If you do as most amateurs do and say *"Oh come on. Was I that good? Did everyone understand everything?"* you release the emotional pressure and the clock starts again.

After I raise my hand, I begin a slow scan of the audience, eyeball by eyeball. I usually start with someone I've bonded to during the event. Typically, they will feel comfortable enough to open things up.

Once that first question comes out, the audience will relax and you'll probably get several hands popping up at once, otherwise simply raise your hand again... *"Any more questions?"* If it's slow, like pulling teeth, simply conclude after two or three questions. Don't drag out a painful moment. If you can't save it...let it go.

And don't take forever answering the questions you DO get. This isn't a mini-seminar here. A long-winded answer is sure to make others reluctant to ask a question. In fact, your verbose style might very well be the reason you're not getting questions in the first place. You've been in many presentations with a speaker who just went on and on. Remember how hard you prayed that it would end and that no one would ask a question.

If you sense that the audience is reluctant to ask questions but someone cracks under your hand-raise pressure technique, your answer to them cannot be a ten-minute soliloquy. A quick, thoughtful response is your best chance to keep the flow going.

Some people recommend that you turn the tables on the audience and cleverly ask *them* a question. That's cute for one of those audience-participation love fests. I think sophisticated audiences see right through this as a cute attempt to drag out the process. Besides, you've just spent an hour convincing them that you're the expert. All you do with this *"ask them"* technique is reduce your stature and arm a potential sniper with a bazooka!

They are testing you

To become a Q&A Session Master, you must understand that audiences are very sensitive about their questions. They view the Q&A as their chance to challenge and test you. Assuming you've done a good job in the body of the presentation, they will be rooting for you to pass the test, but they are eager to test you anyway. It's their right and they take it seriously.

You must listen intently to the question being asked. Not only are you trying to understand the content so that you can answer appropriately, you are also trying to hear the emotional context of the question. As you are listening, the audience is listening too. Part of your test is content. Did you answer the actual question or did you not listen and answer some other question. They hate it when you do that. If you aren't tuned into the question being asked, the audience will pick this up right away. An incomplete or badly delivered answer could create feelings of unease or even disrespect... ***"He's not answering that lady's question! What's the matter with him. We can't trust him!"*** Bang...just like that...you've undone yourself.

Answering the right question is mainly a function of open-minded concentration. Two micro-seconds before the question begins, in that space between the moment you acknowledge a raised hand and the words start to pour out of someone's mouth...you must clear your mind of noise and focus. This takes discipline, but you can do it.

While you're listening for the factual or technical content of the question, watch for clues as to the person's emotional state. Are they nervous? Probably. Are they angry? Are they probing you for truth in an effort to see if they can trust you? Are they trying to trip you up and show the room how much they know? What's the motivation for the question? Is it an academic issue involving some small point of discussion on which there is no right answer or is it a point of clarification on a major topic that may have confused them? Are you being dragged into a debate? Are you headed for a ride down memory lane? What's going on here?

This emotional side is important because one person's state of mind will give you a good picture of how many others in the room are feeling at this point. Your answer needs to be structured and delivered in such a way as to reinforce the positive emotional foundation you've built for the past hour.

Right now, in a minute or two, with your answer, you may find yourself rebuilding confidence, respect, happiness, fear, the whole emotional train ride. This is what makes the Q&A so dangerous and so rewarding. You have a chance to shine brighter than you could in any other part of the event. If you do a solid job, you will have won them over totally. If you mess up...well it's terrifying to imagine!

How to answer questions

The mechanics of answering questions are simple. First, restate each question before you answer. Three reasons for this:

- It shows the asker that you listened carefully

- It gives you time to think

- It gives you a chance to re-phrase the question

We talked about listening carefully. You know why that's important. Time to think is obvious, but it's also important how quickly you think and, in hyper-sophisticated events...what you do and how you look *while* you're thinking.

This is going way too deep for our main purpose here, but some of you might find yourself in a mini-seminar with some very intelligent and sophisticated people who are used to seeing lots of high-level presentations…a Board of Directors meeting might be a good example.

You might be asked a question on a business-critical topic — something you absolutely should know but either don't know or don't want to reveal.

In the space of a few seconds, you will be thinking of an answer. As you're formulating it in your mind, your eyes will give away your secret. The way your eyes move while your thinking can tell a very astute audience who is skilled in the science of Neuro-Linguistic Programming (NLP) whether you're telling the truth or lying — accessing facts from memory or making stuff up. It's scary and it works. It's why professional poker players wear sunglasses.

> *Highly polished communicators like hostage negotiators, intelligence operatives at the FBI or CIA are thoroughly skilled in NLP and can spot telltale subliminal signals a mile away. I learned NLP when I was stationed at Fort Meade, the home of the National Security Agency. It was a fascinating look at a world most people don't even know exists. All I can say is I'm glad they're on our side!*

Rephrasing the question is important for several reasons, and although it seems like it goes against what I just said about answering the question that's being asked, it doesn't.

Often the asker will present the question in such a way that the rest of the audience sort of loses interest. You must make the question meaningful to the whole audience or you run the risk of losing control. You're going to rephrase it so that it is interesting and still acceptable to the asker. You're going to ask permission, either verbally or through gestures to assure that your re-phrased question is OK with the asker before you answer it. Doing this does not violate the earlier rule about listening for content.

Rephrasing the question also allows you to control the emotional sub-text. If, for example, the asker seems hostile or angry, you can bet that the audience is aware of this. You might want to relax the room or lighten him up a bit before you answer. Often a hostile question is a prelude to a sniper attack which we'll discuss in a second. You've got to make a quick determination on how to handle this kind of question and rephrasing allows you a moment to think and gain emotional control.

By the way, you don't always want to tone down an emotionally charged question. Sometimes it can be very powerful to build on this emotion by adding your own complimentary energy to a touchy or troubling subject.

When you're rephrasing the question, you don't need to say *"The question was..."* Simply pause for a second, restructure and repeat the question in your own words to the entire audience. Avoid saying *"That's a good question."* It implicitly obligates you to compliment all the question-askers and leaves you no room to maneuver. What do you say next? *"That's a GREAT question, That's a FANTASTIC question!"* Just skip it.

It's OK to direct part of the answer to the asker, but you don't want it to become a one-on-one conversation, so do not finish with your eyes on him. That gives them permission for a follow-up and this isn't a Presidential press conference. You want everyone to benefit from your answer and have a chance to ask their own questions and you never want to cede too much control to one individual.

What about tough questions?

Tough questions are potential trouble, but there's a specific method to handling them that should render them harmless. If you've ever done a seminar this has happened to you. Someone pops up with a question and you would absolutely swear that she just read some article in Forbes or the Economist and is asking you to comment on some detailed subject. You're at a distinct disadvantage here because the asker is armed with just enough information to sound really smart and you didn't read the article so you haven't got a clue. Sound familiar? Here's how you handle it.

Often, what makes the question tough is the way it was phrased. Start by re-phrasing it with your own words and try to give it a more relaxed and simplified structure. This can be done under the guise of trying to make the question more understandable to the audience who didn't read the article either (or so you hope). What you're really trying to do is take the edges off the question and reduce the level of detail need to answer it in an intelligent-sounding manner.

Try to break a complex question down into smaller chunks and take it one bite at a time. Assuming it's a legit question and not a trap, you should have no trouble answering it and thus demonstrating your ability to think through complex situations. The audience will love this.

When confronted by a particularly tough question on a specific sub-topic that would require a detailed knowledge of items you may not be immediately familiar with, use a pyramid structure to get out of trouble. Start from a narrow focus and work down to the broader subject. Re-state the question giving it a broader perspective allowing you to answer it with a "wider view" by relating it to the main seminar theme. I'll give you an example:

You've just done 55 minutes on global investing. It has gone very well and you feel as though the audience is eager to embrace your ideas...when suddenly...up jumps the Devil!

> "What effect will the decline in the German unemployment rates have on inflation and interest rates in the European community? Isn't this the WRONG time to be buying foreign stocks?"

You just spent the last hour saying it was the RIGHT time to be in Europe and now this Hell Hound is destroying your credibility. What's worse is that this is a completely *legitimate* question. You *should* know the answer. It's not some obscure or irrelevant fact. All eyes are on you. You struggle. Your mind is a blur. Why didn't you read that article? Part of you just wants to race from the room screaming! But then your combat training takes over. You're tough and ready for anything.

> "OK, let's take that one piece at a time because I want there to be absolutely no confusion on this issue."

I'm implying that the questioner may be confused.

Or even better…

> "Did everyone hear this question? This is an interesting question and I'm not sure even you *(the questioner)* realize how important this is. There aren't more than a handful of people who would have picked up on this…I'm impressed!"

I'm going out of my way to make the guy feel really important for asking such an insightful question. The reason is that I don't want a follow-up of any kind and I want him to shut up…so I'm going to build him up so that he couldn't possibly top this moment.

> "This question raises a great teaching point. Let me *expand* on this for a minute just so everyone understand the relationship between inflation, interest rates and unemployment in an economy."

> "What is the risk of rising inflation and what does that mean for the stock markets?

You've restated the question into a broader, less detail-driven problem. Hopefully, you do know the relationships involved and you can answer a much more general issue.

"In any economy there is a concern about the risk of rising inflation because, in general that could signal higher interest rates which could put pressure on the overall stock market. These are exactly the kinds of indicators we watch every day...unemployment, productivity, wage rates, consumer prices - all of that goes into our assessment of every country's economic strength. You can't just go into these markets blindly...we've got to have solid intelligence and a good understanding of what driving these markets and what's going to make them good long-term investments."

"We're NOT seeing any significant long-term trend in unemployment decline anywhere in Europe. There is no inflation anywhere in the system and the stock markets are poised for some dramatic growth. Does that mean we stop watching the indicators...not for one second. The only meaningful trends across a group of economic fronts are very positive."

"Finally, keep in mind that I am NOT recommending that you own stock in every company in every country in Europe. I am buying very selectively. We want those companies that are most likely to grow in excess of the market averages. That's the key to success."

You've handled a difficult question with calm professionalism and you've enhanced the basic premise of your theme. You did not get too deeply drawn into a discussion of German unemployment because you didn't know anything about it. What you knew were general facts that could be applied to any economy and you "pretended" to know a little about the general nature of the statistics noted in the question. Did you lie? Not at all. Could you have been wrong? Sure. But no one pays you to be right ALL the time.

Even in the face of the most bizarre and obscure question this method gives you the ability to extrapolate from broad, well-defined concepts and formulate a plausible answer or explanation. When it comes to your seminar topic, there is no subject or related that you can't discuss intelligently for 30-90 seconds in response to a question. Or, when it gets really tough - there is no question you can't rephrase into something you DO know and CAN answer.

But keep one thought in mind: the Q&A session at the end of your seminar is not the time to solve all the world's financial problems. If you get a question that is so involved and so difficult that it will take more than one or two minutes to answer simply, or a question the answer to which would take you deep into another subject off your main thesis, gently deflect it and move on. It's not fair to the audience to make them sit through a 15 minute dialogue between you and the questioner.

"That's a very tough question. You've opened a subject that has confused many people for years and I'm not sure I can answer that in the few minutes we have left. Let me suggest that we speak after the meeting and we can spend more time on it, because it is important and I want to be able to give it some detailed attention."

I've rarely had that backfire on me. You're being very polite and straightforward. It's not that you can't answer the question but you feel it deserves a more thorough response.

Be sure, however, to follow through on this question. If your seen trying to avoid the issue, it will have negative consequences. Immediately after the seminar, I will make a point to go right up to the person who asked the question and set a time for a meeting. *"Give me three minutes and I'll be right back here to discuss this issue. I just want to say good night to a few people."*

If the asker is serious, he'll stick around and chances are you will have a small audience to hear your answer to this complex question. This can become a mini-seminar with significant benefits if you handle it well.

Is it OK to say..."I don't know?"

I have a problem here...and many of you are going to disagree with my answer. That's OK. You can do whatever works for you.

Most people will tell you that it's OK, even beneficial to say *"I don't know but I'll get back to you,"* when someone asks a tough question. They say that you build trust and confidence by being honest enough to admit you don't have all the answers.

Frankly, I think that's dangerous advice and only partly true!

What's true about that statement is that most intelligent investors know that you, as one person, cannot know all things about the complex world of finance and investing. They fully expect that you will have to research ideas from time to time and confer with your experts. In fact, they like it when you do that!

What's dangerous about "I don't know" is that you *should* know and have anticipated everything they can ask before you decide to get up and do a seminar. You should be able to handle any question ON YOUR SUBJECT that the audience is likely to ask...or are you really expert enough to be giving the seminar in the first place?

It has been my experience that true professionals and top speakers — the people who really command respect and admiration — are never stumped by a question ON THEIR SUBJECT.

Hold your own Q&A session

This puts a lot of pressure on you...doesn't it? I mean...how can you possibly anticipate every question that might come up at an event? Well, start by holding your own Q&A session. Literally, sit down and go through your presentation section by section and brainstorm:

"Given my audience's general age, interests and life experiences, what might they ask me here?" I would even go further..."What would a sniper who wants to show off and make me look bad potentially ask me here?" "What might the CFO of my town's biggest company ask me here?"

Holding your own Q&A session will really make you feel confident and you will begin to distinguish between the two types of questions you'll be facing in the real session. Those are:

Fact questions

Opinion questions

Fact questions are tough because you actually have to know something. The good news is that you already know more facts than anyone in your audience. During your secret Q&A session, look for those areas in your presentation where an important point hangs on a group of facts, statistic or historical economic data. Then research it and make sure you're bulletproof on that issue. Let me give you an example.

I was talking about the future of the markets and how interest rates have steadily declined for the last 18 years and someone rose to challenge me.

"Frank, rates actually went up in the early 90s...so what you're saying isn't really accurate."

The amateur, unaware of interest rate history would probably say,

"Your right...rates did back up in the early 90s but on balance interest rates today are a lot lower than they were 20 years ago...that's all I'm saying."

The professional says,

"Long term government bond rates moved up from 7.4% to 9.3% from April of 1991 to July of 1992, And then again in June of 1994 from 7.3% to 8.1%, but those were market moves unrelated to the action of the Fed."

"In each of those years, the Fed continued to reduce rates, they cut seven times in 92/93 and then five times 94/95. It's important not to get fooled by short-term counter-trend movements in the bond market."

"Those cyclical adjustments have very little impact on the direction of the economy. The key is Fed Funds and for the past 18 years we've seen those critical rates drop from 12.7% to 3.1% and long-term bonds from 16.5% to 5.1% That's the historic trend we're talking about."

Wow! You just took this fact question and smacked it so far out of the park that it's still flying.

How do you get that kind of information? You have to do your homework! By anticipating this question, I knew what research I had to do and I looked up the movement of rates. It's simple…but it's also work — which is why many amateurs won't ever get to the top of the profession and why you will!

Bottom line is I think you should always have an answer for questions related to your topic.

The question from left-field

There will be a time when you get a question from left field that has nothing to do with the subject and for which you cannot be expected to have an answer. **Simply don't answer the question.** No law says you have to deal with every strange question that comes up in a seminar. You're not there to be a sounding board for some stream-of-consciousness rambler who needs to hear himself talk.

As we mentioned earlier, casually laying out the Q&A ground rules or "foul poles" before you start the Q&A can make this an easier task. With an undercurrent of fun and good humor, it goes something like this:

"Before we get into the questions let me set out a few rules. I've found that this helps the process and ensures that everyone gets a chance to cover the issues on their mind. First…I would rather not deal with questions about individual stocks you may own. No one cares about the three shares of American Widget you inherited from your grandfather. I'll be more than happy to stay around after the seminar if you want to talk about portfolios, but not during the Q&A, OK?"

"Second...if your question take more than two minutes to ask...it's a speech...not a question. I'm the only one who gets to make speeches here."

"Third, our topic is retirement planning, but if you have a question about a related issue...just jump right in. I know that there are many aspects of investing in general that may be confusing and that impact retirement, so if you're unclear about anything and you feel as though it's related to our subject...I want to hear from you now. I will tell you if it's too far off the subject. When I do that it usually means I don't have an answer."

You've now set the tone for the process. It's not heavy-handed or too confining. You've used humor to illustrate the common things that audiences hate during the Q&A and you've set yourself up to be able to handle anything that comes your way. By doing this, you've eliminated many of the potential *"I don't know"* responses.

I realize that this may be considered a philosophical issue. In an ideal world you would know everything about your main theme and all peripheral subjects. In the real world you must make a decision between looking less than professional by saying *"I don't know"* when you SHOULD know...or by using your vast array of experience and knowledge to "synthesize" an answer to a tough question in a public presentation environment.

The Q&A nightmares

So what about the really rough question or questioner? I define rough as any question or questioner which may cause me to lose the emotional edge or control of the audience.

Here are three common headaches that pop up during the Q&A part of the seminar and how to deal with them.

"The Sniper"

Every crowd has one — and they are the most dangerous adversary you face as a speaker. I'm not talking about an honest, tough question here. Not everyone is going to agree with your thesis and good probing question is fine. The sniper, however, doesn't really want an answer. He would rather initiate an argument and show everyone else how much HE knows. He is a business-threatening enemy and must be terminated with extreme prejudice.

You never know when a sniper will pop up so be sure and listen to all questions carefully. The sniper generally gives himself away in the tone of the question. Usually, it's very convoluted and complex. It may have nothing to do with your subject and it may come out in a fairly confrontational manner. You will be able to tell pretty quickly that this is a potential problem. Remember, this is NOT just a good, tough question. You must be convinced that the questioner is deliberately trying to undermine your credibility before you resort to the following tactics.

When a sniper starts shooting, you can feel the tension in the room rise….but don't panic. You've got control. If you've done your job for the past hour, this audience thinks you're the expert, they like you and they are ready to side with you in battle with the sniper.

To take out a sniper, use a few simple countermeasures. Start by making a special effort to listen intently to the question with a concentrated focus on the person. Two reasons for this intense listening: First, you want to find a loophole in the sniper's logic — some faulty reasoning that you can use to deflect his fire.

Second, you want the audience to believe that you're really making an effort to understand the sniper. This will generate cooperation from them when the time is right. You want them to believe that you're truly concerned with this individual's question. Now is the time for gestures like taking off your glasses or closing your eyes or walking over toward the sniper to listen more closely. All the time I'm thinking of how I'm going to blow him out of the water. Isn't this fun?

While he's talking, I will take note of the effect he's having on the crowd. Are they getting nervous? Are they angry that he's taking so much time? Do they even understand what he's asking? I need them on my side so I've got to know how they're reacting to him.

I then restate the question in very simple terms while turning away from the sniper completely. So I go from intense direct contact to zero contact in one physical move. Often, you can finesse an inexperienced sniper by giving a direct and brief answer to his question. But if not, I never hesitate to get tough, especially if I know the rest of the room is on my side.

> "I have the feeling that you would rather argue than ask a legitimate question, so why don't you see me after the seminar and we can discuss your problem."

Or my favorite,

> "I'd be more eager to give you a good answer if I thought there was the slightest chance you could understand it."

I am exaggerating. It's extremely rare that you have to get that tough with anyone, but you are in command and you can't appear to lose control if you want to maintain the respect of the audience. Often, the best answer is an exasperated,

"I have no idea what you're talking about!"

This implies that they aren't making themselves clear or the question is so weird as to be invalid.

Using facial expressions and gestures you might want to display mild to overt annoyance at the sniper. It's a signal to your friendly forces in the audience to help out. Maybe someone sitting next to the sniper will chime in and tell him to *"be quiet."* Or a friendly on the other side of the room will jump up with a new question allowing you to make a clean break with the sniper. The audience dynamic when you're under sniper attack is truly amazing, and to the degree you can understand it you can control it toward your own advantage and the ultimate good of the entire room.

Whatever happens, remember this.

Never let anyone take control of your seminar!

You've spent an hour or more building an emotional state in the minds of an audience. A sniper can destroy that and negate all your efforts in a few seconds if you allow it. Again, I stress that we're not talking about the standard tough question. You will learn to quickly recognize the sniper over time. If you come under fire, be firm and keep control at all costs. You are 007 with a license to kill, so use it. After doing this for so long, I now preemptively kill potential snipers just for fun.

A few years ago I was doing a huge meeting for the top producers of a major investment firm. I was the closing keynote speaker on the last day of the conference. This is a tough time slot because everyone was a little brain-dead after three straight days of meetings, but I couldn't pass it up.

I started my talk but out of the corner of my eye, I noticed a person in the very last row reading the paper. That struck me as very rude, but I figured he'd stop after a few seconds so I just let it pass. Unfortunately, he didn't stop. In fact, he started making a lot of noise, shaking the paper up in the air as he folded it.

Now I'm up there thinking…this is too much…I have to do something. But what to do? These were all top producers…the stakes were enormous!

So I started walking to the back of the room. Casually, not wanting to alert him to my presence. I just kept talking as I went, but everyone was turning to watch me as I snuck up on the rude sniper. He never saw me coming. Suddenly, with a lightning fast sweeping motion of my arm…I grabbed the paper from his hands, crumpled it up and threw it to the back of the room and said…"If you want to read the damn paper then get the Hell out of the room. Otherwise sit here and you might learn something!"

People were stunned! The room fell totally silent because what I didn't know was that this guy was the #1 producer in the whole company! For the next 90 minutes all eyes were glued to me. I had total attention. People didn't blink for fear of being the next victim.

At the end of the talk…the crowd rushed the stage and, to my amazement, congratulated me for what I had done to this guy. One person said, "He's been doing that to every speaker for three straight days and you were the only one who had the guts to call him on it!" My credibility with that audience jumped three notches and my preemptive destruction paid off. It could have gone the other way, but I had no choice.

The Griper

This is the client who was *"burned by an advisor"* in a limited partnership or a hot growth stock a few years ago and now all financial advisors are crooks and he's going to make your life miserable. This is a bad one but it can lead you into a fantastic commercial for yourself.

Try to handle his concern as honestly and openly as possible keeping in mind that everyone in that room may have some bad experiences with a advisor in the past, so you can't dismiss him or treat him like a sniper (which he isn't yet). I'll then "confess" that there are some loose cannons in our business. There are some advisors (very few) who abuse this awesome responsibility for personal gain, just like in every profession. But then I'll get into my philosophy which begins with my belief that we in the financial industry have a higher obligation than nearly any other profession including doctors.

Think about it. Doctors take an oath that states as its initial tenet, "Do no harm." We don't have that luxury. "Harm" is not up to us because every investment involves risk, often unseen risks too. As financial professionals in a changing market environment, we must be as well versed in risk as we are in reward.

People only need a doctor or a lawyer when they're sick or in trouble. But people with money need us all the time. They have to do something with it, they have no choice.

Doctors and lawyers all follow universally accepted standards and patterns of treatment or defense based on written laws and guidelines.

Our laws and guidelines change every day with the markets. What was an effective "financial treatment" six months ago may be deadly to the same patient today.

In short, I believe we have a moral obligation to be better, more ethical, more knowledgeable and ultimately more professional than anyone who carries a title. Is that wishful thinking in this industry? Absolutely not.

Back to the unhappy client. Here's a few ideas...

> "Not all investment advisors are cut from that cloth. In fact, very few. Some of us do business very differently, as evidenced by this seminar tonight. Because I know that our relationship is built on trust and that trust takes time."

> "My clients eventually look upon me as their partner. I manage all their assets, their retirement plans, their corporate accounts and they refer me to their friends. That kind of trust is only earned over time."

> "Look, when you think about it, anyone can advise you about your money." (PAUSE) "I try to do things differently. (PAUSE) Is it perfect? I doubt it. Is it better? Yes, absolutely. And ultimately, that's a decision that YOU make."

I love the "Griper" because he can lead me into a powerful opportunity to sell myself to the audience. And you have their attention, because you are mad about the way these unscrupulous advisors do business. Do not dilute the questioner's emotional content, but rather add your own emotional overtones to the answer. It would be OK for you to be even MORE angry than the questioner. This can be a great moment, use it wisely and don't be afraid.

The SOCK (Stream-of-consciousness know-it-all)

In this case, the question usually starts like this:

"Back in 1902, my grandfather bought 10 shares of Pacific Railroad. Now that was a good company. Why I remember a time when that stock split seventeen times in one year."

The question comes out like the Beowulf Tapestry. It can go on for twenty minutes and can cause major gastro-intestinal distress. In an effort to be nice and to let someone talk, you could lose much of the emotional momentum you've so carefully created.

Avoid these kinds of personal/historical questions like these during the Q&A. It's just not fair to the audience. I will often prep the Q&A session with a rule, *"If you have any personal questions, I'll be happy to handle those one-on-one."* This is easy, so be mellow, but don't waste too much time. Q&A is a very uncomfortable experience for your audience if not controlled properly.

Remember, what SOCKs really want is to share the stage...to be up there in the spotlight with you. They're hams and they need attention. They cannot be treated as harshly as snipers, so just give them a little rope and let them hang themselves. Remember, you've still got center stage...let them talk for 20 seconds or so and once you realize they're a SOCK...wait for them to take a breath and simply interrupt...

"I'm sorry...what's the question?   or

"There's a question in there somewhere. Do you think we can get to it before we evolve into a higher life-form?"

Simple and fun! It helps to have the audience on your side, but a little humor is often all you need to reign in those loose SOCKs.

The really dumb question

It has been said that the only stupid question is the one that isn't asked. That's just a polite little platitude you throw an audience who you fear may not have understood a word you've said. There are thousands of dumb questions and some will drive you crazy. *"Wasn't this person listening for the last hour?"*

As dumb as the question may be, if you *treat* it like a dumb question that audience can turn on you in a New York second. Remember, they're very possessive and sensitive about their questions. They empathize with the question-asker, so you've got to give each person all the respect you can muster. Displaying patience and concern for someone who may have misunderstood a simple point will go a long way toward building respect and getting an audience to like you.

This is not to say that you must tolerate overwhelming ignorance. Again, watch the audience. If you sense that they're annoyed with the stupidity of the question being asked, you can handle it quickly and perfunctorily. If, on the other hand, they seem interested, there may be others in the audience who wanted to ask the same question but didn't have the guts. Slam dunking a dumb question could make you feel important but will usually have negative emotional results in the long run.

Chapter 17

THE EMOTIONAL CLOSE

"We know too much and feel too little."

Bertrand Russell

OK…you've finished the Q&A and the Appointment Close…now it's time to wrap up your seminar.

Speak slowly, keep it simple, talk emotions and always end on an upbeat, positive note. Again, eye contact is critical, so memorize your close just as you did with the opening. And don't crowd the ending with administrative stuff like collecting questionnaires or conducting the door prize drawing. If there is anything like this that needs to be done at the end, simply insert a line or two *before* the close:

> "In just a minute, I'm going to introduce my assistant, Laura. She has a few announcements and she's going to give away our door prizes."

Let your final words be ones of emotional, excited, professional enthusiasm. This is also a good time to use some of those gestures we discussed earlier – mopping your brow, rubbing your eyes…something to show that you've given a tremendous physical and emotional effort up in front of that room.

> "Ladies & Gentlemen, I'm very happy you came out tonight. Hopefully, you learned a few things about what's going on in the world of money. This is a very exciting and confusing time in our economic history. Things are changing very fast and many of the old rules are being called into question. Some of you may still be a bit hesitant or a little scared. That's OK. It takes years to really get comfortable with some of these concepts. Maybe tonight, we got you started on that road."

"This is a very exciting time to be an investor. I know times are tough and frightening, but there are things happening all around the world that will make the next few years very rewarding. Most importantly...YOU CAN REACH YOUR GOALS if you're willing to take action. After tonight, you're going to be better prepared, better informed and more ready than ever to make it happen. (PAUSE) Just remember...this is a journey you do not have to take alone. We are here to help you. Thank you and good night."

Don't drag this out too long. The ending needs to be precise, not rambling. Less is more at this point.

The post-game show

Even though the seminar is officially over, there is still a lot of activity going on. This post-game show is a very important part of the total seminar process. It is your chance to mingle with important attendees, top clients and their friends and other centers of influence. A lot of business can be done in the ten minutes following the end of the event.

The challenge is that you might be surrounded by people who want to ask questions, debate something you said, congratulate you or tell you a personal story. All of these things are OK, but they could distract you from the more critical conversations you need to have right now.

The key is to be loose, flexible and nimble. Don't get too deeply engaged with any one person. Here are some basic rules that will make your post-game go very smoothly.

Rule #1 - Leave yourself room to escape.

Here's the scenario: You are trying to make it across the room to shake hands with your top client who came to the seminar with a great referral. You stop for a second and suddenly, you're surrounded by six or seven people who want to debate your stance on inflation. You're trapped and you miss a potentially big introduction.

Don't back yourself into a corner or against a wall. Stand in an open area and have clear eye contact with your assistant in case you need help. I have signals worked out with my team — taking off my glasses and coughing is a Code Red Emergency — they need to rescue me immediately with some major matter that requires my immediate attention.

Rule #2 – Don't get wrapped up in details

At the end of a great seminar you have tremendous emotional momentum built up and it's the perfect time to shake hands with the most influential attendees. But inevitably, someone will corner you and want to dig deep into some subtle point that is interesting to about five people on the planet. It's easy to defer any lengthy discussions for the appointment.

> "You know Bob, that is an interesting point…and I'm sure not too many folks even understood it as well as you did. I would love to discuss this some more with you so let's get together next week if you have some time."

If they come in, that's great…they may be serious clients. If not…you avoided wasting precious time.

Rule #3 – Don't give personal advice

If someone wants to discuss their individual situation in detail I would again try to get them to come in for the appointment. Don't conduct a private class. This isn't the forum to address every stock position or give opinions on all their concerns. If they want your concentrated effort, they have to see you one-on-one. Be nice but firm about this. Any advice you dispense now isn't worth a damn anyway. You've got to review their personal situation in greater detail before you can make a recommendation.

Your next great client

As you meet people during the post-seminar mingle, you might be inclined to make snap judgments about them as in – do they have any money? That's very tough to discern. People these days are reluctant to open up to a new advisor right away and tell them where all the assets are invested. They might prefer to remain low-key and see how you react. If you blow them off too vehemently, you send the message that you're only interested in people based on the size of their wallet. It is better to treat everyone who comes to your seminar as if they could potentially become your next great client. You want to be friendly, respectful, courteous and appreciative…no matter how wealthy you might think someone may or may not be.

Rule #4 Solve a problem to get them off the fence.

Prospect X has listened intently all night but just doesn't seem ready to leap into your pocket. He comes up with a question after the seminar.

> "Frank, what do you think of New York City municipal bonds?"

You may or may not have any opinion on what he's asking but this is the chance to get him in for an appointment. Here's what you say:

> "Well, Bob I like munis in general, but credit analysis has become much more complex these days, especially with the troubles city and state governments are having. I would have your portfolio examined as soon as you get a chance. I would be happy to help you."

Solving a specific problem for them may be the final momentum they may need set an appointment.

Rule #5 Make your key attendees feel special

If you've had a client or an important center of influence come to your seminar...go out of your way to find them during this post-game session. This is the time to cement the bond that is developing between you. This is especially true if your client brought a guest or a referral. Go up to them and greet them warmly.

> "George...it's great to see you! I'm really glad you came tonight. Did you win a door prize? No? Don't worry, I saved a dozen golf balls for you!"

Make them feel important, special, like "Big Dog" in the eyes of their friend. It will go a long way toward locking up their guest as a client and locking your client up as a source of future referrals. And besides...you are genuinely happy they came. These are your clients...your lifeblood. They deserve the best treatment you can provide 100% of the time.

In the category of "Special People to Thank" during the post-game show are any audience members you may have made fun during the seminar. If you use humor like I recommend, these people are already emotionally connected to you in a deeper way than the general audience. If you chose these people carefully, they may be your first and best clients as a result of the seminar. Meet them before they leave and thank them for their participation and great sense of humor. Offer them special help anytime they need you.

Rule #6: Thank the facility staff

Wherever you held your event, someone from the facility helped you get it done. Assuming they did a good job, find them and thank them personally. If you want to drop a few bucks on the wait staff as a tip...go ahead. It's not mandatory, but it's a nice touch. Better yet, find the head person and spread a little folded green joy in their direction. If you're ever planning to be back to this location, a few dead presidents make a big impression. Money or no...a personal word of thanks is a nice gesture between human beings.

Rule #7: Thank your team

Finally, stay until the last person leaves and then give your assistants an envelope with $50 or $100 each in cash IN ADDITION to the normal overtime they are entitled to or any other financial arrangement you may have made with them.

Yes, I know it's part of their job. And yes, I know you give them a piece of the business already or a Christmas bonus...whatever. It doesn't matter. You want to tie a reward and a pleasurable experience to the actual seminar event itself. If they're good and you've used them like I've suggested throughout the planning, preparation and execution of the seminar event...they've put out a lot of extra effort.

Your little gift will bond you with them in a very positive way. They will be eager to help you with your next seminar and they will be the most friendly, smiling faces in the room next time. Remember, you're building a major business here. Think like a winner!

Chapter 18

THE SEMINAR CIRCUIT

"There are two things that are more difficult than making an after-dinner speech: climbing a wall which is leaning toward you and kissing a girl who is leaning away from you."

Winston Churchill

Often known as the "rubber chicken circuit" I like to call this…"doing the mammals."

We're talking about the Lions Club, the Moose, the Elk and the whole host of fraternal and social groups you will have a chance to address in your career — all the clubs and organizations that meet every night of the week in your community. They can be a superb source of business and market recognition as well as a powerful referral network.

Think about it…people who join these groups are highly likely to belong to other groups as well. If you were to map out all the links and connections you are touching by doing a group event, you would be astonished to see how much of the community you're penetrating.

If you're doing any geographic or industry target marketing, this venue will become very valuable to you as a way of building name awareness within the community or group. For a hundred reasons, they are a great market to target with your seminars.

They are also an excellent way to develop your speaking skills. Early in my career, these meetings were my proving ground. As a young broker, I spoke to every club and organization in a tri-state area. If they met…I'd come to speak.

In the Appendix, you will find a letter and a seminar menu that I used to prospect these clubs and organizations. It's often worthwhile to pursue these groups very enthusiastically. They're filled with excellent potential clients and centers of influence in the community.

These groups require a slight modification in presentation style than you would use for your own events. As a **"captive audience"** they are there for some reason other than you, and they can't leave! Your presentation to a group like this is more like a traditional speech than a full-blown seminar. The main differences are:

You have less time

You are probably part of an agenda with one or two more guest speakers and club business. Your talk must be timed to fit their schedule. Run long and not only are you being rude to other presenters but you risk being perceived as an annoyance to the audience and perhaps getting the "hook" from the Program Chairperson. That is very bad form!

The attendees didn't come to hear you

They came to hold a regular meeting and you are their weekly or monthly guest. They will be polite and courteous, but they're not likely to psychologically embrace you as quickly or as intensely as your own crowd would.

A wide range of behaviors

Doing the mammals will expose you to a broad array of strange and disturbing behaviors. All of this is great experience, however, so approach it with an open, adventurous mind.

For example, some folks will view you as an irritant because they have important club business to discuss and you're eating into their agenda. Others will simply want to socialize with their friends and can't wait until you're done. Some are there to drink and have fun…and a boring economics lecture will generate some challenging situations for you. Also, the concentration of snipers is much higher in groups like these, so be on guard. Despite these risks, however, group seminars can be great fun and good business!

The captive seminar

The best way to deliver a presentation to captive audience is to distill your presentation down to its emotional essence. Concentrate the key points into bullets and focus your delivery with as much power, conviction, enthusiasm and humor as you can muster.

It's important to arrive early and mix with the crowd. This will give you valuable intelligence you can use to tailor your talk. Use the old military acronym "SALUTE" to scope out the situation.

S- Size

How big is the group? Can you deliver an informal talk or must your presentation be more structured to fit a larger audience?

A- Activity

What are they doing before and after your presentation? Are they covering serious group business or are they simply socializing. Is alcohol flowing freely? What kind of conversations are they having? Are they talking about you and your presentation or that of another speaker? Is there any group event or characteristic that you can refer to in your talk either for humorous bonding or to enhance a serious part of your discussion?

The most fun I've had as a speaker to a captive group has been when following some important or controversial piece of group business. Which is one great reason to get there early and sit in on the meeting. By doing this, I'm able to tailor aspects of my talk to the issues they just discussed. This has a tremendous bonding effect on your audience and can drive up your credibility several notches.

L - Location

What's the facility like? Are you speaking from a lectern or can you walk around? Are there any distractions? Are waiters scurrying around and making noise or is a meeting going on next door? Can they see and hear you from all points in the room? Are the lights and temperature comfortable or will you have to contend with environmental problems? Where are the exits? That's not for a hasty retreat, but to know where to position yourself after the event to insure maximum traffic flow and individual contact?

U - Unit

This is a military term but in simple, civilian language: who are these people? Do some research prior to the event. When was the group founded? What do they do? Do they have any famous members? Showing a group that you know something about them is a powerful strategy for getting them to like you.

At the event itself you can get more information. I want to get a feel for the kind of personalities in the group. Are they conservative and stodgy or are they a fun-loving crowd likely to respond well to humor? Who are the formal and informal leaders? Who can you make fun of and who should you avoid? Which attendees warrant some special focus? Who are the centers of influence?

T - Time

You will probably know the agenda prior to the meeting, but there may have been changes. Can you expand your talk or must you cut it short? Your "feel" for the audience may also dictate changes in presentation length. For example, you may learn that they *never* have two speakers at the same meeting but tonight they're hosting a surprise visit from their National Chapter Imperial Grand Poobah and he may *"say a few words"* after you're done. They may all be anxious to hear him speak. Go too long and you might make them uncomfortable whereas cutting your talk a bit short would almost certainly garner you recognition as a perceptive professional and might get you back for a follow-up visit.

E- Equipment

Is there a microphone and does it work? What about speakers, a lectern, lighting, a stage or riser. Is there any projection equipment such as an LCD projector and a screen? You should bring your own equipment or be able to do the presentation without visuals if need be.

If you're bringing your own equipment, be sure to get there early enough to set up your stuff BEFORE the meeting begins. There's nothing worse than starting your talk by fumbling with computer equipment. It pretty much eliminates the power of any opening you might have wanted to do. What about handouts...do you have enough?

Be the last speaker

I always recall Shakespeare's Julius Caesar and how unfortunate it was that Brutus chose to speak first. It would have gone a lot better for him and his pals if he could have grabbed the crowd with a few jokes at the end of Marc Antony's speech...

> "Let's hear it for Marc Antony...you know that reminds me of a story. A man walked into a bar with a wooden box under one arm and a duck under the other..."

With very few exceptions, it's best to be the last speaker on the program. The audience will remember best what they hear last. In most meetings, the main attraction is the final speaker on the program. Simply *being* the final speaker will often lend credibility and stature to your presentation.

Going last is also an advantage in situations where the agenda includes only one combined question and answer session at the end of the event. By going last, you usually generate more questions because your talk is fresh in their minds. You should tailor the end of your talk specifically to generate these follow-up questions.

The risk of going last is running out of time. If the first speaker takes too long, you may find yourself cut short. There are few things I hate worse than when the Program Chairperson allows the first speaker to ramble on and then introduces me by saying, *"We're a little short of time, so if you could hurry it up a bit..."*

It takes all my self-control to stop from pinning his wrist to the table Luca Brazzi style. *"Hey pal, I drove two hours to be here, so you just sit down and relax 'cause I'm talkin' now!"*

There are only three times when going first is better:

1 - If you sense that the audience is likely to get impatient or restless with the length of the agenda as planned such as when the Grand Poobah comes to town and will be speaking after you're done.

2 - If you know the other speaker is likely to go long and cut into your time.

3 - If the other speaker is a lot better presenter than you are. It's always hard to follow a polished pro. Even though a real pro would never intentionally blow you out of the water, they can't help it. The ability differential will cause you to look much weaker than you would against ordinary competition. Best to do your thing, make it powerful, sit down and learn from a master. Some day that will be you!

If there are additional speakers on the program, you need to know what they're going to talk about. If it's another financial advisor, someone just like you, always go last! If you're scheduled to go first, get with the Program Chairperson and make up some excuse like *"I have to be on a special conference call with a client in Indonesia at exactly 8:00 PM. It will only last fifteen minutes but could you perhaps re-arrange the order of presenters and let me go last?"*

Time the delay to put you back in the room just after the first speaker has begun. You don't want to miss his presentation, because you're going to watch the crowd's reactions and build on his ideas. The program people usually don't mind the change, and this little ruse lets you land the emotional knock-out punch.

Dangers in the wild

There are a couple of things to watch out for at these "mammal" seminars. Top of the list of dangers is...

The Heckler

You can't handle a captive audience, group heckler the same way you handle a "sniper" during your own seminar. Verbally vivisecting someone may work just fine when it's *your* crowd, but when *you* are the guest...they don't take kindly to that kind of massacre.

The best way to handle a situation like this is to have a few quick-witted comebacks ready for non-lethal delivery if a heckler gets out of hand. Stuff like:

"I guess the wife is away for the week."

"OK no more prune juice for Harry over here!"

Chances are the group knows who the trouble makers are. They probably pop off at every meeting and no one takes them too seriously. What *will* be judged is your ability to handle them with firm but gentle humor. Do it well and they will like you. But take care not to smack old Harry too hard or you risk having the group turn on you.

Eating

Very often there will be some kind of food served at these events. The basic rule of public speaking is: **Do not eat anything thirty minutes before you speak.** The reason for this is spit...saliva. Eating causes a buildup of saliva that lasts some time after you finish eating. This forces you to clear your throat a lot which is very distracting to the audience. Some foods are worse than others. Dairy products like milk, cheese or chocolate are forbidden. You'll sound like you're drowning.

If you are there for a dinner before you speak, eat lightly and avoid the trouble foods. No one will mind and it will make for a better presentation. Also, be aware that the audience is eating and expect some heavy duty throat clearing if they're doing a lot of dairy or sweets. Normally, chortling is a sign that they're losing interest in your talk, but after a big meal, they can't help it.

Handouts

It's not as easy to use complex handouts at a mammal seminar as it is with your own crowd. Keep your handout to one page and keep it non-sales oriented. You might want to have your business card data somewhere on the handout.

If you are talking about specific investments you might need to have prospectuses. Place these on a table in the back and refer to them but do not hand them out.

"Folks, I'm required by FINRA regulations to make the prospectus available for you. I've placed these on a table in the back of the room so please take one on your way out."

Use of humor is more important

As important as humor is in a regular seminar, it's three times as important in a mammal seminar. Two reasons:

1. This a group of people who get together on a regular basis and who know each other as friends in addition to group colleagues. This places them into a more entertainment-oriented mindset.

2. You're dealing with an experienced audience here. They are a regular stop on the regional speaker circuit and they hear from many different kinds of speakers from professional politicians to raw amateurs. They expect a certain humorous delivery and content and will respond to humor very well.

This is not to say that you can't have a serious message. You can! But be aware that these kinds of groups enjoy a good laugh more than a typical seminar audience. You simply need to increase the humor/entertainment content in your presentation by one or two notches.

If that causes you concern, there is another alternative. Rather than upping the humor level, increase the drama level. Give them something to get emotionally involved with as an audience. Be more insightful, dynamic and energetic. Use a greater degree of vocal variety. Make some bold, compelling, even controversial statements and add impact to your message. Give them a little theater.

The best analogy for working with a captive group audience versus your own seminar crowd is something from Broadway theater. Tourists who come to New York once a year all want to see *Cats!* But an experienced Broadway aficionado wants more. They need more substance from their experience to make an impression. That's what group audiences are like.

Remember the goal

To me, the main goal of the captive seminar is NOT to do business with the individual members attending the meeting, but rather to expand my reach in the marketplace. Ideally, you will do such a good job that the centers of influence in the audience will invite you to come speak to their company or other groups. You will be able to parlay this event into others that might lead more directly to bigger business.

This is your chance to leverage yourself and by doing so boost the growth rate of your business to new heights.

Chapter 19

GENERATING ATTENDANCE

"A guy don't walk on the lot lest he wants to buy! They're sitting out there waiting to give you their money."

Alec Baldwin, Glen Gary Glen Ross

All the talent, preparation, speaking skill and content on earth is meaningless if only three people show up to your seminar.

Generating attendance is a vital first step in the seminar process but the good news is that's not as difficult as you might think.

How will you invite people?

There are only a handful of choices when it comes to inviting folks to an event. The big one obviously is direct mail, but you can also use newspaper ads, radio and TV ads, hand-carried flyers, e-mail, word-of-mouth, posters in the library and notices in the church bulletin. I have used all of these and others too bizarre to mention. I think the most effective format today is some combination of direct mail and electronic response capability such as a web-based reply.

Newspaper ads are nice but they're expensive and can't really be targeted to your audience. They are a mass-marketing approach, which may not be the impression you want to achieve.

Radio and TV is great, especially if you have your own show or can afford time slots on upscale programs such as NPRs Talk of the Nation or morning drive. But that's a BIG budget item.

Flyers can work well in a confined area such as in a single building or an office complex. You can use them to invite the other building tenants to a "lunch-and-learn" in your office. I actually did these with great success many thousands of years ago. And it might be worth trying if you have that kind of high-density environment.

When you boil it all down, chances are you will be dealing with direct mail in some format. So let's get into this arena since it's the most common and probably the best bang for your buck.

DIY or farm it out?

Are you willing and able to do all the work needed to invite people to your seminar or would you rather pay an expert to do it for you?

The answer depends on many factors such as budget, experience, time and skill. After many years of doing it myself, my decision and recommendation is to use the pros.

This certainly wasn't always the case. In my early career I had a lot more time than money and I designed all my own mailers, developed all my mailing lists and licked my own envelopes! You do what you must to survive...so I learned how to do these things myself and those skills have never left me.

When I started doing seminars, I went out and bought a knock-off IBM 286 PC clone and a Kyocera black & white laser jet printer for a combined $6,000 and designed my own invitations using embedded printer commands...if you can even imagine that!

Then a client gave me a bootleg copy of a software program called Corel Draw and I thought I died and went to Heaven! With this amazing program I began to do my own desktop publishing and it opened up a whole world of possibilities. I still use it today...12 versions later, of course. There may be other, more sophisticated programs out there today but I will always have a warm spot on my hard drive for Corel Draw...thank you!

But seminars are more competitive today. Prospects in the hottest markets are getting several seminar invitations per month. You can't afford to look less than professional so you should hire a marketing company to do all that for you. It's cheaper in the long run and it will allow you to concentrate on what you do best which is work with clients and give presentations.

Whom should you hire?

As I mentioned earlier, I have had a long relationship with the folks at Response Mail Express (RME) in Tampa, FL. In my opinion, they are the premier seminar marketing firm in the industry. I came to this conclusion in the first edition of this book…long before I became the Dean of Seminar Success University.

They are certainly not the only firm, nor the cheapest, but they have a system that works and they have a massive amount of experience and marketing data. They are the Microsoft of seminar marketing with capabilities that go far beyond mere direct mail. I would encourage you to check them out at **seminarsuccess.com**.

There are many companies that offer different formats including postcard mailers and wedding-style invitations. In the interest of some fairness, I've compiled a brief list below. It is certainly possible to use more than one company for your mailers. Some advisors like to mix it up a bit to test different responses and types of invitations. I admit that that I stopped looking after I found RME, but you are free to make your own decisions here.

- **Acquire Direct Marketing (acquirefinancial.com)**
- **Advisors Marketing (advisorsmarketing.us)**
- **AllPro Printing (allproprinting.com)**
- **CIS (cismarketing.com)**
- **Response Mail Express - RME (seminarsuccess.com)**
- **Seminar Crowds (seminarcrowds.com)**
- **Seminar Direct (www.seminardirect.com)**
- **Seminar Innovations (seminarinnovations.com)**

What about wedding style or postcards?

I like wedding style invitations myself. They have a quality look and feel that resonates with high-net-worth clients and I have used them successfully. They're not cheap but the results are solid.

Postcards, on the other hand, are probably the cheapest form of direct mail piece you can use. Not only are they easy to design, but they have no envelope and the postage is a fraction of a regular mailer.

The problem with postcards is image. In my mind, they reflect a lower-quality brand identity. They suggest to me that this person is somewhat less professional or successful than I would expect from anyone to whom I am entrusting my money. Remember…your invitation is the critical first touch in the relationship process. When clients look at it they want to see success and strength. Creating an image of confident professionalism is a critical element in all personal services marketing.

If you are still unsure, why not experiment and see what works best for you. I've used every form of mailing you could think of from postcards to boxes! I've used one-page flyers with no envelope to wedding style with hand-written addresses and pre-stamped reply mailers. You need a mailer that reflects positively on who you are and is most likely to get opened and read by your target market. All I can say is whatever you do…never cheap out on the invitation! You risk undermining your entire seminar program by trying to save a few buck in this all-important first phase.

I know that marketing and mailing is expensive, and many of you are worried about making back your costs on the seminar. Folks…those days are gone! If you implement the strategies in this book, your events will become massively profitable. So start thinking about seminar marketing as a fantastic investment in your business success. Hey, if I could find you a stock that would return 300% - 500% on every trade…you would trip over yourself to buy it…wouldn't you? Well that's what seminars are going to be for you now.

Pick a great location

As in real estate, a seminar is often a function of location. A great location is defined as an upscale facility as close as possible to the people you are inviting. You probably know the neighborhoods and general area your invitations are going out to, so identify a facility no more than a five or ten minute drive from anywhere in that zone.

Get yourself a map and plot out an area that is within a five minute driving radius of your facility. Don't bother inviting anyone who lives farther away than five or ten minutes max. It's not going to be a perfect circle like this because people take different routes to get to your facility. So you really do need to do this on a map in my opinion. That will tell you specifically where to send your invitations.

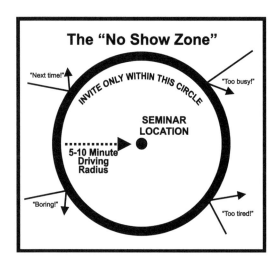

Why a five minute radius? Because that's psychological inner edge of the "No Show" Zone. One hour before the event is when you lose a lot of people. It's then that they realize the seminar is a hike and they come up with a million excuses for not going. The greater the distance, the more drop-outs, particularly in inclement weather environments.

If you're doing a seminar primarily for new prospects, the five minute rule should hold firm. If you're targeting existing clients, they probably all don't live within five minutes of any single spot, so the five minute driving criteria may be too restrictive. Even so, the facility should be as centrally located and as easy to get to as possible for the bulk of your people.

No perfect circles

The real world doesn't work in perfect circles. You will most likely be faced with a situation where the zip codes you are inviting are arranged irregularly around a few potential facilities. You might choose to hold multiple events at different locations to maximize attendance.

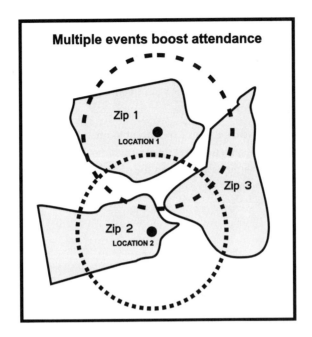

Multiple events boost attendance

I would probably not go with more than two locations myself. It starts to get confusing at some point. If you have a great location, it may still draw some folks from beyond the ten-minute radius. This is not set in stone…it's just a good to remember that the closer they are the higher your attendance will be.

What are some good places to hold seminars?

You have a wide range of choices when doing seminars. Some are a lot better than others, however, so let's examine the options.

- Restaurants

Pros (assuming you pick a good one)
- Easy to find with free or valet parking
- Usually have great appeal to HNW clients
- Food is probably good to excellent
- Puts people in a fun, festive mood
- Possible combo event with wine tasting, cooking demo or cigars and cognac.
- Neutral turf (less perceived sales pressure)

Cons
- Cost can be very high
- May not have the right meeting facility or equipment
- Lots of noise and distractions

- *People may come just for the food*
- *Recent bad press about "free dinner seminars" may make people wary*

I love restaurants, and there is data that confirms they are the best place to hold a seminar. You want one with a good reputation, a separate conference room, good food and a reasonable price ($50-$70 per head.) I would negotiate a package deal based on a certain number of events.

It's also wonderful if you can get a nice restaurant to open up at a special time just for your event. For example, many top restaurants are not open on Saturday mornings, however, you might be able to get the owner to open up with a special brunch menu for your seminar. This can be lots of fun and you would have the place to yourself with no distractions.

- Hotels

Pros
- *Usually easy to find with plenty of free parking*
- *Good meeting rooms with proper equipment (less equipment hauling)*
- *Experienced at hosting meetings (problems solved quickly)*
- *On-site food preparation (easy for you)*
- *Neutral turf*

Cons
- *Not very creative or unique*
- *Possible conflict with lots of other meetings*
- *Not tremendously appealing to High Net Worth (HNW) clients (unless you are using a really nice hotel)*
- *Can be expensive*
- *Need to book far in advance*

- Country clubs

Pros
- *Nice location that has extra appeal to HNW clients*
- *Usually very good food*
- *Easy to invite members*
- *Might have curiosity appeal for non-members*

Cons
- *Cost can be very high*
- *May not have the proper meeting room layout or modern equipment*
- *"Snob appeal" might actually turn off potential attendees*

- Public library or town meeting room
Pros
- Very cheap
- Easy to find

Cons
- Not generally an "upscale" facility
- Lots of distractions (kids running around)

- Art Gallery
Pros
- Unique location with some great HNW appeal
- Cost is not as high as you might imagine
- You can combine events with an exhibition

Cons
- Often in a high traffic area with limited access and not a lot of free parking
- Space is a premium so there's not much room to set up for your event
- Staff may not be used to hosting meetings
- Food needs to be catered in

Art galleries can be fun locations, especially for HNW seminars. If you can work out the logistics of meeting space, parking and food, you might have a great place to host some very special events.

- Theaters (stage or movies)
Pros
- Fun location with easy access and plenty of parking
- Can do combo events with a special movie afterwards
- Good HNW appeal
- Lots of dramatic potential with lighting effects and multimedia capability
- Could serve popcorn and candy instead of dinner
- More of an "event feel."

Cons
- Cost can be high
- No major food capability (some dinner-and-movie venues are great)
- No tables for your audience (hence the term "theater-style seating")

Theaters are potentially great locations for major events. If I were using a movie house I would avoid the Mega-48 Theater Orgasmo-Plex. Stick to the smaller art-film houses or those great dinner-and-a-movie facilities that are sprouting up all over.

I could even imagine hosting a multi-session film retrospective with some classic films after my seminar. These would be invitation only of course, but could attract some interesting clients. You could also get some great free publicity from the local press for such an event. If done well, you could get a huge emotional piggyback effect from such a program.

Legitimate or stage theaters can be even more fun because of the potential for drama in lighting and set design. I could easily imagine creating and producing a one-man-show about money and investing complete with, music, video and lighting effects. The result could be extraordinary. In fact, I may do this myself...so don't try it.

Obviously, the ideal facility should fit within your budget. I would be willing to allocate up to 30% of the cost of the total event to the facility.

Also don't assume that just because a facility is "upscale" it's going to work. I did a Saturday brunch seminar at a beautiful country club. The room had a grand view of the golf course. I previewed the site on a rainy weekday and never anticipated that the golfers teeing off outside would be a major distraction.

This simple seminar facility chart should get you started

Seminar Facility Chart

	#1 Restaurant	#2 Hotel	#3 Country Club	Library	Art Gallery	Theater	School	Your office
Easy to get to	YES	YES	Maybe	YES	Maybe	YES	YES	Maybe
Plenty of free parking	YES	YES	YES	YES	Maybe	YES	YES	YES
Valet parking	YES	Maybe	Maybe	No	No	No	No	No
Upscale feeling	YES	Maybe	YES	No	YES	No	No	Maybe
Appeals to HNW clients	YES	Maybe	YES	No	YES	Maybe	No	No
Unique idea	Maybe	No	YES	YES	YES	YES	No	No
Low cost	No	No	No	Maybe	No	No	No	YES
Few Distractions	Maybe	YES	YES	No	No	YES	YES	YES
Food on site	YES	YES	YES	Maybe	No	YES	No	No
Proper equipment	Maybe	YES	YES	YES	No	YES	YES	YES
Neutral turf	YES	YES	YES	YES	YES	YES	YES	No

Pick an exciting topic

We could discuss the topic issue forever, so let me share a simple philosophy and leave you to decide on what's right for you.

The main purpose of a seminar, besides helping people with valuable information, is to sell yourself...to create or enhance your image in the minds of your audience. So you should pick a topic that allows you to really shine — something that gives you a chance to look really smart and to fully portray those best aspects of your business practice. That means you should...

Pick a topic that gets YOU excited!

If you're fired up about something, the odds are excellent that you will be able to get an audience fired up too.

This may not work all the time. If, for example, you're doing a multi-session seminar where you're going to cover a broad range of financial topics over a few weeks, it's might include stuff like municipal bonds or insurance or other traditionally "boring" areas. There are two alternatives here.

One: find something in your boring topic to get excited about. There is no subject area within the broad category of investing that cannot be brought to life with a little historical knowledge, research or creativity. Everything about this business has some element of excitement in it. Find it and use it. Do not allow money and investing to become mundane or trivial, especially in a seminar presentation.

Two: if you really think that a topic is boring and you can't come up with any sizzle, try to match it up with others that *are* exciting. This creates an agenda in which each event has some sizzle. Do NOT lump all of your boring topics into one presentation. You'll drive them into a coma.

Use the media

The ideal topic should not only be exciting but timely. It helps tremendously to have some recent press discussing your theme. Your chances of getting a SRO crowd really go up when your theme is on the front pages and you can send a recent news or magazine article with your invitation. The media can definitely help you pack a room, so seek out sources that support your seminar effort and use them.

If none exist...create a few yourself. Send out press releases, invitations to local media, sample audio CDs with sound bites from past seminars and articles for publication. Understanding how the media works will help you to work with it in publicizing your events. Take a reporter to lunch and learn about their pressures and challenges. These are professionals with a job to do and to the extent that you can help them do it...you will be helping yourself.

Should you vary the topics?

Let's think about this for a second. Suppose you've found a target audience with good client potential. Your mailing list contains roughly 5,000 names. You've contacted them about a seminar on a strong theme like *"Global Investing."* Chances are you've only reached less than 20% of your potential audience with your initial invitation. Of that 20% who actually saw your invitation, you might have a 10% hit rate, which means 2% of your total target audience actually RSVP'd to your seminar.

Barring extraordinary circumstances, I would try the same seminar five more times over the next year within that target group or until your RSVP rate dropped below one half of one percent. In other words, when you send out 5,000 invitations to a qualified prospect list and fewer than 25 people respond, that would signal the time to change topics.

Notice I said "respond." If you're using a reply-card type mailer, this may mean that they simply requested information, NOT that they actually showed up to the seminar.

As you know, the key to advertising is repetition, but there's an added benefit of doing the same seminar several times within the same market. You begin to build your reputation as an expert on a specific topic. This is another reason I suggest picking a topic with lots of depth. Pick something that would appeal to HNW investors and build a reputation as an expert on that.

The other benefit of repetition is that you really start getting good at the presentation. After one or two seminars, you will begin to notice the audience's reactions to your various delivery styles and content elements. These are things you probably would never see early on because you're too concerned about *doing* the presentation. Repetition allows you to become more comfortable and familiar with the talk...and thus the freedom to expand or alter selected portions of content or delivery in order to achieve maximum audience impact.

Send everyone a ticket

A ticket is an important physical link to the event. (see sample in Appendix) It should have all the pertinent seminar information on it including directions to the facility. It should also have a unique Raffle Number. This will be used in the awarding of the door prize. Have I talked about door prizes yet? No? Well, have some!

People like to get free stuff. If it comes down to a last minute decision between your seminar and a re-run of How It's Made, this might just put them over the top. You can be as creative as you wish. I usually go for books, golf umbrellas or balls, or any of the hundreds of little gift items you have available to you. These make the event fun and ensure that you will get everyone's name and address before they depart.

The ticket should arrive with the invitation and you should include one for each person, not each couple. You should also include extras for guests. This gives you a good reason to confirm with them on the day of the event.

Call to pre-qualify

This is a simple strategy that increases your attendance ratio and the likelihood that you are reaching the right people for your event. Hey when I was doing seminars at Bertucci's Pizza at $10 per head...I didn't really cared who came. But now, at The Palm or Ruth's Chris for $10,000...I want qualified attendees!

Call the people who said they will be coming and say...

> "I just wanted to touch base with you about the seminar coming up tomorrow night. First let me say that I'm very glad you're coming. I think you're going to enjoy the workshop and get some great information you can really use. Second...I wanted to see if you had any general issues that you would like us to explore at the event. Are there any questions that have been on your mind that I might be able to include in the presentation?"

This may get you some valuable information about the people coming. I would not go so far as to ask about their portfolio size on this call. I will rely on my database to have reached the right people demographically. I'm mostly trying to get them excited about the seminar and see if there is potential there.

If I get the feeling that they are brain-dead or coming only for the meal, which is possible, I might try to dissuade them from coming. Conversely, they might have some real concerns...in which case we might even short-circuit the seminar and go right to the appointment. No problem with that!

Do the work

Getting people to come to seminars is not hard…but it is work! Are you willing to do the work necessary to get people to show up? If you hire a marketing company…it becomes their job and they are willing to do it for money. But if you decide to do it yourself, that's fine…just DO IT!

I used to do seminars for advisors back in my wholesaling days. I would ask them, *"How are we looking for our seminar?"* And I would hear, *"Oh we should have fifty people!"* Then I show up and there's three people! When you dig deeper you find they simply did not do the work necessary to get the crowd. They might have made a few calls, sent out a hundred invitations and basically just screwed it up!

Don't do this. Commit to yourself that you are going to make seminars work…then do what's needed to make it happen. This is your business we're talking about. No one can motivate you to succeed…only you can make that decision. You now have the tools and skills necessary. All that remains is the desire. If you want it…you can have it. If not…go do something else because there's nothing worse in life than a half-hearted effort.

The "wrong" crowd

How do you know if you've invited the wrong people? The short answer is you don't…until you meet and talk with them. Obviously you or the marketing company did some demographic list search with age, household income or net worth parameters. So your mailing list is probably pretty accurate. I generally don't worry about the financial capacity of my attendees. In any crowd it tends to balance out around the mean.

Another definition of "wrong" however, is personality fit. I don't care how much money you have…if I don't like you, we are not going to work together. I watch the crowd very carefully before the seminar begins. How are they interacting? What are they talking about and doing?

> *I once had a couple who walked in and start complaining to my assistant about the parking, a typo on the invitation and a stain on the carpet. They told her to send for skim milk because they wouldn't drink cream or regular milk in their coffee. I saw the man pick up three donuts, take a single bite of each and throw them away…that was the final straw! They tried to set an appointment but were turned away by an impossibly high minimum account size. Who needs this headache?*

The reality of seminars is that sometimes, you're going to have people in the room who simply don't qualify for your services. Don't get bent out of shape. You can't pre-qualify so perfectly as to eliminate all "non-quals." To do so would encumber your invitation process too severely and probably tick people off. Not what you're shooting for. So just accept the 10% to 15% excess and move on. It's just the cost of doing business.

What about the "lunch bunch?"

I hate the phrase "plate-lickers" but in some parts of the country, people actually shop seminar menus! *"What are you serving?"* is the standard question in Florida, Arizona, North Carolina, Orange County, parts of Long Island and the Chicago suburbs.

> *I actually had a group of women come to a seminar and celebrate a birthday party right there in the room! I was so stunned when the cake came out during my talk that I had to laugh. I stopped and we all sang Happy Birthday!*

There are two ways to handle the "buffet bunnies."

One is to try to pre-qualify very strictly and ask them to bring financial data to the event. This usually knocks them out, but it can turn off potentially good clients as well.

I have a totally different philosophy for these folks. I want them to come…in fact, I love them because I'm going to win them over and get all their money and their friends.

I have special plastic bags made up with my company logo and my name on it and tell them to take all the food they can carry! They love it and we have a great time. It's all about being different and fun and exciting. They're coming for the food. They're going to do business because of me!

I've had a lot of fun with this:

"Folks...I know why many of you came today. You knew we were going to have a nice meal and you wanted to stock up on rolls, sugar packets, cookies and anything else that looked good. Believe me I've done enough seminars in Florida to know the routine. You came because of the food...so I want to give everyone their own plastic doggie bag. Please fill these with anything that isn't nailed down!"

"But I make you one promise...because I understand what you're feeling. These are scary times. And many of you may be reminded of other scary times you experienced earlier in your life and you're determined never to feel that sense of scarcity, deprivation and fear again. After today...after you learn and understand what we are talking about...you will never need this plastic bag again. This bag represents fear...and I know how to make all the fear go away!"

All I can say is it works!

Chapter 20

STAGE FRIGHT

"It's not that I'm afraid to die. I just don't want to be there when it happens."

Woody Allen

Doctor, I have this recurring dream.

I am standing back stage of a major theatrical production. I have a leading role and it's seconds before my entrance. Suddenly I realize that I can't recall any of my lines. I'm frantically grabbing for a script and trying to memorize my lines for this crucial scene...but it's hopeless...there's no time...I'm on...and no words will come out. Then I wake up. What does it mean?

We all get butterflies

Public speaking is one of the biggest fears most people have in life...but let's be honest...that's not you. You are probably not someone who quivers, shakes, vomits, or faints at the thought of having to stand up in front of a group of people and speak. Chances are you love the idea or you wouldn't be reading this book. But you might still have a few butterflies.

Believe me - ALL speakers get butterflies. They never go away totally. I don't know a single person who doesn't get a little twinge, a jolt of adrenaline just before they go on. There is a nervous energy involved with the act of public speaking that manifests itself in a very physical way. It may be different for each person but you can feel it in your gut.

This is a totally normal phenomenon and it becomes much less distracting over time. I actually enjoy the rush right before I go on stage…it's a great joy of excitement and anticipation.

But for some folks it's actually a feeling of fear — a certain type of public speaking tension that usually comes from two main sources: ***"Administrative or Presentation Anxiety"***

Administrative anxiety is easy to minimize by being totally organized. Presentation anxiety can only be overcome by solid preparation, rehearsal and mastery of the techniques we're discussing in this book. Fears like:

- What am I going to say?

- What if I forget something important or make a mistake?

- What if they ask me something I can't answer?

…are very controllable and quickly dispersed with the confidence that comes from having delivered your talk a few times.

Some older public speaking books will tell you to picture the audience naked, or some other mental trick to reduce the tension or diminish the importance of the event. Frankly, that can be too distracting and it's not congruent with reality. This IS an important event. Instead, use this checklist to help you overcome stage fright.

Reducing anxiety

1. Organize

Lack of organization will kill you. It will sap your emotional strength and reduce your effectiveness dramatically. Knowing that your thoughts are well organized and that your presentation flows smoothly from one point to the next in a logical fashion will give you more confidence, which will allow you to focus energy into your delivery and on the audience. Make sure you have all the seminar details covered well in advance and that you have contingency plans for emergencies. And get a good assistant!

2. Visualize

Imagine walking into a room, delivering your presentation with enthusiasm, fielding questions with confidence and leaving the room knowing you did a great job. Mentally rehearse this sequence with all the details of your particular situation, and it will help you focus on what you need to do to be successful.

Visualization may sound corny, but every great athlete, especially the ones who compete in mentally intensive sports like tennis or golf, will tell you that success visualization plays a major role in their training, pre-game preparation and actual game execution.

3. Practice

Many speakers rehearse a presentation mentally or talk through it inside their heads. Instead, you might want to practice out loud, standing up, as if an audience were in front of you, and with your visual aids if you have them. At least two dress rehearsals are recommended. If possible, have somebody critique the first one and/or have it videotaped. For many people, this is the best form of preparation.

For some of us, however, this tactic could work in reverse. I tend to get more nervous with practice which is why I rarely rehearse my talks. Of course, I write all my own material, so that makes it easier because I know what I'm going to say at all times. If I were doing a pre-packaged seminar, I would have to do it a few times to get comfortable.

4. Breathe to relax

When your muscles tighten and you feel nervous, you may not be breathing deeply enough. The first thing to do is to stand up and inhale deeply a number of times. Instead of thinking about the tension, focus on relaxing. As you breathe, tell yourself on the inhale, *"I am"* and on the exhale, *"relaxed."* Proper breathing will get those butterflies in your stomach to all fly in one direction and it will give you an oxygen boost to clear your head and increase alertness.

5. Release tension

As tension increases and your muscles tighten, nervous energy can get locked into the limbs. This unreleased energy may cause your hands and legs to shake. Before standing up to give a presentation, it is a good idea to try to release some of this pent up tension by doing a simple, unobtrusive isometric exercise. Starting with your toes and calf muscles, tighten your muscles up through your body finally making a fist. Immediately release all of the tension and take a deep breath. Repeat this exercise until you feel the tension start to drain away.

6. Move

Speakers who stand in one spot and never gesture often experience physical tension. In order to relax, you need to release tension by allowing your muscles to flex. If you find you are locking your arms in one position when you speak, then practice releasing them so that they do the same thing they would if you were in an animated one-on-one conversation. Keep your gestures relaxed and natural and be sure they support your content.

Moving with your feet is important as well. You should take a few steps, either side-to-side or toward the audience. When speaking from a lectern you can move around the side of it for emphasis. Don't hide behind it. If you're comfortable, you can move throughout the audience. When tied into the context of your presentation, this level of dramatic movement adds a bold tone to the event.

7. Make eye contact with the audience

Remember the "Audience Mind Meld." Make your presentation similar to a one-on-one conversation. Relate with your audience as individuals. Look in people's eyes as you speak. Connect with them. Make it personal and personable. The eye contact should help you relax because you become less isolated from the audience and learn to react to their interest in you. Their enthusiasm will encourage you and the effect is very positive.

8. Watch or listen to talk shows on money

One of the best ways to develop confidence in your expertise is to hear for yourself how little the investing public knows about the world of money and how desperate they are for good information. This will also remind you to structure your presentation so that it's understandable to the public, not a roomful of portfolio managers.

Whenever I'm nervous, I remember listening to a radio call-in programs on investing. I have a vivid recollection of the questions being asked by the public and how basic they were. These people were obviously motivated enough to actually call a radio show, so I assume they felt that their problem was important. I remember thinking how little the public knows about investing – even the largest and most sophisticated investors know virtually nothing except their own portfolio and investment history.

This thought has helped me in speaking situations that would drive most financial professionals insane. I once spoke before the San Diego Chapter of the American Association of Individual Investors. These are the people who day-trade with the deep discounters for a penny a share. They truly think that they're smarter than most advisors. I wondered, *"What in God's name am I going to tell these people? How am I going to impress them given their level of knowledge and understanding?"*

On the way to the seminar, I tuned into one of those radio talk-shows, purely by accident. It was inspiring. It left me with the confidence that compared to *"the public"* I was Warren Buffett! The feeling was extraordinary and I blew the audience away. It's all about confidence and you should have tons of it…because you're good!

Chapter 21

THE INSTINCTIVE SPEAKER

"My definition of success is the freedom to be yourself."

Kathy Kolbe

We are all creatures of instinct…those hard-wired characteristics that define us, drive us and operate every day below the level of consciousness.

These instincts have a profound effect on all aspects of the seminar process…and indeed your total performance in this profession. Let's spend a few minutes on this important topic.

The Three-Part Mind

There are three parts of the human mind. These are known as:

- **The Cognitive Mind (thinking, intellect and learned abilities)**
- **The Affective Mind (feelings, desires and personality)**
- **The Conative Mind (actions, behaviors & instincts)**

The conative mind and the instincts it contains have been and always will be with us, but unlike personality and learned abilities, instincts change very little throughout our lives.

I first learned about instinctive strengths back in the military. It was in an experimental training program that attempted to identify and quantify advanced leadership qualities in junior officers. This was fascinating stuff and cutting edge for its time, but I didn't find a practical use of this information until decades later when I attended The Strategic Coach® program with Dan Sullivan.

It was there I took the Kolbe A Index® which is the only APA (American Psychological Association) validated instinct test in existence. When I got my scores back it was like someone lifted a blanket from in front of my face and said, *"Now do you see?"* Every great thing and every stupid thing I ever did came flooding back into my mind. I was filled with tremendous joy that I had the science to verify who I thought I was. And at the same time, I felt massive regret that I didn't know these things about myself decades earlier. It could have made such a huge difference to understand my natural strengths.

The Kolbe Index was a revelation for me and I had to learn more, so I studied with Kathy Kolbe and now I teach this to thousands of financial professionals each year. It's a simple and inexpensive tool that helps focus your energy and clarify your efforts – a 20 minute test that could change your life! You can take the test right on my website and if you do, I will personally analyze your scores for you in terms of what they mean for this business. This is a very valuable conversation. Go tofrankmaselli.com to learn more.

Kolbe and seminars?

Your instincts drive every aspect of your behavior each day, and they have a gigantic impact on the kind of presenter you will be, how you will prepare for a seminar, how you will handle questions, preparation, follow-up…the entire seminar process. Knowing your instincts, specifically your Kolbe Action Modes, and how they drive you, will go a long way toward making you a more effective presenter.

Kolbe measures four instincts and you will score between 1 and 10 in each "Action Mode." Despite the numerical scale however, there are no "high" or "low" scores. The numbers just represent a different use of your instinctive energy along a continuum of behaviors and actions. There are also no "good" or "bad" instincts. I have found that the only bad instincts are the ones you don't know…because they are operating inside you all the time whether you are aware of them or not.

Fact Finder

This is the way you handle data, work with information and details, do analysis. On the 1, 2, 3 end of the spectrum you are what Kolbe calls a "Simplifier." You like to cut to the chase, get the essential facts and boil them down into a few key points. You are not instinctively drawn to excruciating details and deep research before a seminar. When asked a question, you will probably respond in broad generalities and "bottom-line" kind of statements.

As a presenter in the 1 – 3 Fact Finder zone you might run into situations where certain people in the audience (like engineers) need more information. If you fail to dig deeply enough, they could walk out of your presentation thinking that you are light on the facts – more fluff and not enough substance…which is not good. Knowing your Kolbe scores allows you to prepare levels of detail in specific areas so that you can drill down during the seminar and appeal to the most intense Fact Finders in the room.

In the 7-10 range of Fact Finder, you "Specify" – you do intense analysis and probably need to know everything about a topic before you would even feel comfortable *giving* a presentation. Details and historic justification are your world and in a seminar, you come across as extremely knowledgeable…a real expert witness. The potential seminar risk here is giving too much info. You may think it's critical but the audience may not be able to handle it. You may also have a tendency to "talk past the sale." By the time you get to the twentieth floating bar chart the audience will have checked out. So you may need to streamline and synthesize data into critical elements that drive home key points.

Follow-Thru

This is your instinct for process, structure, organization and discipline. On the 1, 2, 3 side you are "Adaptable" or a "Multi-Tasker" which I have found translates most simply in our industry into "disorganized."

You may have a lot of trouble even *planning* a seminar and coordinating what seems like a million different tasks required to succeed. You definitely need a good administrative assistant to keep you on track, or at least a simple process where you hire a marketing company to do the work so you can just show up.

As a speaker, you run the risk of jumping around a lot with the stream of consciousness rambling. Following a detailed outline or a script would probably not work for you. Also, putting together handouts, gathering necessary paperwork and compliance approvals, all the back-office minutia that goes into getting things done would be an instinctive challenge.

On the 7 – 10 side, you are a "Systematizer" – someone who injects discipline and structure into situations. You could parachute into a chaotic world and have things running smoothly in minutes. You not only follow procedures…you *create* procedures!

As a presenter, you are a disciplined, step-by-step professional who does things by the book. It would never occur to you to skip a bullet point on a slide and it could inflame you to have a typo on your handouts.

The risk you run as a presenter might be a lack of flexibility and spontaneity. You would be driven to complete each segment of the talk before moving on and this instinctive need to follow the planned path may conflict with the audience's desire for a change in pace or a shift into a new topic.

Quick Start

This is the Kolbe Action Mode that deals with risks and unknowns. On the 1, 2, 3 end you are instinctively drawn toward proven ideas, consistent and reliable strategies. You deal with unknowns by trying to reduce the risk and uncertainty in the equation. You are a "Stabilizer."

As a presenter, you would likely practice a script and need to know exactly what you're going to say before the event. Making stuff up off-the-cuff is not your strong suit and if you get thrown a curve ball during the presentation you could be stressed. Ironically, this fear of the unknown may be preventing you from embracing seminars at all…which would be sad because you can succeed with any set of Kolbe scores.

In the 7-10 range, you are an "Innovator," an ad-libber, someone who embraces risk and experiments with new ideas to see how things will turn out. As a speaker you could be very dynamic and entertaining with the ability to comfortably handle any situation that pops up. You are not likely to practice or rehearse your talk in advance preferring the spontaneity of the moment to the memorization of lines.

I am a 10 in Quick Start…what a surprise! In my mind, there is nothing I can't do in front of a room…any room…any topic at any time! This instinct has been with me since birth. In my High School yearbook the editor wrote, *"Frank can expound fluently on any subject!"* I love to talk and I'm pretty good at it…or at least I think I am.

> *Is there a potential downside to this QuickStart level? Oh yes! I was the young Army Captain who decided to "wing it" during a briefing to then Vice President George H.W. Bush during an unscheduled inspection of my unit's deployment at Fort A.P. Hill in Virginia. My casual attitude and relaxed, style seemed to appeal to the Veep who laughed and joked…but it horrified my superiors. They almost stroked out when I strolled from behind the lectern and sat on the edge of a table with a "let's just chat" informality. One bird colonel came up to me*

afterwards and locked my heals. He said, **"Captains are not supposed to have a personality!"**

Knowing my Kolbe scores now…I can anticipate those moments, plan for them and if necessary, control them. Although to this day, I swear that Bush loved my briefing.

Implementor

This has nothing to do with implementing a strategy. In Kolbe-land, this is the Action Mode that deals with your instinct for working with physical objects, getting tangible and tactile, touching and handling things, or using tools.

On the 1, 2, 3 end you "imagine" things which means you see them in your mind or can deal with them abstractly. You don't need to handle or touch them. On the 7-10 end you will get physical and handle objects. You will build things, sculpt granite, mold clay, shape wood, dig in dirt or use a surgeon's scalpel.

I have done thousands of Kolbe tests with financial services professionals and I've run into only 15 who scored 7-9 in Implementor…and I've never met a 10. We don't seem to attract these folks. They find it instinctively uncomfortable sitting at a desk all day long. They have a deep drive to move around, stay active and fix stuff. Staring at a computer and talking on a phone does not ring their bell. So I would be surprised if you are in this category.

In presentations, however, it can be very useful to get physical. We talked earlier about using props and tangible items to illustrate key points. It works like a charm. That's partly because there are a lot more Implementors in your audience. The general population has a more balanced distribution of this Action Mode than we do. So try it and see what happens.

You can also move people around. This is a basic teaching technique used by many meeting facilitators who are trying to create some excitement and get a spirit of team building going in the audience. For example, they may have a room full of executives compete to build a car out of plastic pipes, wood and duct tape. First team to race across the finish line wins. It's a lot of fun and you learn a great deal about the way people work together, or not. Generally you are not going for this kind of result, so getting physical isn't likely to play a big role in the typical seminar.

Middle of the fairway

If you have a score of 4, 5 or 6 in any Kolbe category (and most people do) you actually are in great shape. This means you have the instinctive flexibility to go in either direction when the need arises. In Fact Finder you can get specific or stick to generalities. In Follow-Thru you can be highly disciplined or extremely flexible. In quick Start you can innovate or stabilize when needed. And in Implementor, you can probably fix the copier and change a flat.

The middle ground can be a good place to be also because you get along with a broad range of different people. I don't have time to get into this too deeply, but Kolbe will actually tell you the kinds of people who are likely to rub you the wrong way. These can be clients, colleagues, partners…even your spouse.

You may have heard me tell the story about my wife who is the Kolbe opposite of my 3-3-10-3. Rebecca is an 8-8-2-2. Our only instinctive common ground is our mutual hatred of power tools. It makes for some interesting times.

If you have these kind of extreme scores in any Kolbe category there are some things you're going to need to do in your seminars to guard against alienating entire segments of the room. That's a very personal issue that I would be happy to discuss on an analysis call with you.

To learn more

Go to **www.kolbe.com** and pick up Kathy's book, "Powered By Instinct." Also, contact me any time. I love to talk about this and can really help you and your team navigate these instinctive waters. This is one of those rare tools that can boost your business and personal success with a very small effort. Kudos to Kathy and her staff for their tremendous work!

Chapter 22

COURAGE & CONVICTION

"No man is worth his salt who is not ready at all times to risk his body...to risk his well-being...to risk his life in a great cause!"

Teddy Roosevelt

OK...you are now as ready as any book can make you to take on the perils and thrills of public presentations.

Some final advice remains before you go.

Adapt to fit your style

This whole discussion is not about turning out thousands of copies of any one style or delivery. It's about giving you the tools to find your own style and empowering you to be yourself. These tools and techniques I've shared with you will work differently for each person who uses them. You will find yourself modifying, altering, tweaking almost everything I've said and that's wonderful!

Have conviction

Whatever you decide to do, please remember that clients today desperately need your help....perhaps more than at any other time in history. You have all the expertise and the tools to help them. The only thing that's missing today is conviction. Unfortunately, it's the most important thing.

Seminars are symphonies of conviction! Find something you believe in – an idea, philosophy of investing, a money manager...whatever – and run with it until you can't run anymore. People will flock to you and you will build the greatest life you can imagine in this wonderful industry!

Pick one thing and try it

Above all, don't let this go to waste as an academic exercise. Try one or two techniques at your very next event. The positive feedback you receive will spur you on to try more ideas and the whole process will begin to snowball.

Then you need to commit to doing at least one seminar per quarter for the next year. That's four events spaced out with plenty of prep time even for the busiest schedule. Only by speaking more will you give yourself a chance to become excellent at it. There is simply no substitute for being on stage in front of a crowd.

Above all...please have some fun! The business is tough, downright brutal at times. But seminars can be a tremendously pleasurable experience. If you enjoy giving a presentation, the audience will read that in your total delivery and they will enjoy *you*. That's when magic happens!

OK...I'm done!

I hope this book has helped you. If you ever want to talk about seminars, share some ideas, or ask some questions about building your business...please get in touch with me anytime. Working with advisors is my deepest passion and I am always eager to help people get better at this wonderful profession. Visit **frankmaselli.com** for more info.

I want to wish you "good luck," but you NEVER do that in theater, so in keeping with tradition...

"Break a leg!"

Appendix 1
Marketing to Clubs & Organizations

I have always enjoyed speaking to groups such as the Kiwanis, Rotary, Lions, Moose, Elk, etc. Here are the basic elements of a marketing kit I send to clubs and organizations in my region marketing myself as a an expert speaker in financial matters.

Mr. Joe Slate
Grand Poobah
The Water Buffalo Lodge
123 Flint Street
Bedrock, USA 12345

Dear Mr. Slate,

As a leader in your organization, one of your jobs may be involve arranging for guest speakers on topics of particular interest to your members. I would like to offer my help.

I am an expert in the field of investing and financial planning. This topic is certainly on the minds of many people faced with serious questions about their financial future. Many people today are asking:

- How can I survive these chaotic markets and continue to grow my retirement nestegg?

- How can I protect my portfolio income from severe market downturn?

- How can I take advantage of the growth potential in new industries and new markets worldwide?

I have prepared a series of entertaining and informative talks on a wide variety of investment related topics that your group is sure to find enjoyable, informative and thought-provoking. These are not sales presentations and no products will be discussed.

I have enclosed some comments from recent seminars in your area. I think you will see that these sessions have been very well received. I've also enclosed a topic menu. You may select from one of these talks or we can customize one for your group.

If you are interested or would like more information, please contact me at 800-231-5272. My business card is attached.

I look forward to meeting with you and your organization.

Sincerely,

Joe Tentpeg

P.S. If you ever need a last-minute replacement for a program or a speaker who has cancelled, please call me. I live in the area and will make every effort to help!

Use comments from other seminars

I would attach a one-page sheet of my favorite ten or fifteen comments from previous seminars. The power of this is enormous. A club president or a program chairperson runs a big risk when they invite an unknown guest speaker to a meeting. If the members don't enjoy the presentation the leader is going to catch hell.

If you have actual comments from leaders of other clubs and organizations…all the better! Also, a DVD of one of your events may be a great tool. When you get serious as a speaker…that's a must-have item.

Depending on the group you're marketing to, you might want to highlight different aspects of your talks. Some groups are more interested in having fun than in learning the details of advanced investment management. Find out as much as you can about the group and use quotes that support the appropriate marketing message.

This would also be a great place to use your Personal Profile Interview. For more information on this, please visit my website at frankmaselli.com.

Seminar Topic Menu

These are some of my favorites. You can augment this list with anything that makes sense for your business. Please don't call me asking for a copy of these seminars. The best ones are the seminars you build yourself.

Protecting Your Retirement

Saving for the "golden years" has become the greatest challenge facing Americans today. Learn some simple and proven strategies that will protect your nestegg even in the face of chaotic market volatility.

The Seven Secrets of Professional Investors

In this talk we will discuss methods used by today's top investors to grow their portfolio and reduce risk. These techniques were once reserved for the wealthiest families and corporations...but now they can be used by any investor with the knowledge!

The New Technology Boom

Recent advances in several key technologies may find us at the doorstep of an incredible new boom for the next decade and beyond. Learn about some of these advances and what they could mean for you and your money.

Global Investing in the New World Economy

All the countries of the world are connected economically and to succeed as an investor you need to know the new rules of the international market. We will discuss several key strategies that could increase your growth and income potential and decrease your risk.

Doing Well by Doing Good

Can you translate your personal and family values into a viable investment strategy? The answer is yes! Learn how as we discuss "socially conscious" investment strategies

Women & Investing

Many women today face special challenges when it comes to money and investing. This discussion goes beyond the basics and addresses the critical strategies women need to implement for success.

Estate Planning 101: Life After Death

Many of us may be at a stage in our lives when we start thinking about what we leave behind and how it will affect those we love. The estate plans and decisions you make today will have a tremendous impact on the people and institutions about which you care most. Learn a few simple strategies that can help your hard work live on forever!

Never Retire

The old rules of retirement are gone. Chances are you have no intention of sitting in a rocking chair for thirty years. You need and want to stay active, physically, mentally and professionally. In this program we will discuss several ideas for a changing retirement and how you can make it the most exciting time in your life.

Appendix 2

Sample Evaluation Form

I use a simple evaluation for after my seminar. It gives you some potentially valuable feedback and it gives your audience a chance to tell you the subjects they might be interested in learning more about.

Seminar Evaluation

Name_____

Address _____
_____

Phone_____   E-mail_____

Please circle your answers to the questions below.

	NO		Neutral		YES
The seminar information was valuable.	1	2	3	4	5
I found the presentation interesting.	1	2	3	4	5
I understood most of the key points.	1	2	3	4	5
The food was good.	1	2	3	4	5
The room was comfortable.	1	2	3	4	5
I would be likely to attend a future seminar.	1	2	3	4	5
I would tell my friends about these seminars.	1	2	3	4	5

I would like more information about:

☐ Retirement planning   ☐ Global investing
☐ Growth investing   ☐ Estate planning
☐ Safe income ideas   ☐ College savings
☐ Tax-reduction ideas   ☐ Other _____

Comments (Please tell us what you really liked or disliked about this seminar.)
_____
_____
_____
_____

(See reverse side for sample comments.)

On the back page of the Evaluation form, I list several super-hyperbole "seed quotes" that get them chuckling a bit. It lets them know the kind of comment I am looking for regarding my seminar. If you've done a great seminar, people will often want to reward you with some particularly clever feedback. These serve to get the creative juices flowing.

Sample comments *(feel free to check off one of these if you prefer)*

☐ "This was the greatest seminar since Moses came down from the mountain!"

☐ "Wonderful, incredible and awe-inspiring!"

☐ "An event unlike anything I've ever witnessed!"

☐ "I laughed...I cried...it was a spectacle!"

☐ "An Oscar-winning performance!"

Appendix 3

Confidential Seminar Profile

This form may be used to gather more detailed information if you prefer.

Confidential Seminar Profile

Name _____   Home Phone _____

Address _____   Work Phone _____

_____   E-mail addr: _____

Employer or company name: _____

● Rank your major investment or financial concerns today: (1-HIGH, 10-LOW)
(You can have more than one HIGH priority!)

- [ ] Providing for a more enjoyable retirement
- [ ] Providing for child's (grandchild's) education
- [ ] Minimizing or reducing income taxes
- [ ] Diversifying the risk of closely help company stock or options
- [ ] Increasing my current investment income
- [ ] Maximizing the growth potential of my portfolio
- [ ] Reducing the risk of my current portfolio
- [ ] Developing a comprehensive financial plan
- [ ] Reviewing my insurance and estate situation
- [ ] Exploring ways to sell or restructure my business
- [ ] Providing long-term care to aging parents or grandparents
- [ ] Other _____
- [ ] Other _____

● How satisfied are you with the financial advice you're getting today?
(People often have multiple advisors. Check the boxes as appropriate for you.)

- [1] [2] [3] Extremely satisfied: I'm getting the best advice and service imaginable!
- [1] [2] [3] Very satisfied:.I'm getting good advice and service
- [1] [2] [3] Somewhat satisfied: I'm happy but things could be better
- [1] [2] [3] Not satisfied: I need more than I'm getting
- [1] [2] [3] Very unsatisfied: These people have some major problems
- [ ] I do not have an advisor

Appendix 4

Customized Note Paper

Place this at each seat or in your handout booklet. It's a nice professional touch that people will appreciate.

The 7 Secrets
of Professional Investors

Tuesday, Oct. 19 2010
Rumson Country Club
Featuring
Joe Tentpeg
Senior Vice President
Blowhard & Boggle
800-231-5272

NOTES

"Uncertainty is the friend of the long-term investor."

Warren Buffett

Appendix 5
Storyboard Workbook

This is an example of a handout workbook that you would give out at the seminar. I don't often use these because people will read ahead in the slideshow, but sometimes you may have to. PowerPoint will actually print these for you!

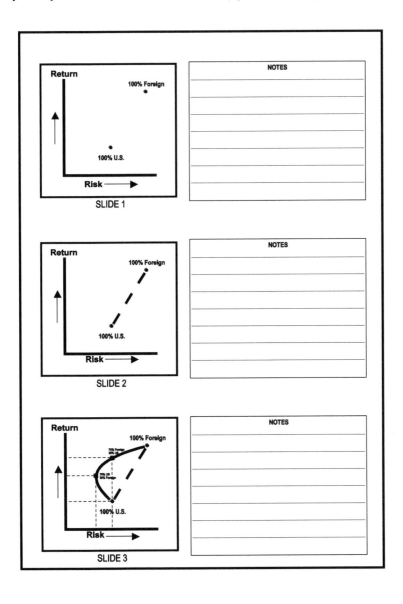

Appendix 6

Seminar Ticket

I like sending tickets with my seminar invitations. It tells people that something special is going to happen and begins to create that positive expectation. Here's a sample front and back view.

Name _____

Address_____

_____

Daytime Phone _____

Evening Phone _____

E-Mail Address: _____

Appendix 7

5 Week Seminar Planner

This planning checklist assumes you are doing all the work yourself. If you are using a seminar marketing firm like Response Mail Express, to handle the process, your workload is dramatically reduced. Also, you may need to increase the time for compliance review depending on your own company's policy.

5 weeks before the seminar

- Decide on demographic and geographic market to be targeted for this event.
- Choose date, time and topic of seminar. (Check for conflicts or holidays.)
- Select and reserve the location
- Order hand-out materials (i.e., brochures, reprints, research reports, etc.)
- Notify your advertising department and order ad materials if you are using print ads.
- Select and book any guest speakers.*
- Determine your budget and request additional support as required.
- Begin script outline
- Begin developing your storybook (gather research, data, articles, etc.)
- Design seminar invitation, tickets, note sheets and other marketing material.
- Contact all free sources of advertising (i.e., company newsletters, church bulletins, local newspaper calendar of events, radio and cable TV events listings, community websites, etc.)
- Check all your electronic equipment (i.e. LCD projector, microphone, etc.)

*Some guest speakers will require two or three months of advanced notice, so plan accordingly. Most fund and annuity wholesalers work in a standard five or six week rotation.

4 weeks before the seminar

- Deadline for making major changes in date, time, location or topic.
- Submit script outline for compliance approval if necessary.
- Follow-up on budget support requests.
- Organize list of potential invitees.
- Finalize your invitation and get it to the printer.
- Notify your team of upcoming overtime requirements if necessary.
- Plan for postage needs.

3 weeks before the seminar

- Send out invitations (bulk mail 18-20 days prior)
- Run print ads if necessary
- Notify clients and send them tickets for their friends
- Continue working on presentation
- Edit and print handout materials

2 weeks before the seminar

- Send out first class invitations if any
- Begin calling the people on your invitation list
- Practice the presentation and determine the overall length
- Cut out half of the slides and reduce the run time
- Prepare for the Q&A session by anticipating all possible questions
- Memorize the power opening, appointment close and emotional close
- Confirm with guest speaker

1 week before the seminar

- Continue calling to invite people
- Begin confirmation/qualification calls
- Prepare attendance roster and sign-up sheet
- Confirm room setup with the facility
- Finalize headcount with the facility (usually 72 hours needed for any free changes)
- Videotape a dress rehearsal of the presentation if necessary
- Double check your electronic equipment
- Scan all news stories for the latest information pertinent to your topic

The day before the seminar

- Get a good night's sleep
- Avoid alcohol
- Rest your voice
- Finalize handouts and prepare kits

Day of the seminar

- Meet with your staff to finalize plans
- Arrive 90 minutes early

- Don't eat anything 30 minutes before speaking
- Avoid excessive caffeine
- Greet guest speaker and go over any program changes
- Do some light vocal warm-ups and physical stretching
- Take 10 deep breaths and get excited
- Knock them dead!

Immediately after the seminar

- Thank guest speaker, facility staff, your team
- Greet any top clients you haven't had a chance to talk with yet
- Do a quick de-briefing with your team to determine any immediate follow-up opportunities and audience intelligence while it's still fresh in their minds.
- Do NOT critique your performance or watch the video...relax

The day after the event

- Do a more detailed de-briefing with team for any operational items that could be improved
- Send thank-you note to guest speaker
- Confirm appointments
- Begin meeting with attendees

Two weeks after the seminar

- Review the video if you did one
- Critique your presentation
- Begin preparation for your next event

About The Author

Frank Maselli brings a unique combination of experiences and abilities to the subject of investment seminars. He graduated from Lafayette College in 1978 with a degree in Biology and spent the next five years as a U.S. Army Officer in command of a modern M*A*S*H* hospital.

After leaving the Army, Frank began his investment career in 1983 at Dean Witter in Baltimore, MD where he opened one of the nation's first Sears Financial Centers. It was here that he learned the incredible power of face-to-face marketing and found his calling – conducting hundreds of public seminars.

Frank joined PaineWebber in 1986 and served for ten years in a variety of sales and managerial roles. He conducted over a thousand seminars for reps nationwide and began to train other advisors in the art and science of presentations.

In 1996, Frank went to Boston to become the National Sales Manager for what was then called New England Funds (now Natixis Global Asset Management). While there he created The Advisor Academy and expanded his training expertise to offer a wide variety of advanced skill programs to advisors, wholesalers and managers.

In 2006, Frank published his second book called **Referrals The Professional Way** and started his own training company. He currently teaches an entire spectrum of skill programs to advisors, wholesalers and managers including:

- **The Psychology of Advising**
- **Taking the Hill: The Combat Leader's Guide to Victory**
- **The 12 Disciplines of Professional Wholesaling**
- **Breakout Branding: Creating & Telling the Story of YOU**
- **The Instincts of Success: Finding and Using Your Deepest Strengths**

He has also become one of the most popular keynote speakers in the industry today. Some of his exciting programs include:

- **An Industry Reborn: The New Financial Services Profession**
- **Conviction & Passion: Building the Twin Pillars of Success**
- **The Lighthouse in the Storm**
- **Aspire: Your Journey to the Top**
- **Thriving on CHAOS: Five Strategies for Growing Your Business in the Toughest Times**

Frank's deepest passion lies in helping financial professionals be the best they can be and empowering them to help their clients reach the most critical life goals. He does it with a blend of enthusiasm, humor, intelligence and experience that is hard to duplicate. He is a member of the FPA, IMCA, MENSA, and the National Speakers Association. You can learn more about his programs at **www.frankmaselli.com**.